SOCIO-ECONOMIC PROFILE OF RURAL INDIA [SERIES III]

Volume Two

Socio-Economic Profile of Rural India (Series I)

VOLUME 1 : **South India,** *Edited by* V.K. Agnihotri

VOLUME 2 : **North East India,** *Edited by* C. Ashokvardhan

VOLUME 3 : **Western and North Central India**
Edited by Rajendra Vora

VOLUME 4 : **Eastern India—Bihar, West Bengal, Orissa and Uttar Pradesh,** *Edited by* C. Ashokvardhan

Socio-Economic Profile of Rural India (Series II)

VOLUME 2 : **North East India (Assam, Manipur, Tripura and Nagaland),** *Edited by* S.C. Patra, Ashish Vachhani

VOLUME 4 : **Eastern India (Orissa, Jharkhand, West Bengal, Bihar and Uttar Pradesh)**
Edited by C. Ashokvardhan, Ashish Vachhani

VOLUME 5 : **North and Central India (Punjab, Haryana, Himachal Pradesh and Madhya Pradesh)**
Edited by Raj Mohini Sethi

Socio-Economic Profile of Rural India (Series III)

VOLUME 1 : **Haryana, Punjab, J&K, Rajasthan and Himachal Pradesh,** *Edited by* C. Ashokvardhan, Varunendra V. Singh

---

ABOUT THE EDITOR

Professor (Dr.) Sucha Singh Gill, M.A. (Economics), Ph. D., Punjabi University, Patiala Former Director-General, CRRID, Chandigarh. Former Professor & Head, Department of Economics, Punjabi University, Patiala; Former Dean, Academic Affairs, Dean, Social Sciences; Dean, Research, Punjabi University, Patiala; Vice-President of Indian Association of Social Science Research Institutions (IASSI); Elected President for Annual Conference for Indian Society of Labour Economics.

Areas of Specialization: Development Economics, International Economics, Punjabi Economy.

Dr. Varunendra Vikram Singh, Faculty, Centre for Rural Studies: Ph.D., Sociology Department, Lucknow University, Lucknow. Awarded Junior Research Fellowship and also Senior Research Fellowship by Anthropological Survey of India, Government of India, Kolkata. Did Certificate Course in 'Computer Basics & Internet'. Passed National Stock Exchange's Certification in 'Financial Markets with expertise in Derivative & Capital Market.' Did an International Course on Management of 'Common Property Resources' from IIM, Ahmedabad. Organized and contributed to several seminars and workshops of national importance. Worked as Researcher in National Institute of Administrative Research, LBS National Academy of Administration, Mussoorie. Has several Reports and Research papers published in scientific journals and also edited published and Co-authored books to his credit. Areas of Interest are in the field of Land Reforms, Land Markets, Elementary Education, Tribal Development, Common Property Resources, Financial Management and Land Resources Management in India.

SOCIO-ECONOMIC PROFILE OF RURAL INDIA

[Series III]

VOLUME TWO

(Maharashtra, Karnataka, Kerala, Andhra Pradesh, Telengana, and Bihar)

Edited by

Sucha Singh Gill

Varunendra Vikram Singh

Published for

LBSNAA

Lal Bahadur Shastri National Academy of Administration

Centre for Rural Studies

Lal Bahadur Shastri National Academy of Administration

Mussoorie

by

CONCEPT PUBLISHING COMPANY PVT. LTD.

NEW DELHI-110059

ISBN-13: 978-93-5125-249-8 (Series-III)
ISBN-13: 978-93-5125-251-1 (Vol. II)

First Published 2017

Published and Printed by

Since 1974

Concept Publishing Company Pvt. Ltd.
Regd. Office:
A/15-16, Commercial Block, Mohan Garden,
New Delhi-110059 (INDIA)
Phones : 25351460, 25351794, *Fax* : 091-11-25357109
Email : publishing@conceptpub.com
Website: www.conceptpub.com

Cataloging in Publication Data—DK Courtesy: D.K. Agencies (P) Ltd. <docinfo@dkagencies.com>

Socio-economic profile of rural India. Series III / edited by Sucha Singh Gill, Varunendra Vikram Singh.
volumes cm
Includes bibliographical references and index.
Contents: volume 2. Maharashtra, Karnataka, Kerala, Andhra Pradesh, Telengana, and Bihar
ISBN 9789351252498 (series-III)
ISBN 9789351252511 (vol. II)

1. India—Rural conditions. 2. India—Economic conditions—1947- 3. India—Social conditions—1947- I. Gill, Sucha Singh, 1949- editor. II. Centre for Rural Studies (Lal Bahadur Shastry National Academy of Administration), issuing body.

HN683.5.S63 2017 DDC 307.720954 23

Dr. Prem Singh, IAS
Centre Director,
Centre for Rural Studies,
LBS National Academy of
Administration, Mussoorie

Foreword

This volume is the outcome of the Socio-Economic Assignments submitted by IAS Officer Trainees of Lal Bahadur Shastri National Academy of Administration, Mussoorie. Five eminent scholars has compiled the assignments from the year 2003 to 2010 and written State papers on the basis of these assignments. The States covered under these assignments are Maharashtra, Karnataka, Kerala, Andhra Pradesh (including Telengana) and Bihar. These State papers bring out the present status of the rural development of the States covered and also demarcate the strength and weakness in the development process. I would like to appreciate the cooperation and contribution made my the Officer Trainees, scholars and especially Dr. Sucha Singh Gill who accepted the task of editing the volume. The initiative taken by Dr. Varunendra Vikram Singh, faculty, Centre for Rural Studies are also accredited. I hope that this volume will attest to be of immense importance for reference readings of the planners, policy-makers and academicians.

Dr. Prem Singh, *IAS*

Lal Bahadur Shastri National Academy of Administration (Govt. of India) Mussoorie - 248179
EPABX : (0135) 2222000, 2632374, 2632489, 2632405, 2632236, 2632367 Fax : (0135) 2632350, 2332720
Website: http://www.lbsnaa.gov.in

Preface

The Socio-Economic development of India is experienced very fast especially during the last three and half decades. The tempo of development is different for different sectors of economy as divided into primary (agriculture and allied activities), secondary and tertiary sectors. The pace of development of agriculture and allied activities has been very slow compared to that of secondary and tertiary sectors. Consequently, the weight of agriculture and allied activities has gone down in GDP from nearly 30 per cent in 1991-92 to less than 14 per cent in 2012-13. The fall in the share in GDP of agriculture is not accompanied by the corresponding fall in the share of employment in the country which is still close to 50 per cent (2011-12). This has made people living in the rural areas at the position of comparative disadvantage compared to the population living in the urban areas. This development trend has set in motion the process of massive migration from the rural to urban areas.

The Centre for Rural Studies, LBSNAA has been bringing out publication of Socio-Economic Profile of Rural India series in this context to look at the impact of socio-economic development on the overall rural development of the country.

Sucha Singh Gill

Varunendra Vikram Singh

Acknowledgements

I would like to express my gratitude to the many people who provided support, offered comments and assisted in the proof reading and design of the volume. It would not have been possible without the kind support and help of many resource persons. This volume is an outcome of the socio-economic assignments submitted by the IAS Officer Trainees during the year 2003 to 2010. I am highly thankful to all these IAS Officer Trainees. I would like to extend my sincere thanks to Sri Padamvir Singh, the Director and Chairman of the Centre for Rural Studies, LBS National Academy of Administration, Mussoorie. I am also thankful to Dr. Prem Singh, Centre Director, Centre for Rural Studies, who motivated and provided all support beginning with compilation of socio-economic reports, selection of resource persons for writing the state papers to the final design of the volume and its publication.

Finally, I would like to acknowledge with gratitude the support and cooperation of my colleagues from the Centre for Rural Studies.

Dr. Varunendra Vikram Singh
Centre for Rural Studies,
LBS National Academy of Administration,
Mussoorie, Uttarakhand

Contents

List of Box

List of Figures

List of Tables

List of Contributors

C.E. Ajith Kumar, Department of Agricultural Extension, College of Agriculture, Vellayani-685 522, Thiruvananthapuram, Kerala.

Prof. Qamar Ahsan, Professor of Economics, Magadh University, M-2/7, Sri Krishna Puri, Boring Road, Patna-800 001, Bihar.

Prof. S.N. Tripathy, Professor of Economic Gokhale Institute of Politics & Economics, Pune-411 004, Maharashtra.

T. Prabhakara Reddy, Senior Research Officer Regional Centre for Urban and Environmental Studies, Osmania University, Hyderabad (Telengana).

Prof. Tamanna Maqbool Shah, Former Assistant Professor, Centre for Rural Studies, LBS National Academy of Administration Mussoorie-248 179, Uttarakhand.

1

Socio-Economic Development of Rural India

An Introduction

SUCHA SINGH GILL

The overwhelming majority of people of India live in the rural areas. Without improving the quality of life and living standards and provision of protection of vulnerability of the rural masses, the country cannot make a legitimate claim to inclusive growth. During the period of planned development India has taken several initiatives to make rural areas as a part of her development process. It began with the new thrust of rural development with four major pillars in early 1950s. They were: (i) land reforms, (ii) community development programme, (iii) cooperative credit societies, and (iv) public investment in multi-purpose projects for irrigation, flood control and power generation. The main responsibility of the rural development was given to village panchayat as an agency to provide the necessary leadership. This was followed by introduction of green revolution technology in 1960s to meet food scarcity. In view of prevailing massive poverty among the weaker sections in the rural areas especially agricultural labourers, marginal and small farmers got attention of the policy planners and two agencies were born in 1971. They were: (i) Marginal Farmers and Agricultural Labour Agency (MAFALA) and Small Farmers Development Agency (SFDA). They were merged into Integrated Rural Development Programme (IRDP) in 1978. Later on a large number of programmes were started and at present seven flagship programmes are operating in the rural areas. They are: (i) Mahatma Gandhi National Rural Employment Guarantee Act (MGNREGA), (ii) National Rural Livelihood Mission (NRLM), (iii) Indira Awas Yojana (IAY), (iv) National Rural Drinking Water Programme (NRDWP) and Total Sanitation Programme (TSP), (v) Integrated Watershed Development Programme (IWDP), (vi) Pradhan Mantri Grameen Sadak Yojana (PMGSY), and (vii) Rural Electrification and Rajiv Gandhi Grameen Vidyutikaran Yojana (RGGVY). Along with the development programmes the 73rd Amendment of the Constitution has made Panchayati Raj Institutions as the statutory third tier of the government. The elections to PRIs are held after every five years with statutory reservations for SCs/STs and women for elected positions. The PRIs especially Gram Panchayats have been made nodal agencies for implementation of the rural development programmes. Along with the rural development Gram Panchayats are involved in identification of the target groups for social protection measures such as old age pension, beneficiaries under IAY, PDS, NRLM, TSP (renamed as Swatch Bharat Mission) etc. (Planning Commission, 2012). This volume contains five state papers written by scholars based on IAS probationers/Trainees village reports and data from other sources. These scholars have been identified by Centre for Rural Studies of the LBSNAA for this purpose. These papers cover the states of Maharashtra, Karnataka, Kerala, Andhra Pradesh and Telengana, Bihar to bring out the socio-economic profile of these states.

The working of socio-economic system for the last sixty five years or more and interventions by the government have raised the level of expectations of the rural people and their response to various policy initiatives. There has been shift from the subsistence rural economy to commercialized economy. This has weakened community feeling and support with breakup of Jajmani system. In the working of rural economy private economic interests, viz. profits and wages, dominate decision-making. There is great awakening of economic interests both among employers and the workers in farming and non-farm activities in rural India. There is awakening among the SCs/STs and women towards their rights and participation in social and economic activities. The rural economy's capacity to absorb labour is diminishing in view of increasing mechanization of agriculture. This has set in motion the process of both seasonal and long term migration of workforce to urban areas in India and abroad. The weakening of economic and caste bonds have contributed significantly to the mobility of workforce from the rural areas. The links of rural areas are fast expanding with urban India through exchange of commodities and mobility of population through better and increased connectivity. The penetration of mobile phones, social media, electronic and print media along with personal mobility of the workforce and rural population have brought a new awakening in the rural areas. The new awakening and diminishing economic opportunities have weakened the hold of traditional dominant classes and castes over the rural society. A new power balance in the rural economy and society is in the process of transition and making. Rural population is aspiring and demanding urban facilities in the rural areas. At this juncture it is worth to record the changes which are taking place in the rural India. India is a large country with vast variations in the pace and level of rural transformation, it provides an opportunity to record changes in the various parts of the country. This has been attempted by the scholars in the state papers.

Chapter on Maharashtra by S.N. Tripathy is largely based on secondary data along with data from the 20 village reports of IAS trainees. The state belongs to the one of highest per capita income state in the country. It is more industrialized and urbanized compared to all-India average. In 2001 the rural population was 57.6 per cent of the total compared to urban population of 42.4 per cent. In literacy also the state has higher rate compared to the All India average. Around 55 per cent of the working population depends on agriculture, but the share of agriculture in the GSDP is just 12 per cent. The incidence of poverty (31.7%) especially rural poverty is high and it is close to all-India average. There is lot of inter-district variation in the incidence of rural poverty ranging from 72.00 per cent of the households in Nandurbar district and 15.97 per cent in Sitara district. Our districts fell in this range in incidence of rural poverty. There is also variation in concentration of backward population (SC/ST) and districts of Nasik, Thane, Nandurbar, Ahmednagar, Yavatman and Amravati show high concentration of this population. Similarly, the lowest literacy is found in Nandurbar (56%) followed by Gadchiroli (60%) and Jalana (64%). Thus, Maharashtra presents a paradox of richness and poverty in the state both between rural and urban areas and across different districts spread in the three major regions, namely Konkan, Marathwada and Vidarbha.

Agriculture is the major source of livelihood for rural population. Agriculture is mainly rain-fed and area under irrigation is only 17 per cent of the total compared to 41 per cent for India as a whole. About one-third of the state area falls under rain shadow where rainfall is very less. The rain-fed agriculture shows very low level of crop yield compared to other states. But cropping pattern is changing from cereals to non-cereal cash crops such as sugarcane and horticulture crops. The holding size in agriculture of the state is dominated by the small and marginal cultivators and they account for 73.7 per cent of the holdings. Another 10 per cent are nearly landless households. These cultivators are poor and majority of them are unviable and lack resources for investment in agriculture. Thus, the benefits of agricultural growth are not equally distributed across social groups and regions which partly explains the incidence of high poverty in rural Maharashtra. Agricultural labourers are another major category of workers engaged in agriculture. In the off season, they face acute shortage of work and migrate to the cities and also to other state to supplement their earnings. But in some villages there is emergence of non-farm employment due to diversification of activities in the rural areas especially in agro-processing, transport and construction activities.

The author also brings out that Maharashtra has secured the better position in the country for effective implementation of Panchayati Raj System in the rural areas and was among the first to implement 33 per cent reservation for women in local bodies elections. The state stood ahead of others in its implementation of Pradhan Mantri Gram Sadak Yojana, empowerment of women and MGNREGS. But major flaw in the rural development of the state remains disproportionate distribution of benefits across different social groups and geographic regions. The regional disparity is found in incidence of rural poverty and there are critical gaps in health care delivery system, infant mortality rate, maternal and child health. There is also disparate need for better staffed primary health centres and schools. There is an urgent need to concentrate efforts especially on the backward communities such as SCs and STs. It is noted by the author that rural employment programme or poverty alleviating rural development schemes could not get success due to several reasons. It is observed that the allocated amount is not wholly spent, there are leakages and misappropriation of funds at different stages and only 20 per cent of the funds percolate to the grassroots level. These factors have created disparity in the distribution of income and wealth in the rural areas as less investment is made than the allocated investment. Thus, investment does not create sufficient income and employment for the poor. The misappropriation of funds leads to increase in the income of those who are not entitled for benefits from such programme. The main reason for this is that unlike Andhra Pradesh villages there is not the sufficient mobilization of the poor to collectively assert for their rights and check corruption in the implementation of the poverty alleviation programmes (Reddy, 2016). The village reports mention unemployment in the villages as a major problem for the poor farmers and agricultural labourers leading to their migration to the cities and rural areas of other regions within Maharashtra and also to the neighbouring states. This indicates a large scope for further implementation of poverty alleviation programmes in the villages of the state.

Chapter on Karnataka by Temanna M. Shah begins with the history of formation of the state in 1956 by including some areas of Hyderabad State, Bombay Presidency, Madras Presidency and Coorg, Mysore and host of small states and was named as Mysore state. Its present name was given in 1973. After discussing the geography and history of the state, the author brings out disparity in literacy rates and educational infrastructure, availability of water supply and agricultural productivity between Hyderabad-Karnataka (dry region) and Southern Karnataka. The growth of employment is largely concentrated in Bangalore Urban, Dakshina Kannada, Dharwad, Kopal, Mysore and Raichur districts. The districts of Bidar, Bijapur, Gulbarga and Raichur have shown negative growth. All the districts with negative growth are located in north Karnataka. The study of livelihood conditions brings out that the economic activities are dominated by agriculture in the rural areas. The possession of land and other assets determines the nature of employment. The land is an important production asset and its owners are in self-employment and landlessness leads to casual or regular agricultural labour employment. The occupation-wise analysis of employment in households in villages shows self-employment is dominant in agriculture. A large proportion of sample households are employed as either cultivators or agricultural labourers. The small and marginal farmers generally combine cultivation with wage employment to get minimum livelihood. Small and marginal holdings account for 75 per cent of the total holdings and they operate 37 per cent of the area. The semi-medium, medium and large holdings together account for

25 per cent of the total holdings and operate 63 per cent of the area. The average size of the holdings is 1.63 hectares and the holdings operating less than 1.0 hectare account for 42 per cent of the total holdings. A large number of holdings are becoming unviable and land areas are turning from agricultural to non-agricultural uses and a large number of farmers and agricultural labourers are now entering non-agricultural activities. This is giving rise to low productivity, degraded soil in cultivation and eventually shrinkage of land under agriculture. The village studies by IAS trainees also point towards shrinkage of employment opportunities leading to out-migration from the rural areas. The shrinking role of tanks and canal irrigation and increasing role of bore-wells and tubewells, introduction of machinery are leading to decline in employment in agriculture. In some of the villages, especially in the Cauvery delta area water intensive crops like paddy are still predominantly sown over large area causing land degradation and also fall in ground water level. Some of the farmers especially along the roads are resorting to floriculture and palm oil as alternative to water intensive crops. If the state is considered as a whole agriculture continues to be a major source of livelihood in the rural areas and primary sector (including allied activities) account for 17.20 per cent of GSDP and agriculture employs more than 56.8 per cent of the workforce in 2009-10. This is in spite of the fact that Karnataka has done well in horticultural crops like coffee, cocoa, spices and fruits and has taken large number of initiatives in storage, cold chains and marketing institutions. Karnataka has made a rapid strides in its literacy level compared to many other states in India—and all-India average. Among the southern states (including Karnataka) which are front runners in literacy in the country, Karnataka lags behind Kerala and Tamil Nadu but is ahead of Andhra Pradesh (including Telengana). Notwithstanding such an achievement, nearly one quarter of its population is illiterate as per 2011 Census. There is gender bias in literacy as about one-third of females in the state have remained illiterate. Three districts, namely Chamarjanagara, Raichur and Yadgir have literacy rates below national average. The village reports point out deficiency in the infrastructure such as shortage of classrooms, lack of toilets, lack of proper functioning of Mid-Day Meal programme leading to high dropout rates. It is also reported that literacy rates are low among SC/ST communities and their children experience high dropout rates due to poverty, migration, child labour, parent apathy and lack of interest among the children. It is

reported that Karnataka has taken several initiatives in rural sanitation and water supply, such as the Karnataka Ground Water Act, 1999, Swajaldhara, Nirmala Grama Yojana, Swachh Grama Programme, National River Conservation Plan and Sampurana Nairmalya Yojana. Still more than 50 per cent of the rural households in seven districts have less than 55 litres per capita per day water supply. In the drought prone 9 districts more than 30 per cent of rural habitations do not have access to 55 litres of per capita per day water. The village reports point towards deficiencies in the public health facilities due to shortage of power supply, leading to problem of storing of medicines and injections, and absenteeism of staff. This has led to marked presence of quacks in the villages. Poverty alleviation remains one of the objectives of rural development of Karnataka. This has also resulted in marked decline in poverty in the state. The state has started Swarnjayanti Swarozgar Yojana (SGSY) to promote asset endowment of the poor, Sampoorna Grameen Rozgar Yojana (SGRY) to provide employment opportunities and PDS to provide subsidised foodgrains to the poor. This has been supplemented by the efforts to provide affordable housing to the poor. In order to weed out the fake beneficiaries the State Government carried out an elaborate exercise to verify the ration cards and enhance the targeting of PDS. These measures have achieved some success over time. However, the reduction in poverty has not been uniform across districts. The city of Bangalore alone contributes around 22 per cent of GSDP. Bijapur along with Bidar, Gulbarga and Raichur districts continues to be poorest in terms of per capita income with high incidence of poverty. Some of the village reports point towards involvement of contractors in the schemes for employment generation and discrepancies in BPL lists and roll book of employment, suggesting better monitoring and evaluation of schemes. Karnataka is ahead of many states in terms of the powers and functions delegated to the PRIs. The listed 29 functions in the Eleventh Schedule of the Constitution have been devolved to panchayats in three separate schedules each for gram panchayat, taluk panchayat and zilla panchayat. They prepare annual plans, annual budgets, sectoral schemes for agriculture, animal husbandry, rural housing, drinking water, roads and bridges, rural electrification, education, public health, sanitation, women and child development, social welfare, maintenance of community assets, promotion of libraries etc. The working of PRIs is less constrained and is more flexible for innovations. There is reservation for SC/ST and women in elected positions. Due to proper devolution of functions and funds on scientific basis PRIs are functioning much better than in most of the states in the country. In gram panchayat meeting members of women SHGs try and assert their position. But distortions in some villages have been pointed out in village reports. They pertain to discharge of duties of elected women in panchayats by their husbands, overlooking identification of beneficiaries at the margin above the fixed earning level, use of money and liquor in elections and consequently improper implementation of schemes leading to corruption or providing benefits to non-eligible persons on partisan basis. Some of these problems have also been observed by some scholars working on Karnataka (Kadekodi 2011:141-155; Deshpande and Raju, 2011: 499-522). These drawbacks can be eliminated by proper monitoring and evaluation of the implementation especially through social audit and by mobilization of beneficiaries through enhancement of their awareness of rights for assertion in the Gram Sabha meetings. Generally speaking, the author concludes that Karnataka has succeeded in affecting significant improvement in the living conditions of the rural people.

The chapter by C.E. Ajith Kumar covers rural development of Kerala. It starts with the Constitutional position that all persons have the right to an adequate means of livelihood, distribution of material resource in a manner as best to subserve the common good and operation of economic system does not result in the concentration of wealth and means of production to the common detriment. The evolution of various rural development programmes over the last 50 years has been traced and fast rate of decline in poverty in Kerala is recorded in comparison to all-India level. The number one position of Kerala in HDI in the country is brought out in terms of various indicators.

The author traces the history of formation of Kerala state in 1956 on linguistic basis by merging the Malayalam speaking regions such as Thiru-Kochi state, Malabar district of Madras Presidency and South Kanana taluk of Kasaragod. Details of administrative structure in terms of number of districts, revenue divisions, taluks, community development blocks and revenue villages have been provided and description of topography and quality of soil have been stated as a background to agriculture development and food security. It is stated that Kerala has high per hectare yield in foodgrains compared to all-

India average still the area under foodgrains is shrinking and it has continued to remain as food deficit state. The state has moved away from the foodgrain (rice) cultivation to plantation crops, such as coconut and rubber. Southern districts are richer compared to the northern districts of the State. The high level of human development indicators in the state is attributed to the legacy of public action. This has been crucial to the Kerala's inclusive development. Kerala Land Reforms (Amendment) Act, 1969 was a landmark legislation that abolished long established landlordism in the State. It provided for vesting in private land in excess of a prescribed limit to the government for distribution among the landless population in the rural areas. It also prohibited tenancy in land cultivation. The author has provided a detailed chart of evolution of land settlement since 1738. The revenue administration of the village has been described elaborately and it is stated that the record of the land of the village is maintained at the village level office. The village level offices in Kerala are housed in well constructed offices. In view of emerging problem of the space, computerization of land records is going on at a fast pace. The recent experiments of democratization is qualified as a direct attempt at deepening democracy in the state with augmentation of the space for public action and people's participation in the rural Kerala. These changes were brought under Kerala Panchayati Raj Act, 1994 and its amendments in 1999 as recommended by S.B. Sen Committee in 1996. The Amendment Act of 1999 and People's Plan Campaign ushered in a new phase of decentralization of governance in Kerala. It was a process which devolved functions and resources of the state to the elected local self-governments to facilitate direct participation of citizens in fixing local priorities, identification of the schemes, selection of beneficiaries and monitoring of implementation of these schemes. The entire process was completed by the end of Eleventh Five Year Plan ending on 31st March, 2012. According to the author, 20.65 to 33.33 per cent of the state's plan funds are transferred in the form of grant in aid to the local self-governments, i.e. PRIs and ULBs. The average of 15 years (1997-98 to 2011-12) works out to be 24.98 per cent. This is a unique feature of decentralized governance and development specific to Kerala and is not observed in any other state in India. Although the target of transfer of 30-40 per cent of the funds envisioned in the PRI Act of 1994 and Amendment Act of 1999 is not achieved yet the level achieved in Kerala (25%) is not a mean achievement when one compares it with other states in the country.

Apart from the state transfers as grant-in-aid, the panchayats are empowered to impose professional tax, entertainment tax, vehicle tax, license fee on shops, market fee, rent on government buildings, sale proceed on plantation at public lands and stamp duty on transactions of lands. The panchayats pay salaries to its employees and spend nearly 50 per cent on establishment expenditure head. The rest is spent on roads, services like public health/sanitation-water supply, drainage, street lights. Thus, panchayats in Kerala are autonomous for power to collect taxes, receive grant-in-aid from the state plan fund and also to decide and spend the financial resources as per local priorities and preferences of the citizens. This model is worth emulation in other states of the country.

There are 15 village study reports by IAS probationers which have provided some information on the various aspects of rural development. But many of these reports are not comparable in information. The data have been used from other sources to make observations on rural development. The village studies did not cover all the districts in the state. The studies covered four panchayats each from the Ernakulam and Kozhikode, two from Kollam and one each from Kannur, Palakkad and Thrissur while two probationers repeated studies in the Kannur and Ernakulam districts. Some of the village studies have provided information on living conditions of some specific section of village population in true colour and detail so that these cases are models to replicate in a developing society. These reports bring out that all villages except one have favourable sex-ratio to women but child sex-ratio is favourable to males in all villages. The employment pattern in the villages brings out that very few persons take up cultivation. Workforce in agriculture as cultivators and agricultural labourers is only a miniscule presentation in the workers population in the state. All villages have more than two-third of population of non-workers. Female participation in workforce is considerably lower than males in all occupations. The share of women non-workers is almost double compared to their male counterparts. The village reports have presented a high incidence of morbidity and malnourishment. Kerala being located in the humid tropical region with two annual monsoons leading to heavy rainfall for 5-6 months in a year, the incidence of water borne seasonal diseases is high and hospitals record a large number of such diseases in these months. Kerala has achieved high indicators of social and economic development as reflected in high (number one) rank of the state in the country. The rural areas of Kerala have better public health care facilities compared to other states in the country. It is reported that slowly the preference for government health care is declining and people are shifting towards private healthcare system. This is also happening in case of school education where a large number of children from the rural areas are opting for private (unaided) English medium schools. This can be explained by high level of income which Kerala has achieved in the wake of out-migration to Gulf countries (Kannan, 2011: 157-176). The SHG of women has presence in most of the villages in the form of institution of Kutumbashree. They are engaging women in self-employment activities such as catering, traditional arts and trainings. This has helped in empowerment of women and increased their participation in decision-making. The mobilization of rural population and their participation in PRIs has put Kerala on top position in HDI. This has also increased their assertion in decision-making especially of women. The PRIs are collecting a large amount of resources on their own through tax collection as well as from the State Government through statutory devolution of funds, functionaries and functions. This has made PRIs as formidable institutions. It is worth mentioning that although there is scope of improvement yet the state presents a model of social and economic transformation of rural areas (Isaac and Frank, 2000: 286-303).

Chapter on Andhra Pradesh by T. Prabhakara Reddy covers both the present state of Andhra Pradesh and state of Telengana. The author begins with a positive note that Andhra Pradesh (including Telengana) is blessed by a bounty of natural resource and is endowed with fertile land and conducive agro climatic conditions. It is opined that it is an agriculturally prosperous state and ranks as among the largest producer of foodgrains, vegetables, cotton, maize, dairy and poultry products and is leading state in agro-based industries such as sugar, edible oil, sea food etc. The state is also ranked second in the country in mineral resources. This chapter helps in understanding the rural development in the state in the light of some policy initiatives started by the Union Government. The author has examined the rural development status by dividing it into three units, viz. Telengana, Coastal Andhra and Rayalaseema. Most of the observations are based on 24 village reports of IAS trainees. It is brought that there is a spatial variation in the land use and agriculture in the state. In Telengana and Rayalaseema the land use pattern is skewed and net sown area is limited due to lack of proper irrigation facilities, but land used for agriculture is large and intensive in coastal Andhra because of assured and proper irrigation facilities. In all the three regions of the state tenancy is in vogue but it is largely oral in nature. The tenants are vulnerable and face threat of eviction and pay fixed cash rent followed by share cropping in Telengana and Rayalaseema, but pay largely cash rent in coastal Andhra. In the case of crop failure due to natural calamity they do not get compensation from the government. They are also unable to access credit from the banks. The Land Licensed Cultivators Act, 2012 was passed in Andhra Pradesh to protect and help the tenants and also to protect the land owner, who has faced the problems of implementation. The dynamism of capitalist agriculture has made small and marginal farmers unviable, many of them are leaving agriculture and becoming agricultural labourers. Many among these farmers when fall in debt trap commit suicide. There is alienation of land from the poor land allottees. There are reports of continuous alienation of tribal land by the non-tribals and also by the state for private industries, mining and infrastructure projects.

There is improvement in the literacy in the rural areas and in villages literacy rate is above the national average. It is commonly observed that in many villages the schools are functioning but there is a shortage of teachers and teachers lack commitment. Earlier there was lack of toilets especially for girls in the school but facilities have improved under SSA (Sarva Shiksha Abhiyan). The situation is relatively good in coastal Andhra, relatively bad in Rayalaseema and mixed in Telengana. The same is the story of health facilities and sanitation. These facilities are good in Coastal Andhra villages but they are poor in Telengana and Rayalaseema. The people incur heavy out of pocket expenditure to access private healthcare.

On poverty alleviation programmes, the Andhra Pradesh has done well due to the commitment of the government and social mobilization in the state. A large number of programmes such as SGSY, IAY, Old/ Widow/Disabled Pensions, SHGs, MGNREGS, Rajiv Arogyasri, Scholarships and fee reimbursement, Rs. 2 per kg. Rice, free power to small and marginal farmers and issue of *patta* to the landless have immensely benefited below poverty line population. They have obtained facilities like housing, employment and health among others. The village reports have brought out that SGSY self-help groups (SHGs) have been formed, nurtured and linked to banks for obtaining loans for livelihood purposes. It is reported that SHGs are functioning like movement in all the villages of the state leading to empowerment of women in taking decisions, spending their earning and saving for the future. SHGs in the state have displayed sustainable model in poverty reduction. The strength of this model lies in commitment of the government and social mobilization of the beneficiaries in the state. The successful implementation of MGNREGA all over the state has helped in arresting the distress migration from the rural areas especially in the Rayalaseema region. It has increased the bargaining power of the agricultural labourers and brought equality in the wage rate of men and women. The SC and ST families have benefited substantially. In some areas ground water table has improved; there is also improvement in road connectivity, afforestation and tanks have been renovated for improving irrigation efficiency. Some of the village studies bring out that selection of works and allotment works to job card holders have been done in Gram Sabha in a transparent manner. But in some villages in Coastal Andhra a few problems have been observed both in implementation of MGNREGS and IAY leading to less than expected achievement in these programmes. The functioning of panchayats is reported to be varying across different regions of the state depending upon the local conditions. Generally, the financial position of panchayats is good and many panchayats have shown surplus budget due to tax compliance of the people. Gram Sabhas are held regularly in some panchayats while in others there is irregularity. In some panchayats male members of families of elected women perform panchayat functions on behalf of the women. Although functioning of panchayat display a mixed bag in performance yet mobilization of the beneficiaries in the state for poverty alleviation has produced good result for rural development in the state. Andhra Pradesh (including Telengana) is emerging as a model for the rest of the country for effective implementation of rural development programme. These conclusions are supported by other scholars from Andhra Pradesh (Reddy, 2013: 117-163; Vijay, 2013: 164-204).

The chapter by Qamar Ahsan attempts to capture socio-economic profile of rural Bihar. This chapter begins by providing historical background to separation of the state from Bengal in 1912, carving out Orissa from it in 1935 and Jharkhand in 2000. Using comparative sectoral share in the state gross domestic product, the author has presented the position of agriculture and allied activities in Bihar from 1950-51 when its share was 63.34 per cent. This share declined to 51.77 per cent in 1979-80 and 36.5 per cent in 2003-04 and stood at 22.1 per cent during 2008-11. Such a fall in the share of primary sector mainly that of agriculture in income, it absorbs 78 per cent of the workforce. This makes people engaged in agriculture poor and vulnerable. As per Tendulkar Committee Report, 55.7 per cent of rural households in Bihar are estimated to be below poverty line. Most of the small and marginal peasants from the OBC and agricultural labour households mainly from SCs/STs and Muslims are living below poverty line. The higher poverty and vulnerability have worsened the human development indicators. This demands state intervention to moderate poverty in the rural areas. This chapter is primarily based on the village reports of 38 IAS trainees from Bihar. These villages are spread over diverse economic and agro-climatic zones and provide a representative profile of the rural economy of the state. Bihar state is highly rural as 88 per cent of its population live in the rural areas and urban population is just 12 per cent of the total. There is a common pattern of study based on structured questionnaire for collection of information specifically on (i) rural infrastructure, (ii) agrarian relations, (iii) social structure, (iv) economic activities (livelihood), (v) poverty alleviation and rural development, and (vi) Panchayati Raj Institutions. Most of the village reports are written around these sub-themes.

In rural infrastructure rural road connectivity, electricity, education, health facilities, sanitation and integrated child development schemes have been discussed. Investment in the rural infrastructure is a precondition for development of productive activities. The availability of all-weather roads is essential for connectivity of rural production with the market and towns both for output disposal as well as acquisition of inputs for commercial agriculture and access of urban services for the village people. The status of rural roads in Bihar is a matter of serious concern. Not only the per capita availability of road is very low but quality is extremely poor. A large number of villages especially in North Bihar remains cut off with other parts during the monsoon. This is also the case with villages located at greater distance from the national highways. Although there has been some improvement during the last one decade or more, the road connectivity of the rural areas remains very poor. Similarly, electricity connectivity has improved under Rajiv Gandhi Grameen Vidyutikarana Yojana (RGGVY) and it is reported that 65 per cent of the villages in Bihar are connected with electricity. But, the supply of electricity is irregular forcing many farmers to use costly diesel pump sets, denying access to the small and marginal farmers. In the villages it is reported that electricity connections are mostly in *pucca* houses of upper castes or the landed OBCs. The SCs and landless labourers usually have low or no electricity connections in their houses. Bihar has made a significant progress in literacy rate which has increased from 22.0 per cent in 1961 to 63.8 per cent in 2011. The gender gap in literacy has also decreased but there remains very low literacy rate among SCs and STs. There also remains high inter-district differentials in literacy rate. While Rohtas district has a literacy rate of 75.6 per cent for Purnea it is just 52.5 per cent. There is also progress in the narrowing down of rural-urban differentials in the literacy rates. The village studies bring out that although enrollment ratio has gone up in the rural schools yet dropout rate is very high especially among the OBCs, SCs and minorities. The reported dropout rate at the primary level is 42.5 per cent in 2009-10 and very high at 58.8 per cent at upper primary level during this year. Three main reasons are reported for high dropout rate of the students: (i) parents do not consider schools as learning centres due to high absenteeism among the teachers; (ii) discouraging social and economic environment at home especially for girls; and (iii) deficiencies in school infrastructure. Like other parts of the rural India private schools have come up in several Bihar villages where children from upper castes and upper class study but are beyond the reach of lower caste poor people. In the area of rural health Bihar has done well during the last decade and half. There is significant reduction in death rate and infant mortality rate. Despite limitations of infrastructure the crude death rate has fallen below all-India average and infant mortality rate has nearly achieved national level in 2011. These improvements are due to increase in coverage of immunization, more institutional deliveries, better use of healthcare facilities and increased investment flows for NRHM and other schemes of the State Government. But inadequacies in the rural healthcare and huge gap in the health delivery, the people are now spending a large amount to access private healthcare from private practitioners and poor among them borrow from the money-lenders for accessing private healthcare. This is accompanied by poor sanitation conditions and most of the people defecate in the open. The practice of open defecation is influenced by social conditioning, lack of awareness and high cost of toilets especially for poor households. This is one of the causes of spread of diseases and infection. This requires a widespread campaign for sanitation supported by financial help to construct private and community toilets in the villages. Similarly, there are ICDS (Integrated Child Development Services) and AWCs (Anganwari Women Centres) established in the state for improving health, nutrition and skill of women. But inadequacy in the ICDS and AWCs in far-flung areas is not fulfilling this purpose. Bihar remains a state where highest proportion of the poor live in the country. The proportion of rural households as per Tendulkar Committee report in the rural Bihar was 55.7 per cent compared to 41.8 per cent at all-India level in 2004-05. The poverty count is more complex as there exists regional variation in the level of deprivation indicating acute poverty in North Bihar and Seemanchal compared to Central and Western Bihar. The incidence of poverty and deprivation is very high among SCs/STs, Muslims and landless labourer households. It is distressing to note that at national level poverty shows declining trend but it is rising in Bihar. This requires special consideration for policy-makers. The field reports suggest that rural poverty and unemployment are intertwined with dismal growth, low productivity and subsistence nature of agriculture. The poverty alleviation schemes like the Swarnjayanti Gramin Swarozgar Yojana (SGSY) through self-help groups (SHGs) is not properly working in the state. MGNREGS is also performing poorly in the state. The impact of these two flagship schemes is very low due to large scale corruption and insufficient monitoring. A concerted effort is need to reverse the trend of rising poverty in Bihar.

The introduction of decentralized governance in the state through Bihar Act of 2006 has improved the awareness among different sections of rural population and the level of their participation has increased. The government has entrusted village panchayats with planning and implementation of schemes but hardly any proper planning takes place. The implementation takes place through the nexus of heads of PRIs at different levels, bureaucracy and contractors. The decisions are taken without consultation with Gram Sabha. Corruption is rampant and partisan nature in implementation is evident at grassroots level. But, with increasing participation of SCs and women in panchayat affairs, it is expected that grassroots democracy will be strengthened and PRIs will play positive role in achievement of decentralized development. The winds of change are blowing in the rural Bihar especially in agricultural development, rural connectivity, access to electricity and also consumption pattern (Rodger *et al.*, 2013: 199-216; Gupta Shekhar, 2015: 16-19).

The chapter in this volume bring out variations between different states on the socio-economic rural profile. On one end there is Kerala state which has experienced fast rate of economic change and attained highest HDI in the country, whereas Bihar remains lowest in per capita income and HDI. Other states fall in between the levels of development. Within each state including Kerala and Bihar there are districts which show better performance and compared to low performing districts. The scholars present not only on spatial dispersion but also reflect different perspectives on recording change. Similarly, there is a large variation in the coverage and quality of data covered by IAS probationers/trainees in their reports. This is also reflected in the quality coverage of recording of socio-economic change in different state papers. At the same time the state papers reflect a vast variation in the level of awareness and awakening of the rural people and their assertion for rights and share in rural development. Again contrast seems far greater between Kerala and Bihar while other states fall in between. In spite of state differences it is evident that change is visible in the rural development across states in the form of road connectivity, electrification, employment generation, social protection in the form of old age pension, housing support and participation in PRIs decision-making. This can be made more effective and better managed by committed political leadership, awakened bureaucracy and mobilized beneficiaries at local level. In the absence of any of these elements change become slow and chaotic. The collection of these papers can be useful for policy-makers, scholars of rural development and mobilisers of rural masses at grassroots level.

BIBLIOGRAPHY

Isaac, T.M. Thomas with Franke, Richard W. (2000), *The Local Democracy and Development: People's Campaign for Decentralized Planning*, Leftword, New Delhi, pp. 286-303.

Deshpande, R.S. and K.V. Raju (2011), "Monitoring Poverty and Human Development Indicators", in R.S. Deshpande *et al.* (Eds.), *Development Windows*, Academic Foundations, New Delhi, pp. 499-522.

Gupta, Shekhar (2015), "Gen Gana Mana of Youth", *Outlook*, November 16, pp. 16-19.

Kannan, K.P. (2011), "Kerala's Turn Around in Growth Role of Social Development, Remittances and Reform", in R.S. Deshpande *et al.* (Eds.) *Development Windows, op. cit.*, pp. 157-176.

Kedekodi, Gopal K. (2011), "Some Recent Developments on Measures of Quality of Life" in R.S. Deshpande, *et al.*, (Eds.), *Development Window, op. cit.*, pp. 141-155.

Planning Commission (2012), *Twelfth Five Year Plan*, Vol. II, Government of India, New Delhi, pp. 286-287.

Rodger, Gerry, *et al.*, (2013), *The Challenges of Inclusive Development in Rural Bihar*, Manak Publications, New Delhi, pp. 199-216.

Reddy, D.N. (2013), "Functioning of NREGS in Andhra Pradesh", in K.P. Kannan and Jan Breman (Eds.), *The Long Road to Social Security*, OUP, New Delhi, pp. 117-163.

Vijay, G. (2013), "The Business of Healthcare and the Challenge of Health Security: The Case of Rajiv Aarogyasri Community Health Insurance Scheme in Andhra Pradesh", in K.P. Kannan and Jan Breman, Eds. *op. cit.*, pp. 164-204.

2

Rural Development in the State of Maharashtra

S.N. TRIPATHY

This chapter makes an effort to outline briefly the demographic, health and education profile of rural Maharashtra. Besides, it encompasses agrarian relations and cropping pattern, occupational and social structure in the framework of existing rural poverty in the state, the performance of Panchayati Raj, the impact of anti-poverty and rural development programme through Government initiative in the state of Maharashtra.

INTRODUCTION

In fact, the Maharashtra state paper is documented on the basis of secondary sources of data, literature available from books, journals, reports, statistical hand book and substantially supported by village survey papers prepared by young IAS officers during 2003-09, who have made field visits to such villages.

Apparently, those IAS officers/probationaries were not professional researchers and therefore, the reports submitted by them as a part fulfilment of their assignments have some limitations, which one has to reckon with.

MAHARASHTRA STATE SITUATIONAL ANALYSIS

Demographic Profile of the State

The state of Maharashtra is located in western India, with a geographical area of 3.08 lakh square kilometres and size is 9.4 per cent of India's geographical area, consisting 35 districts. It is the third largest state in India. As per the census of 2001, the state has a total population of 96.8 million, that is, 9.42 per cent of India's total population. Historically known for its industrialization, the state of Maharashtra has achieved higher economic growth as compared to many other Indian states. The state ranks fourth in terms of per capita income and second in terms of industrial growth during the year 2007-08. Since its formation in 1960, the state per capita NSDP grew at 4.73 per cent till 1999-2000 and after that the rate has slightly declined to 2.43 per cent.

A comparison of the state with India in some demographic and socio-economic features across two time points (1991 and 2001) in Table 2.1 exhibits that in Maharashtra density of population has been lower than the national average, but decennial population growth rate has been 25.7 per cent in Maharashtra whereas it was 23.9 per cent at all-India level during 1990s.

The level of urbanization in 2001 at 42 per cent for Maharashtra is not only higher than the all-India average, but the percentage point difference with the all-India average has also been increasing over the years. The district Gudchiroli has the least urban population of 6.9 per cent followed by Sindhudurg (9.4%) and Ratnagiri (11.33%). There is 100 per cent of urban population in Mumbai, Mumbai sub-urban or its adjacent areas including Thane. The comparatively high population growth in Maharashtra when compared with the all-India average is largely due to its urban component. Decadal increase in population for urban Maharashtra was almost 20 percentage points higher than that for rural Maharashtra in 1980s as well as in the 1990s. The decadal growth of population was 22.6 in Maharashtra which is slightly more than the national average of 21.3 per cent (Tables 2.1 and 2.2).

The proportion of Scheduled Castes (SCs) at 10 per cent was lower by 6 percentage points from the all-India average in 2001 whereas the proportion of Scheduled Tribes (STs) at 9 per cent was greater than the all-India average by 0.5 percentage points. The sex-ratio for Maharashtra declined compared to its increase at the all-India average between 1991 and 2001 (Table 2.1).

It is further revealed from Table 2.2 that Latur has the highest concentration of SC population (19.4%) followed by Bhandara

Table 2.1: Selected Socio-Economic Indicators in Maharashtra and India

Socio-Economic indicators	*1991*		*2001*	
	Maharashtra	*India*	*Maharashtra*	*India*
Geographical area (lakh sq.km.)			3.1	32.9
Total population (millions)	78.9	846.4	96.9	1028.7
Population density (persons per sq.km.)	257.0	267.0	314.0	324.0
Urbanization rate (%)	38.7	25.7	42.4	27.8
Decadal increase, Total (%)	25.7	23.9	22.6	21.3
Decadal increase, Rural (%)	18.6	20.0	15.2	17.9
Decadal increase, Urban (%)	38.9	36.5	34.3	31.2
Proportion, Scheduled Caste (%)	11.1	16.3	10.2	16.2
Proportion, Scheduled Tribe (%)	9.3	8.0	8.9	8.2
Literacyrate, 7+ years (%)	64.9	52.2	77.3	65.4
Gender gap, literacy (%age points)	24.3	24.8	18.8	21.7
Urban-rural gap, literacy (%age points)	23.8	28.4	15.1	21.2
Life expectancy at birth, Female (years)[#]	65.8	60.9	69.8	65.4
Sex ratio (females per '000 males)	934	927	922	933
Sex ratio, 0-6 age (females per '000 males)	946	945	916	927
Birth rate (per '000 persons)[$]	28.0	30.9	19.9	24.8
Death rate (per '000 persons)[$]	9.3	10.6	7.2	8.0
IMR (per '000 live births)[$]	69	87	42	60
Per capita income, current prices (Rs.)[@]	8083	5596	29204	20989
Proportion Below Poverty Line, BPL (%)[†]	36.9	36.0	25.0	26.1
Human Development Index, Value	0.45	0.38	0.52	0.47
Human Development Index, Rank**	4		4	

Note: *Literacy rate for 1981 is for 5+ years of population.

$ The latest data for Birth Rate, Death Rate and Infant Mortality Rate are for the year 2003. IMR indicates infant mortality rate.@ Per Capita Income are for the years 1990-91 and 2003-04 with latest year being provisional estimates for Maharashtra and quick estimates for India.

** Ranks are across 15 major states.

Source: www.indiastat.com and *Economic Survey of Maharashtra*, 2004-05.

(17.7%) and Nanded (17.3%) while the state average for SC population is 10.2 per cent of the total population. Similarly, Nadurbar has the highest percentage of ST population (65.5%) followed by Gadchiroli (38.3%) and Dhule (25.9%) while the state average for ST population is 8.8 per cent of the total population.

Table 2.3 presents the village level data relating to the total population, male and female population, sex-ratio of some of the villages under review. The percentage figure in the parentheses shows

Table 2.2: District-wise Rural-Urban Population and Percentage of SC and ST Population to the Total Population

Sl. No.	*Name of Districts*	*Total Population*			*Percentage of Scheduled Castes to Total Population*	*Percentage of Scheduled Tribes to Total Population*
		Total	*Urban*	*Rural*		
1.	Ahmednagar	4040642	803697 (19.89)	3236945 (80.11)	484685 (12.00)	30325 (0.75)
2.	Akola	1630239	627497 (38.49)	1002742 (61.51)	168447 (10.33)	100088 (6.14)
3.	Amravati	2607160	899579 (34.500	1707581 (65.50)	446623 (17.13)	356533 (13.68)
4.	Aurangabad	2897013	1087150 (37.53)	1809863 (62.47)	376181 (12.99)	100416 (3.47)
5.	Bhandara	1136146	175728 (15.47)	960418 (84.53)	201949 (17.77)	97718 (8.60)
6.	Beed	2161250	387070 (17.91)	1774180 (82.09)	281240 (13.01)	24193 (1.12)
7.	Buldhana	2232480	473383 (21.20)	1759097 (78.80)	241623 (10.82)	115156 (5.16)
8.	Chandrapur	2071101	665067 (32.11)	1406034 (67.89)	296927 (14.34)	375256 (18.12)
9.	Dhule	1707947	445885 (26.11)	1262062 (73.89)	109102 (6.39)	443564 (25.97)
10.	Gadchiroli	970294	67261 (6.93)	903033 (93.07)	108824 (11.22)	371696 (38.31)
11.	Gondiya	1200707	143431 (11.95)	1057276 (88.05)	167699 (13.97)	196455 (16.36)
12.	Hingoli	987160	154030 (15.60)	833130 (84.40)	100697 (10.20)	86898 (8.80)
13.	Jalgaon	3682690	1052794 (28.59)	2629896 (71.41)	286777 (7.79)	435951 (11.84)
14.	Jalna	1612980	307865 (19.09)	1305115 (80.91)	181017 (11.22)	32103 (1.99)
15.	Kolhapur	3523162	1050353 (29.81)	2472809 (70.19)	449641 (12.76)	21387 (0.61)
16.	Latur	2080285	490261 (23.57)	1590024 (76.43)	404251 (19.43)	47836 (2.30)
17.	Mumbai	3338031	3338031 (100)	0	183469 (5.50)	20666 (0.62)
18.	Mumbai Suburban	8640419	8640419 (100)	0	401569 (4.65)	70454 (0.82)
19.	Nagpur	4067637	2613751 (64.26)	1453886 (35.74)	696461 (17.12)	444441 (10.93)
20.	Nanded	2876259	689064 (23.96)	2187195 (76.04)	498196 (17.32)	253596 (8.82)
21.	Nandurbar	1311709	202673 (15.45)	1109036 (84.55)	92150 (7.03)	859574 (65.53)

(Contd.)

Sl. No.	Name of Districts	Total Population			Percentage of Scheduled Castes to Total Population	Percentage of Scheduled Tribes to Total Population
		Total	Urban	Rural		
22.	Nashik	4993796	1937556 (38.80)	3056240 (61.20)	426516 (8.54)	1194271 (23.92)
23.	Osmanabad	1486586	233256 (15.69)	1253330 (84.31)	245790 (16.53)	27857 (1.87)
24.	Parbhani	1527715	485186 (31.76)	1042529 (68.24)	152463 (9.98)	35210 (2.30)
25.	Pune	7232555	4200837 (58.08)	3031718 (41.92)	761857 (10.53)	261722 (3.62)
26.	Raigarh	2207929	534835 (24.22)	1673094 (75.78)	53667 (2.43)	269124 (12.19)
27.	Ratnagiri	1696777	192209 (11.33)	1504568 (88.67)	24515 (1.44)	20102 (1.18)
28.	Sangli	2583524	633218 (24.51)	1950306 (75.49)	313474 (12.13)	17855 (0.69)
29.	Satara	2808994	398121 (14.17)	2410873 (85.83)	246110 (8.76)	21896 (0.78)
30.	Sindhudurg	868825	82319 (9.47)	786506 (90.53)	38536 (4.44)	4952 (0.57)
31.	Solapur	3849543	1225284 (31.83)	2624259 (68.17)	578123 (15.02)	68989 (1.79)
32.	Thane	8131849	5902473 (72.58)	2229376 (27.42)	339720 (4.18)	1199290 (14.75)
33.	Wardha	1236736	325041 (26.28)	911695 (73.72)	158630 (12.83)	154415 (12.49)
34.	Washim	1020216	178445 (17.49)	841771 (82.51)	162663 (15.94)	70987 (6.96)
35.	Yavatmal	2458271	457211 (18.60)	2001060 (81.40)	252802 (10.28)	473370 (19.26)
	Total	**96878627**	**41100980 (42.43)**	**55777647 (57.57)**	**9881656 (10.20)**	**8577276 (8.85)**

***Note*:** Bracket Value is indicating Percentage to total Population.

Source: www.censusofindia.gov.in

the percentage to the total. It is seen that except the village Madalmuthi (Sangli) and Titwa (Akola) all the villages have higher male population as compared to female population. The village Hingni (Wardha) has the highest male population (55.3%) followed by Ozare Khurd (Ratnagiri) (54.2%). The village Sirpalli (Nanded) has the lowest sex-ratio of 906 followed by Kawahta (Akola) 937.

District-wise the net enrollment ratio (NER) and dropouts in Maharashtra is presented in Table 2.4. The literacy rate for Maharashtra has remained higher than the national average while the

Table 2.3: Demographic Structure in Surveyed Villages (As per Census 2001)

Sl. No.	Name of the Villages	Total	Population		
			Male	Female	Sex ratio
1.	Sirpalli (Nanded)	904	495 (54.7)	405 (45.3)	906
2.	Nimgaon (Ahmednagar)	3173	1650 (52.0)	1523 (48.0)	958
3.	Pipara (Nagpur)	1930	1022 (52.9)	908 (47.1)	—
4.	Jamgaon (Ahmednagar)	671	352 (52.4)	319 (47.6)	—
5.	Lamkani (Dhule)	6150	3125 (50.8)	3025 (49.2)	—
6.	Pokhra (Aurangabad)	1859	956 (51.4)	903 (48.6)	944
7.	Hingni (Wardha)	2235	1238 (55.3)	997 (44.7)	—
8.	Madalmuthi* (Sangli)	1558	737 (47.3)	821 (52.7)	—
9.	Dhanora (Wardha)	1619	848 (52.3)	771 (47.3)	—
10.	Titwa (Akola)*	1447	714 (49.3)	733 (50.7)	—
11.	Ambarde (Kolhapur)	589	297 (50.4)	292 (49.6)	983
12.	Randivevadi (Solapur)	850	454 (53.4)	396 (46.6)	—
13.	Telkamptee (Nagpur)	3317	1753 (52.8)	1564 (47.2)	—
14.	Jalgaon (Ratnagiri)	7317	3753 (51.2)	3564 (48.8)	—
15.	Nilewadi (Kolhapur)	1679	897 (53.4)	782 (46.6)	—
16.	Gojore (Jalgaon)	2122	1084 (51.0)	1038 (49.0)	957
17.	Motha (Amravati)	827	420 (50.7)	407 (49.3)	—
18.	Belura Khurd (Akola)	1136	576 (50.7)	560 (49.3)	—
19.	Dhamangaon Gavali (Nagpur)	652	338 (51.8)	314 (48.2)	—
20.	Chichkhede (Jalgaon)	1273	687 (53.9)	856 (46.1)	—
21.	Ozare Khurd (Ratnagiri)	1620	879 (54.2)	741 (45.8)	—
22.	Kawahta (Akola)	1080	570 (52.7)	510 (47.3)	937
23.	Bhopara (Nanded)	755	383 (50.7)	572 (49.3)	—

* Shows higher percentage of females as compared to males.

Note: Figures in brackets are in percentage.

Source: Village Study Reports, LBSNAA, Government of India, Mussoorie, 2003-2009.

Table 2.4: District-wise net enrollment ratio and dropouts in Maharashtra (as on 30th September, 2007)

Sl. No.	*Districts*	*6-11 years Age Group*		*11-14 years Age Group*	
		NER	*Cohort Dropout*	*NER*	*Cohort Dropout*
1.	Ahmednagar	96.78	12.36	99.9	14.44
2.	Akola	99.22	14.25	99.48	7.79
3.	Amravati	99.87	10.28	88.43	9.44
4.	Aurangabad	92.85	4.9	97.24	9.27
5.	Beed	99.78	19.12	99.53	11.2
6.	Bhandara	96.92	2.04	87.36	7.46
7.	Buldhana	99.93	3.55	99.9	2.55
8.	Chandrapur	99.94	10.1	99.91	9.73
9.	Dhule	99.81	6.75	99.73	8.04
10.	Gadchiroli	99.68	15.15	99	11.26
11.	Gondiya	99.96	2.27	99.97	1.18
12.	Hingoli	99.63	12.16	99.52	19.66
13.	Jalgaon	99.75	8.39	99.65	3.94
14.	Jalna	98.75	17.24	96.64	30.45
15.	Kolhapur	99.81	13.65	99.9	16.84
16.	Latur	99.74	18.25	99.67	15.65
17.	Mumbai	86.32	4.63	95.46	–2.45
18.	Mumbai (Suburban)	89.12	9.11	86.45	13.55
19.	Nagpur	98.95	2.88	99.47	2.04
20.	Nanded	96.73	4.54	89.15	4.98
21.	Nandurbar	99.74	13.28	99.27	13.19
22.	Nashik	99.41	8.7	99.4	17.15
23.	Osmanabad	99.97	19.75	99.96	7.24
24.	Parbhani	99.9	9.7	100	25.01
25.	Pune	99.36	0.23	99.54	0.07
26.	Raigarh	99.83	26.9	99.89	2.86
27.	Ratnagiri	92.86	0.07	90.57	10.36
28.	Sangli	99.61	5.78	99.39	7.68
29.	Satara	97.89	4	94.36	4.31
30.	Sindhudurga	99.65	5.65	99.04	8.8
31.	Solapur	99.75	9.26	98.36	11.97
32.	Thane	99.75	9.34	98.25	16.23
33.	Wardha	97.08	1.12	99.84	2.78
34.	Washim	99.95	7.33	99.88	10.97
35.	Yavatmal	89.83	26.02	99.92	16.14
	Total	**97.95**	**9.68**	**97.54**	**10.05**

Source: Government of Maharashtra (In Financing Human Development– VIII) National Institute of Public Finance and Policy, New Delhi. p. 26).

gender gap and the urban-rural gap in literacy rate has been lower than the corresponding national average. In the age group of 6-11 years, the districts of Osmanabad, Gondia, Washim and Parbhani have reported above 99 per cent in comparison with NER respectively. In the same age group, the dropout percentages are as high as 30.45 per cent in Jalna, 25.01 per cent in Parbhani, Nashlk 17.15 per cent, 16.23 per cent in Thane district. The lowest dropout are manifested in Pune (0.07%), followed by Gondia 1.18 per cent and Nagpur (2.04%).

Table 2.5 depicts the literacy percentages among the males and females in the surveyed villages and the educational facilities available

Table 2.5: Status of Literacy and Educational facilities in villages covered/surveyed (Percentage of Literacy as per Census 2001)

Sl. No.	*Name of the Villages*	*Male*	*Female*	*Angan-wadi centre*	*Primary School*	*ME*	*High School*	*Secon-dary School*
1.	Gojori (Jalgaon)	77	71	—	One	One	—	—
2.	Nilewadi (Kolhapur)	75	58	One	One			
3.	Telkamptee (Nagpur)	84	92	—	One	—	—	—
4.	Wadi Sutanda (Aurangabad)	68	56	—	One	One	—	—
5.	Randivevadi (Solapur)	74	55	—	One	—	—	—
6.	Ambarde (Kolhapur)	63	37	—	One	—	—	—
7.	Takarkhede (Jalgaon)	57	43	—	One	—	—	—
8.	Kawatha (Akola)	74	53	—	One	One	—	—
9.	Titwa (Akola)	79	55	—	—	One	—	—
10.	Dhanora (Wardha)	83	66	—	One	One	—	—
11.	Madalmuthi (Sangli)	74	54	—	One	—	—	—
12.	Khaseli (Ratnagiri)	59	33	—	Two	—	—	—
13.	Jalgaon mete (Aurangabad)	57	53	—	One	—	—	—
14.	Sukali (Akola)	74	55	—	One	One	—	—
15.	Lamkani (Dhule)	77	75	—	Three	One	One	One
16.	Pipara (Nagpur)	68	56	—	—	One	—	—
17.	Jamgam (Ahmednagar)	85	64	One	One	One	—	—
18.	Chinkhkhede* (Jalgam)	74	81	One	—	—	—	—
19.	DhamangaonGavali (Nagpur)	68	56	One	One	—	—	—
20.	Mothe (Amaravati)	57	48	—	One	One	One	—
21.	OzareKhurd (Ratnagiri)	81	72	—	One	One	—	—
22.	Varhane (Nashik)	54	33	—	One	One	One	—

* Higher female literacy compared to male literacy, relatively contradictory to the State as well as National trend.

Source: Village Study Reports, LBSNAA, Government of India, Mussoorie, 2003-2009.

Table 2.6: District-wise Minority Religions Population of Maharashtra (Census, 2001)

Sl. No.	Districts	Christians	Muslims	Sikhs	Buddhists	Jains
1.	Mumbai City	106240 (10.04)	734484 (7.15)	16330 (7.58)	161417 (2.76)	159021 (12.22)
2.	Mumbai Suburban	340166 (32.14)	1488987 (14.50)	53271 (24.74)	464354 (7.95)	319339 (24.53)
3.	Thane	242101 (22.88)	880827 (8.58)	31709 (14.73)	309630 (5.30)	149331 (11.47)
4.	Raigarh	10163 (0.96)	170003 (1.66)	4332 (2.01)	93251 (1.60)	10680 (0.82)
5.	Rantagiri	2866 (0.27)	175672 (1.71)	712 (0.33)	120855 (2.07)	4227 (0.32)
6.	Sindhudurga	16001 (1.51)	23668 (0.23)	284 (0.13)	24320 (0.42)	1437 (0.11)
7.	Nashik	22849 (2.16)	525983 (5.12)	8766 (4.07)	84044 (1.44)	35135 (2.70)
8.	Dhule	4902 (0.46)	149466 (1.46)	1439 (0.67)	14613 (0.25)	13099 (1.01)
9.	Nandhurbar	17953 (1.70)	71215 (0.69)	580 (0.27)	5161 (0.09)	5949 (0.46)
10.	Jalgaon	5424 (0.51)	455288 (4.43)	2758 (1.28)	126136 (2.16)	27369 (2.10)
11.	Ahmednagar	25961 (2.45)	264145 (2.57)	5850 (2.72)	35893 (0.61)	38561 (2.96)
12.	Pune	116661 (11.02)	452397 (4.40)	21938 (10.19)	321948 (5.51)	104073 (7.99)
13.	Satara	3759 (0.36)	125661 (1.22)	1107 (0.51)	128570 (2.20)	12156 (0.93)
14.	Sangli	9696 (0.92)	203524 (1.98)	1312 (0.61)	35142 (0.60)	85160 (6.54)
15.	Solapur	9625 (0.91)	377579 (3.68)	2752 (1.28)	38497 (0.66)	27904 (2.14)
16.	Kolhapur	16078 (1.52)	236875 (2.31)	2082 (0.97)	37932 (0.65)	147285 (11.31)
17.	Aurangabad	15558 (1.47)	569516 (5.55)	4452 (2.07)	247222 (4.23)	26782 (2.06)
18.	Jalna	12438 (1.18)	211531 (2.06)	1515 (0.70)	121033 (2.07)	8960 (0.69)
19.	Parbhani	1368 (0.13)	243935 (2.38)	789 (0.37)	153231 (2.62)	5698 (0.44)
20.	Hingoli	468 (0.04)	103199 (1.00)	474 (0.22)	147927 (2.53)	5245 (0.40)
21.	Beed	1380 (0.13)	256582 (2.50)	746 (0.35)	65122 (1.12)	8628 (0.66)
22.	Nanded	3734 (0.35)	385081 (3.75)	12645 (5.87)	302161 (5.18)	5003 (0.38)

(Contd.)

Sl. No.	Districts	Christians	Muslims	Sikhs	Buddhists	Jains
23.	Osmanabad	765 (0.07)	151181 (1.47)	818 (0.38)	28356 (0.49)	5029 (0.39)
24.	Latur	1494 (0.14)	292996 (2.85)	1435 (0.67)	74351 (1.27)	6123 (0.47)
25.	Buldhana	2545 (0.24)	285387 (2.78)	1501 (0.70)	306503 (5.25)	12254 (0.94)
26.	Akola	3494 (0.33)	296272 (2.88)	1201 (0.56)	293184 (5.02)	10313 (0.79)
27.	Washim	1211 (0.11)	111863 (1.09)	500 (0.23)	150580 (2.58)	8504 (0.65)
28.	Amravati	7315 (0.69)	347250 (3.38)	2940 (1.37)	350403 (6.00)	11932 (0.92)
29.	Yavatmal	3997 (0.38)	196909 (1.92)	1632 (0.76)	221793 (3.80)	11098 (0.85)
30.	Vardha	2559 (0.24)	47605 (0.46)	1825 (0.85)	169579 (2.90)	5990 (0.46)
31.	Nagpur	31682 (2.99)	296709 (2.89)	19633 (9.12)	589218 (10.09)	22608 (1.74)
32.	Bhandra	1844 (0.17)	23324 (0.23)	739 (0.34)	144541 (2.48)	975 (0.07)
33.	Gondiya	1292 (0.12)	21980 (0.21)	1745 (0.81)	119618 (2.05)	1471 (0.11)
34.	Chandrapur	11301 (1.07)	76050 (0.74)	4922 (2.29)	274067 (4.69)	4135 (0.32)
35.	Gadchiroli	3423 (0.32)	17341 (0.17)	603 (0.28)	78058 (1.34)	369 (0.03)
	Total	**1058313 (1.09)**	**10270485 (10.60)**	**215337 (0.22)**	**5838710 (6.03)**	**1301843 (1.34)**

Note: Bracket figures indicates percentage with regard to minority religions to the total Population.

Source: *Statistical Abstract of Maharashtra State* 2000-01, p. 58, and *Handbook of Basic Statistics of Maharashtra State 2007*, p. 40.

in the villages. It is found that the male literacy is the highest in Jamgam (Ahmednagar) 85 per cent followed by Telkamptee (Nagpur) (84%) and Dhanora (Wardha) 83 per cent. Similarly, the lowest percentage of male literacy is seen in the village Varhane (Nashik) 54 per cent followed by both Jalgaon mete (Aurangabad) 57 per cent and Mothe (Araravati) 57 per cent.

It is found that the female literacy is the highest in Telkamptee (Nagpur) 92 per cent followed by Chinkhkhede (Jalgam) 81 per cent. Similarly, the lowest percentage of female literacy is seen in two villages Khaseli (Ratnagiri) and Varhane (Nashik) 33 per cent

Table 2.7: District-wise percentage of Disabled and Able Population of Maharashtra

Sl. No.	Districts	Blind	Crippled	Speech	Hearing	Mental	Total of Disabled Population	Total Population	Able Population
1.	Mumbai City	28928	12020	3706	1696	7617	53967 (1.62)	3338031	3284033 (98.38)
2.	Mumbai Sub-urban	58714	28326	8146	3571	17053	115810 (1.34)	8640419	8524190 (98.66)
3.	Thane	18348	28115	6349	3911	13684	70407 (0.87)	8131849	8061593 (99.13)
4.	Raigarh	8890	10792	2438	1851	3824	27795 (1.26)	2207929	2180205 (98.74)
5.	Rantagiri	9556	8794	2166	2487	4225	27228 (1.60)	1696777	1669772 (98.40)
6.	Sindhudurga	3932	4094	1328	785	2669	12808 (1.47)	868825	856192 (98.53)
7.	Nashik	23316	28512	4795	4394	9103	70120 (1.4)	4993796	4923880 (98.60)
8.	Dhule	9834	11717	1960	1623	3195	28329 (1.66)	1707947	1679671 (98.34)
9.	Nandhurbar	13174	6344	1209	909	1952	23588 (1.8)	1311709	1288412 (98.20)
10.	Jalgaon	15945	26496	4175	3692	6956	57264 (1.55)	3682690	3625736 (98.45)
11.	Ahmednagar	35509	27841	5537	4630	10043	83560 (2.07)	4040642	3957440 (97.93)
12.	Pune	26853	36091	7160	4920	16258	91282 (1.26)	7232555	7141718 (98.74)
13.	Satara	9386	15874	3310	2252	6635	37457 (1.33)	2808994	2771543 (98.67)
14.	Sangli	8735	13208	3394	1448	6157	32942 (1.28)	2583524	2551058 (98.72)
15.	Solapur	21436	26234	5733	3236	9445	66084 (1.72)	3849543	3783916 (98.28)
16.	Kolhapur	13512	17083	4180	1595	7456	43826 (1.24)	3523162	3479174 (98.76)
17.	Aurangabad	23181	21712	3718	3366	6603	58580 (2.02)	2897013	2838420 (97.98)
18.	Jalna	16702	13428	2283	2417	3966	38796 (2.41)	1612980	1574204 (97.59)
19.	Parbhani	11186	13837	2313	2520	3411	33267 (2.18)	1527715	1494733 (97.82)
20.	Hingoli	7947	8259	1351	1779	2205	21541 (2.18)	987160	965459 (97.82)
21.	Beed	12223	17913	2810	2416	4880	40242 (1.86)	2161250	2120758 (98.14)
22.	Nanded	40967	20929	4744	3817	6872	77329 (2.69)	2876259	2798671 (97.31)

(Contd.)

Sl. No.	Districts	Blind	Crippled	Speech	Hearing	Mental	Total of Disabled Population	Total Population	Able Population
23.	Osmanabad	12911	13648	2267	2079	4152	35057 (2.36)	1486586	1451943 (97.64)
24.	Latur	14656	18652	3211	2927	5372	44818 (2.15)	2080285	2035182 (97.85)
25.	Buldhana	11596	18178	2697	3993	5310	41774 (1.87)	2232480	2190226 (98.13)
26.	Akola	9346	11633	1992	2459	3712	2 9142 (1.79)	1630239	1600858 (98.21)
27.	Washim	5275	7917	1295	1709	2015	18211 (1.79)	1020216	1001789 (98.21)
28.	Amaravati	27921	18805	3863	3802	7070	61461 (2.36)	2607160	2545539 (97.64)
29.	Yavatmal	14826	15644	3180	3063	5264	41977 (1.71)	2458271	2416023 (98.29)
30.	Wardha	7677	7963	1401	1899	3252	22192 (1.79)	1236736	1214808 (98.21)
31.	Nagpur	19234	24329	4262	3463	11185	62473 (1.54)	4067637	4005527 (98.46)
32.	Bhandra	6261	8277	1135	1494	2644	19811 (1.74)	1136146	1116189 (98.26)
33.	Gondiya	11832	9118	1149	1809	2822	26730 (2.23)	1200707	1174270 (97.77)
34.	Chandrapur	16892	12767	2556	2836	4463	39514 (1.91)	2071101	2031486 (98.09)
35.	Gadchiroli	4229	5395	1230	1542	1804	14200 (1.46)	970294	955800 (98.54)
	Total	**580930**	**569945**	**113043**	**92390**	**213274**	**1569582 (1.62)**	**96878627**	**95310418 (98.38)**

Note: Bracket Value is indicating Percentage to total of disabled and able population.

Source: *Statistical Abstract of Maharashtra State 2000-01*, p. 58; and *Handbook of Basic Statistics of Maharashtra State 2007*, p. 36.

followed by Ambarde (Kolhapur) 37 per cent. Further, it is also manifested in the Table that baring a few there is inadequate educational facilities/infrastructure in the study villages.

Table 2.6 outlines the district wise the minority population in Maharashtra. The close observation of the Table reveals that Muslims are more concentrated in Mumbai sub-urban (14.5%), followed by Aurangabad (5.55%) and Thane (8.58%). In the Mumbai city Muslims constitute 7.15 per cent of the total population, while in Nasik the percentage of Muslims is 5.12. In other districts the Muslim population

Table 2.8: District-wise Rural Health Indicators in Maharashtra

Districts	*Infant mortality rate*	*Rank*	*District*	*Birth rate*	*Rank*	*District*	*Death rate*	*Rank*
Wardha	37	1	Ahmadnagar	24.5	1	Sindhudurg	9	1
Gadchiroli	22	2	Gadchiroli	22.7	2	Ratnagiri	7.4	2
Washim	18	3	Nashik	20.3	3	Wardha	7	3
Nanded	16	4	Bandhara	19.7	4	Bandhara	6.7	4
Yawatmal	16	5	Sangli	18.1	5	Gadchiroli	6	5
Amaravati	14	6	Nagpur	17.4	6	Sangli	6	6
Latur	14	7	Chandrapur	17.3	7	Kolhapur	5.6	7
Sindhudurg	14	8	Dhule	16.8	8	Chandrapur	5.3	8
Buladhana	12	9	Ratnagiri	16.2	9	Nagpur	5.3	9
Jalagoan	12	10	Jalagoan	16	10	Satara	5.3	10
Jalana	12	11	Buladhana	15.9	11	Jalagoan	5.1	11
Osmanabad	12	12	Solapur	15.9	12	Raigad	5.1	12
Thane	11	13	Sindhudurg	15.4	13	Amaravati	5	13
Beed	9	14	Wardha	15.1	14	Nandurbar	4.6	14
Chandrapur	9	15	Satara	15	15	Dhule	4.5	15
Nagpur	9	16	Raigad	14.9	16	Akola	4.4	16
Raigad	9	17	Nandurbar	14.8	17	Nashik	4.4	17
Akola	8	18	Latur	14.6	18	Solapur	4.3	18
Aurangabad	8	19	Amaravati	13.9	19	Ahemdnagar	4.2	19
Nandurbar	7	20	Pune	13.4	20	Buladhana	4.1	20
Ahmednagar	6	21	Aurangabad	12.8	21	Pune	4	21
Dhule	6	22	Akola	12.3	22	Thane	4	22
Nashik	6	23	Kolhapur	12.2	23	Aurangabad	3.8	23
Pune	6	24	Thane	11.8	24	Latur	3.8	24
Satara	6	25	Yawatmal	11.4	25	Yawatmal	3.8	25
Kolhapur	5	26	Parabhani	10	26	Osmanabad	3.5	26
Solapur	5	27	Osmnabad	9.9	27	Parbhani	3.2	27
Sangli	4	28	Washim	9.3	28	Washim	3.2	28
Ratnagiri	3	29	Jalana	9	29	Jalana	2.5	29
Bandhara	N.A.	N.A.	Beed	7.9	30	Beed	2.4	30
Gondia	N.A.	N.A.	Nanded	7.1	31	Nanded	2.3	31
Hingoli	N.A.	N.A.	Gondia	N.A.	N.A.	Gondia	N.A.	N.A.
Parbhani	N.A.	N.A.	Hingoli	N.A.	N.A.	Hingoli	N.A.	N.A.

Source: Statistical Abstract of Maharashtra State 2000-01, p.135.

varies in the range of maximum below 3 per cent to minimum below 1 per cent of the total population. With regard to Christians, Mumbai suburban has the highest percentage of 32.14 per cent followed by Thane (22.88%) and Pune (11.02%). Similarly, the Sikhs are also heavily concentrated in Mumbai suburban (24.74%) followed by Thane (14.73%) and Pune (10.19%). The other minority population like the Buddhists and Jains are also highly concentrated in Mumbai suburban whose percentage are 7.95 per cent and 24.53 per cent respectively.

With regard to district-wise distribution of disabled population, Nanded has the highest percentage of 2.69 per cent followed by Jalna (2.48%) and both Buldhana and Osmanabad with 2.36 per cent. The

Table 2.9: District-wise Health Facilities in Maharashtra

Sl. No.	Districts	Govt. Hospitals	Private Hospitals	Rural Hospitals	Dispensaries	PHCs	Blood banks
1.	Ahmednagar	240					9
2.	Akola	NA	7				7
3.	Amaravati	210					8
4.	Aurangabad	81					36
5.	Beed	17					2
6.	Bhandara	3					1
7.	Buldhana	1					NA
8.	Chandrapur	3					4
9.	Dhule	1					3
10.	Gadchiroli	5	10				1
11.	Gondia	1		9		39	NA
12.	Hingoli					20	NA
13.	Jalgaon	45					2
14.	Jalna	3					19
15.	Kolhapur			13	29	66	3
16.	Latur	3			9	11	2
17.	Mumbai and Mumbai Suburban	19	455		8100	52	165
18.	Nagpur	11					19
19.	Nanded	2					2
20.	Nandurbar			14		49	NA
21.	Nashik	7					8
22.	Osmanabad	2	24				1
23.	Parbhani	1	2				2
24.	Pune	31					26
25	Raigad	1					NA
26.	Ratnagiri	4	2			43	2
27.	Sangli	2					5
28.	Satara	1	3	10		69	3
29.	Sindhudurg	3	25				4
30.	Solapur	14	32			66	1
31.	Thane	33				22	8
32.	Wardha	11	4				5
33.	Washim	1	14	7		24	NA
34.	Yavatmal	7					3

Data Recompiled.

Source: Compiled by IGIDR (2005) in *State of Environment Report: Maharashtra (Final Draft)*, p.28.

districts Parbhani and Hingoli both have 2.18 per cent of disabled population while Latur reports 2.15 per cent of such population (Table 2.7).

Health is an important indicator of economic development. Table 2.8 unfolds the district-wise population of infant mortality rate, birth rate and death rate in the State of Maharashtra. From the available data it is revealed that the highest infant mortality is seen in Wardha (37) followed by Gadchiroli (22) and Washim (18). With regard to birth rate Ahmednagar ranks first (24.15%) followed by Gadchiroli (22.7%) and Nashik (20.3%). Similarly, Sindhudurg has the highest death rate (9) followed by Ratnagiri (7.4%) and Wardha (7%).

Table 2.10: Status of Health Facilities in villages surveyed/covered

Sl. No.	*Name of the villages*	*Sub PHC*	*PHC*	*Anganwadi*	*MPW*	*ANM*
1.	Gojore (Jalgaon)	One	—	—	—	—
2.	Jalgaon (Ratnagiri)	One	—	—	—	—
3.	Telkamptee (Nagpur)	One	—	—	—	ANM one
4.	Takarkheda (Jalgaon)	—	—	One	—	ANM one
5.	Kawatha (Akola)	—	—	One	One	—
6.	Dhanora (Wardha)	—	—	One	—	ANM one
7.	Madalmuthi (Sangli)	—	—	One	One	ANM one
8.	Ingrul (Sangli)	One	—	One	One	ANM one
9.	Sukivalli (Ratnagiri)	One	—	—	—	ANM one
10.	Lamkari (Dhule)	One	One	One	—	—
11.	Pipra (Nagpur)	—	—	—	—	ANM one
12.	Jamgaon (Ahmadnagar)	One	—	One	—	—
13.	Sirpalli (Nanded)	One	—	One	One	ANM one
14.	Motha (Amaravati)	One	—	—	—	ANM one
15.	Ozarekhurd (Ratnagiri)	One	—	One	—	—
16.	Sulibhanjan (Aurangabad)	—	—	—	—	ANM one
17.	Ambawade (Kolhapur)	—	—	—	—	ANM one
18.	Ajnpur (Jalgaon)	One	—	Three	—	—
19.	Bawakalwadi (Satara)	—	—	—	—	ANM one

***Note*:** PHC = Primary Health Centre, MPW = Multi-Purpose Worker, ANM = Auxiliary Nurse Midwife.

Source: Village Study Reports, LBSNAA, Government of India, Mussoorie, 2003-09.

With regard to availability of health facilities there is great disparity across the state while Mumbai and Mumbai-suburban have 19 government hospitals, 455 private hospitals, 8100 dispensaries, 52 primary health centres, 165 blood banks and other districts have inadequate facilities (Table 2.9).

Maharashtra's female infant mortality rate was 69 per cent more than the male infant mortality rate in 2003 and the excess of female over male infant mortality rate in absolute numbers (57 – 32 = 25) is the highest across 15 major states. It is interesting to point out here that even though the infant mortality rate in urban areas is two-thirds of the rural infant mortality rate, yet the excess of female infant mortality rate is almost similar (60 for girls as against 37 for boys in rural and 43 as against 23 in urban). This brings forth another paradox. Maharashtra is a state with relatively greater female literacy rate and female life expectancy, yet it is also a state with relatively much greater discrimination against the female foetus/child.

Table 2.10 unfolds the non-availability of Primary Health Centre and Primary Health Sub-Centre in most of the surveyed villages. Even from among the total 39 villages surveyed in different districts of Maharashtra, the village study reports depicts the ground reality that there has been non-availability of Primary Health Centre and Primary Health Sub-Centre in 29 villages. These villages are Bawakalwadi (Satara), Ambawade (Kolhapur), Sulibhanjan (Aurangabad), Varhane (Nagpur), Ozarekhurd (Ratnagiri), Belura Khurd (Akola), Dhamangaon Gavali (Nagpur), Chinkhkhede (Jalgam), Nimgaon (Aurangabad), Pipara (Nagpur), Sukali (Ratnagiri), Jalgaon *mete* (Aurangabad), Pokhri (Aurangabad), Ingrul (Sangli), Hingni (Wardha), Sukali (Akola), Khaseli (Ratnagiri), Madalmuthi (Sangli), Dhanora (Wardha), Titwa (Akola), Bhopara (Nanded), Kawatha (Akola), Takarkheda (Jalgaon), Ambarde (Kolhapur), Maldoli (Ratnagiri), Randivevadi (Solapur), Telkamptee (Nagpur), Wadi Sutanda (Aurangabad) and Newadi (Kolhapur).

Economic development is attributed to the development of infrastructure, human resources and availability of basic necessities of life. Table 2.11 presents the ranking of districts according to the road connectivity, concentration of SC/ST population, rate of literacy and houseless population. With regard to backward population (SC/ST) the district Nashik, Thane, Nandurbar, Ahmednagar, Yavatmal and Amaravti have the corresponding rank of 1, 2, 3, 4, 5,

Table 2.11: District-wise Development Indicators for Maharashtra

Districts	Lakh population road length (Per 100 Sq. Km.)$	Rank	Districts	SC/ST population* (Actual Number)	Rank	Districts	Literacy rate@	Rank	Districts	Houseless** (number of Persons)	Rank
Gadchiroli	38	1	Nashik	1298862	1	Jalana	1	60.75	Thane	51888	1
Buldhana	43	2	Thane	1092817	2	Nandurbar	2	63.01	Nashik	25421	2
Jalana	45	3	Nandurbar	857027	3	Gadchiroli	3	63.54	Solapur	18112	3
Washim	48	4	Ahmadnagar	667894	4	Hingoli	4	64.92	Jalgoan	16879	4
Yawatmal	50	5	Yavatmal	642287	5	Beed	5	65.43	Pune	16316	5
Wardha	50	6	Amravati	640774	6	Osmanabad	6	65.59	Raigad	14607	6
Amaravati	51	7	Nanded	628892	7	Nanded	7	65.97	Ahmadnagar	10494	7
Akola	55	8	Jalgaon	601841	8	Solapur	8	67.65	Wardha	10434	8
Hingoli	58	9	Dhule	495726	9	Latur	9	68.40	Amaravati	9904	9
Thane	60	10	Chandrapur	493471	10	Parbhani	10	70.16	Yawatmal	9581	10
Dhule	62	11	Gadchiroli	462293	11	Aurangabad	11	70.42	Nagpur	8995	11
Raigad	63	12	Nagpur	458918	12	Washim	12	70.98	Satara	8843	12
Chandrapur	65	13	Solapur	454902	13	Dhule	13	71.45	Chandrapur	8139	13
Parbhani	66	14	Pune	447528	14	Jalgoan	14	71.59	Kolhapur	7416	14
Latur	68	15	Latur	365952	15	Buldhana	15	72.14	Aurangabad	7132	15
Osmanabad	69	16	Kolhapur	347158	16	Ahmadnagar	16	73.23	Sangli	6402	16
Nagpur	69	17	Gondiya	329695	17	Yawatmal	17	73.70	Ratnagiri	6294	17
Ratnagiri	74	18	Buldhana	301700	18	Pune	18	73.73	Sindhudurg	6172	18
Beed	75	19	Aurangabad	289119	19	Sangli	19	73.91	Akola	5842	19
Ahmadnagar	75	20	Raigarh	276687	20	Kolhapur	20	73.92	Beed	5811	20
Solapur	77	21	Bhandara	254684	21	Nashik	21	73.95	Nanded	5600	21
Jalgoan	82	22	Beed	252946	22	Chandrapur	22	74.32	Jalana	5525	22
Kolhapur	82	23	Sangli	245149	23	Satara	23	75.25	Buldhana	5340	23
Gondia	83	24	Wardha	244911	24	Ratnagiri	24	75.72	Osmanabad	5337	24
Satara	84	25	Osmanabad	236106	25	Sindhudurg	25	76.21	Nandurbar	4044	25
Nandurbar	87	26	Satara	220690	26	Akola	26	77.46	Dhule	3620	26
Pune	88	27	Washim	209179	27	Raigad	27	78.32	Gadchiroli	3476	27
Nashik	88	28	Akola	200169	28	Wardha	28	79.42	Latur	3308	28
Nanded	94	29	Jalna	179752	29	Bhandara	29	79.62	Parbhani	2653	29
Sangli	94	30	Hingoli	168842	30	Thane	30	79.63	Washim	2593	30
Bhandara	96	31	Parbhani	135861	31	Gondia	31	79.96	Bhandara	2472	31
Aurangabad	100	32	Sindhudurg	39795	32	Amaravati	32	80.55	Gondia	1914	32
Sindhudurg	103	33	Ratnagiri	38739	33	Nagpur	33	83.49	Hingoli	1286	33

Source: *Statistical Abstract of Maharashtra State* 2000-01, pp. 436$, 24-25*, 61-62@, 172**.

Table 2.12: Land holding pattern of the surveyed villages in different districts of Maharashtra

Sl. No.	Name of the villages	Total land	Land under cultivation	Area under forests	Village grazing and fallow land	Waste land	Home stead
1.	Sirpalli (Nanded) (in hectares)	389.46	373.41	Nil	8.93	4.13	2.99
2.	Pokhri (Aurangabad) (in acres)	2149.87	2108	Nil	38.87	Nil	3
3.	Randivevadi (Solapur) (in hectares)	771	709	NA	5.42	56.58	NA
4.	Ambarde (Kolhapur) (in hectares)	186.44	127.44	48.76	1.17	6.54	2.17
5.	Maldoli (Ratnagiri) (In acres)	1878.16	562.5	23.64	Nil	615	666.52
6.	Kawatha (Akola)						
7.	Titwa (Akola) (in acres)	581	432	Nil	5.42	143	Nil
8.	Dhanora (Wardha)						
9.	Madalmuthi (Sangli) (in acres)	1278	975	Nil	303	Nil	Nil
10.	Khaseli (Ratnagiri in acres)	1568	1124	Nil	0.23	392	2.15
11.	Jalgaon mete (Aurangabad) (in hectares)	514.07	435.6	NA	87.07	52.57	25.9
12.	Sukali (Akola) (in hectares)	731	693	NA	NA	32.5	5.4
13.	Lamkani (Dhule)	2578.81	1630.41	633.99	127.22	182.88	4.31
14.	Pipara (Nagpur) (in hectares)	4060	1640	1762	622.40	35.5	NA
15.	Jamgam (Ahmadnagar)						
16.	Chinkhkhede (Jalgaon) (in hectares)	577	573.3	Nil	0.59	2.40	NA
17.	Ingrul (Sangli) (in acres)	1780	1552	Nil	46	98	11.5
18.	Mothe (Amravati) (In acres)	1520.70	1390.18	116.43	129.83	129.83	10.18
19.	Ozare Khurd (Ratnagiri) (In acres)	6909	4065.75	242.5	812.5	NA	NA
20.	Jalgam (Ratnagiri) (in acres)	3930.90	375.75	13.50	641.77	67.30	NA

Source: Village Study Reports, LBSNAA, Government of India, Mussoorie, 2003-2009.

6 in the descending order. Similarly in terms of literacy rate, the lowest literacy rate of 56 is noticed in Nandurbar followed by Gadchiroli (60) and Jalana (64).

AGRICULTURE AND LAND HOLDING

Table 2.12 reflects the landholding/utilization pattern in the surveyed villages. Table 2.12 highlights the data for 20 villages. It is exhibited that only 7 villages have forest cover and thus, most of the villages have no forest cover.

Secondly, as illustrated in Table 2.12, there is lower proportion of agricultural land available for cultivation and therefore, there is pressure on land resources. The rural people, particularly the rural women view forests and its resources as wealth creating and livelihood supporting assets. In addition rural households through the use of forest resources derive many benefits and numerous opportunities that help to improve their welfare. The forests and the benefits they provide in the form of food, income and medicinal materials play important role in enabling rural households to be in a state of good health and well-being.

In the light of the afore-said analysis it is inferred that:

1. Most of the cultivated land in the surveyed villages suffers from soil erosion, water logging, and salinity. Groundwater Tables are falling fast and forest cover is under threat. The inter-relationship and inter-dependencies among water, land, vegetation and animal resources determine the nature and kind of livelihood support systems particularly in rural areas.
2. Depletion of natural resource base and increased biomass demand for human and livestock population are major threats to livelihoods of the small holder farmers from rain-fed villages under review. The degeneration of natural resources land, water and forests, particularly in rain-fed areas has assumed alarming proportion.
3. The increasing impoverishment of farming had a cascading effect on all sections of people living off agriculture including agricultural workers and tenant farmers and it is also correlated to food and nutritional insecurity.

4. In this context, there is need to continue efforts to improve the livelihoods portfolio of farming households not only from agriculture but also through agri-allied sectors such as animal husbandry, fisheries, horticulture and non-farm sector.
5. There is need to emphasize on management of natural resources such as water, soil, plants and animals, with a particular focus on how management affects the quality of life for both present and future generations.
6. Further, there is imperative need for waste land development and change in the policy paradigm promoting social forestry, integrated farming and agro-forestry.

AGRICULTURE AND CROPPING PATTERN

Table 2.13 makes it clear that the study villages cover a total of ten districts scattered over 18 villages [(Ahmednagar (two villages), Dhule (one village), Ratnagiri (two villages), Kolhapur (two villages), Solapur (one village), Akola (two villages), Jalgaon (four villages), Aurangabad (two villages), Wardha (one village), and Nagpur (one village)].

A close observation of Table 2.13 brings to light the following conclusions:

1. Table 2.13 shows that in the villages of Maharashtra the cropping pattern has reflected major crops mainly cash crops, depending on the sources of irrigation and climatic conditions.
2. A wide-range of crops consisting of items like sugarcane, wheat, cotton, *bajra, moong*, soybean, sunflower, oilseeds, and pulses. *jowar*, cashewnut, banana, mango, vegetables etc. are produced in different villages of Maharashtra.
3. Agricultural lands are mostly dependent on rain water and therefore, the output is subject to fluctuations depending on the monsoon/climatic conditions. Irrigation facilities available in the villages comprises of well, canal, tanks, river water, small dams and minor irrigation projects.
4. Cropping pattern in the surveyed villages is dependent on the availability of rain fall or assured sources of irrigation

Table 2.13: Agriculture, Land Holding and Cropping Pattern in surveyed Villages of Maharashtra

Sl. No.	*Name of the Villages*	*Main features of cropping pattern and land holding*
1.	Jamgaon (Ahmednagar)	(a) Mostly rained agriculture with limited facilities of canal irrigation and main crops shown are sugar cane, wheat, vegetables etc.
2.	Nimgaon (Ahmednagar)	(a) In this village due to rain-fed agriculture, lack of modern technology there is low productivity in the yield. Single crop is grown in a year mainly cotton, *bajra, moong*, wheat, *jeera*, and castor.
3.	Lamkani (Dhule)	(a) Colluvial calcareous soil is found in the village which is suitable for the cultivation of paddy, wheat, sugar cane, vegetable, papaya, chillies, onion, ground nut, moong, *turdal*, plantain, coriander, cotton, *bajra* and *jowar*.
		(b) Irrigation facilities available in the villages comprises well, canal, tanks and small dams.
4.	Ozare Khurd (Ratnagiri)	(a) Extensively dependent on monsoon the agriculture in this village comprises paddy, *ragi*, vegetables, mango, and cashew nut with the use of low technology.
5.	Maldoli (Ratnagiri)	(a) With rain-fed agriculture, the important crops raised are paddy, cashew nut, and mango.
		(b) The land holding pattern of the village indicate that there is dominance of marginal and small farmers (about 64%) having less than 3 acres' of land as an average.
		(c) Farmers are having land holding in the range of 3 to 5 acres constitute 17.2 per cent, in the range of 5 to 10 acres there are 15.8 per cent of farmers and a meagre percentage of 02.2 constitute above 20 acres category farmers.
6.	Ambarde (Kolhapur)	(a) Rain-fed agriculture leads to single crop mainly sugar cane, rice, *jowar* with moderate yield. There are frequent occurrences of drought in the village.
		(b) Ninety eight per cent of land is under ownership cultivation.
		(c) The distribution of land holding pattern is skewed. Fifty two per cent of operational holding have an area of less than one acre, 29 per cent have land between 1 and 3 acres' and only 2 per cent have more than 5 acres of land.
7.	Nilewadi (Kolhapur)	(a) Due to alluvial soil the land of the village is conducive for sugar cane, cotton, ground nut and paddy cultivation. There has been limited application of better and modern technology, and high yielding varieties of seeds.
		(b) Mostly there are small/marginal farmers having the facilities of Warna river water.

(Contd.)

Sl. No.	Name of the Villages	Main features of cropping pattern and landholding
8.	Randivevadi (Solapur)	(a) Cropping pattern is mainly cash crops like sugar cane, jawar, turdal are main crops grown. (b) Canal irrigation from the Ujni reservoir through pipeline connections is adopted.
9.	Sukali (Akola)	(a) Agriculture mostly non-irrigated and rainfed. Main crop is cotton, *jowar*, *turdal*. (b) There is vulnerability of farmers in times of failure of crops due to scanty rainfall or untimely rain falls.
10.	Kawahta (Akola)	(a) Cropping pattern of the village under reference is mainly cotton, sunflower, oilseeds, and pulses. (b) Dominance of small and marginal farmers is the phenomena of landholding pattern in the village.
11.	Chichkhede (Jalgaon)	(a) Both irrigated and non-irrigated lands are found in this village. The sources of irrigation are the Manyad and Girna projects. (b) The *kharif* crops undertaken for cultivation by the farmers are *jowar*, cotton, pulses, sugarcane and the *rabi* crops sown are *bajra*, groundnut, gram and wheat. Besides, horticulture comprises fruits, banana, lemon are being cultivated. (c) Kitchen garden is manifested in the households for meeting their daily consumption requirements. Drip irrigation, spraying of pesticides, herbicides, fungicides, use od bio-fertilizers are familiar among the cultivators.
12.	Anipur (Jalgaon)	(a) Usually double cropping is seen in the village. During monsoon kharif crops mainly *jowar*, *bajra* and during winter, *rabi* crops like wheat, cotton, banana are grown. (b) Export quality banana are produced with the use of modern technology like sprinkler irrigation, fertilizer, drip irrigation, pesticides.
13.	Takarkheda (Jalgaon)	(a) The village has black alluvial soil; land used mainly for agriculture, less than one per cent of land has forest cover. (b) The main crop is cotton, banana, *jowar*, maize. (c) Ninety per cent of land have single crop and only 10 per cent of agricultural land have double crops.
14.	Gojori (Jalgaon)	(a) Agriculture is largely rainfed, no assured source of irrigation except wells constructed by farmers in their own land. There is neither water-harvesting structure nor also any watershed development programme. Lands are mostly under ownership cultivation and tenancy is non-existent in the village. (b) Fifty per cent of landholding are very small ranging from 1 to 3 acres. (c) The main crops raised are cotton, jowar, and moong. Eighty per cent of land produce single crop.

(Contd.)

Sl. No.	*Name of the Villages*	*Main features of cropping pattern and land holding*
		(a) Use of high-yielding varieties and manual labour makes the production unremunerative. (e) The village is drought-prone as per the climatic condition and its location, i.e. close to tropic of cancer. (f) Hardly any forest cover is found in the village literally burns from March onwards (probably, i.e. what Jalgaon implies).
15.	Wadi Sutanda (Aurangabad)	(a) Mostly rainfed land but to a limited extent there are provisions of well and minor irrigation. (b) The main crop is cotton but soybean, jowar, sugar cane and banana are also cultivated. (c) While in the rainfed area single crop is grown, but in the irrigated land multi-cropping is done.
16.	Sulibhanjan (Aurangabad)	(a) Agriculture in the village is mostly rainfed with limited irrigation facilities through a small irrigation project. (b) The main crops grown are cotton, soybean, jowar, *turdal* etc.
17.	Dhanora (Wardha)	(a) Due to rainfed agriculture, single cropping is grown mainly cotton, followed by *channa*, soybean, wheat, *turdal* and orange. (b) No modern technology or high yielding varieties are adopted and the yield fluctuates depending on water availability to the farm land.
18.	Pipara (Nagpur)	(a) Though mostly dependent on rain fall, there are facilities of medium irrigation project and well irrigation in this village facilitating for multiple cropping pattern and use of high yielding varieties of seeds. Main crops are cotton, soybean, *jowar*, and vegtables.

Source: Village Study Reports, LBSNAA, Government of India, Mussoorie, 2003-2009.

and as such, mostly single crops are raised. Where ever, such irrigation or water supply is present we find the adoption of double crops.

5. The overall picture that has emerged is that the distribution of landholding pattern is skewed and uneven. Mostly no modern technology or high yielding varieties are adopted and the yield fluctuates depending on water availability to the farm land.
6. There is dominance of marginal and small farmers having less than an average of 3 acres of land.

In this context, it will be appropriate to mention as has been aptly pointed out and suggested by Ms. Sampada Mehta, IAS, 2008 batch, that in Anipur village (Jalgaon) due to lack of storage facilities of banana and manual loading of tonnes of banana in the railway wagons, major losses occur in handing of this delicate fruit.

Due attention needs to be accorded for value additions through food processing units like banana chips, banana-wine, banana pulp and giving banana flavour to various preparations.

OCCUPATIONAL PATTERN

An attempt has been made to study the occupational pattern of the members of the households with a view to understand their occupational status on the one hand and the extent of unemployment on the other. Occupational pattern of the members of the households, with and without land, has also been focused as landless labourers and marginal farmers predominate in the rural society. Due to seasonal nature of agricultural activities they remain unemployed during a major part of the year. The members of the households can be broadly classified into four occupational groups, *viz.*, (i) agricultural labour, (ii) non-agricultural labour, (iii) other occupations, and (iv) no occupation.

Occupation in the surveyed villages (Table 2.14) reflects the base of the socio-economic culture prevalent in rural districts of Maharashtra. The main occupation types in the villages as reflected in the surveyed villages are agriculture, fishing, weaving, cottage industry, handicrafts etc.

There are 18 villages covered in this analysis of occupational pattern, employment and economic activities of the surveyed villages, scattered over eight districts, namely Ahmednagar (one village), Kolhapur (three villages), Nanded (two villages), Akola (one village), Jalgaon (one village), Wardha (one village), Ratnagiri (five villages) and Nagpur (4 villages).

The following inferences pertaining to the economic activities/ living conditions of rural people as well as suggestions/policy implications have emerged from the study:

(1) It is evident from Table 2.14 that people in the rural Maharashtra are engaged in wide range of economic activities as their occupation and employment to maintain their livelihood for generating income.

Table 2.14: Occupational pattern, Employment and Economic activities of the surveyed villages of some selected districts of Maharashtra

Name of the district and the villages	*Occupational pattern, Employment and Economic activities of the surveyed villages of some selected districts of Maharashtra*
Ahmednagar district 1. Nimgaon gangarda village	(a) Agriculture and agricultural labourers constitute the major portion of employment to the people followed by animal husbandry and dairy activities mainly cattle, buffaloes, sheep and some hove camels. (b) During lean season after the transplantation and agricultural operations are over, people prefer to migrate to cities for employment and income. (c) It is revealed that majority of the members of households were without occupation.
Kolhapur district 1. Nilewadi village	(a) Agriculture is the main occupation. Farmers produce mainly sugarcane, groundnut and paddy. (b) Dairy, floor mill, shops, motor mechanics, brick manufacturing units are some other avenues of occupation and employment.
2. Ambawade village	(a) Occupation pattern is predominantly agriculture and farm-based. (b) It has been revealed that 43 per cent of people in the village are engaged in agriculture, 35 per cent as agricultural labourers, 17 per cent in small household industries and the rest are engaged in petty trade, poultry and vending. (c) However, majority of the members of households were without occupation
3. Ambarde village	(a) Occupation pattern is predominantly agriculture and farm-based. Most of the villagers own some land even though the land holding is small. Farmers produce mainly sugarcane and paddy. (b) Dairy and milk production is another economic activity of the people with large number of milch cattle available in the village. (c) Some are employed in brick-kiln industries, carpentry, masonry, civil work contacting, handloom and unskilled labourers. (d) It is also seen that majority of the members of households were without occupation
Nanded district 1. Sirpalli village	(a) Main occupation of the people is agriculture and allied activities like dairy farming, fishing and animal husbandry or livestock. (b) Usually people migrate for their income and employment to neighbouring state of Andhra Pradesh for plucking the cotton from the cotton fields and other construction activities.

(Contd.)

Name of the district and the villages	*Occupational pattern, Employment and Economic activities of the surveyed villages of some selected districts of Maharashtra*
2. Bhopara village	(a) Agriculture is the prime occupation which employs about 34 per cent of population in the village. Besides, horticulture, cottage industries in making blankets, candles etc, diary and milk products, (b) People in large-scale migrate in search of employment to construction sector, sugarcane cutting fields and sugar industries, mainly to Pune, Kolhapur, Sangli etc.
Akola district 1. Kawatha village	(a) Agriculture is the main occupation of the people followed by non-farm employment in brick-kiln industries, livestock. (b) A small segment of population is engaged in cottage industries like *papad* making, pickle making, petty trade and other services.
Jalgaon district 1. Ajinpur village	Agriculture provided employment to about 45 per cent of population, horticulture about 30 per cent, trade, service sector about 12 per cent (fruit shake stalls, transportation, tourist activities, cyber café, Xerox shop, kirana store etc.) and a negligible percentage of 4 are engaged in cottage and small industrial enterprises and the rest are unemployed.
Wardha district 1. Dhanora village	(a) Agriculture and agricultural labour is the dominant occupation of the people in the village. (b) The agricultural operations during the peal–season are performed by labourers from other states due to scarcity of labour and reluctance of the villagers to perform such work. (c) In times of drought and failure of crops people move to cities for search of employment and hence, migration of rural labour is seen.
Ratnagiri district 1. Khaseli village	(a) Mainly employed in agriculture, mango cultivation and harvesting. (b) Non-farm employment is available to a limited extent. Baring a few employed in service sector with in the village as teacher, wireman, local bodies and approximately 30-40 people employed outside the village in Mumbai Nagar Palika, mostly people prefer to migrate to Mumbai as unskilled labourers to eke out their living.
2. Sukivalli village	(a) Occupation pattern is predominantly agriculture and agricultural labourers. (b) In the absence of assured source of employment mostly people prefer to migrate to Mumbai as unskilled labourers and the remittance constitute an important source of income of the village.
3. Maldoli	(a) Mainly employed in agriculture, mango cultivation and harvesting. Majority of the members of households were without occupation

(Contd.)

Name of the district and the villages	Occupational pattern, Employment and Economic activities of the surveyed villages of some selected districts of Maharashtra
	(b) For seeking employment mainly unskilled labour in the construction sector and other activities people prefer to migrate to Mumbai as unskilled labourers and the remittance constitute an important source of income of the village.
4. OzareKhurd	(a) Mainly agricultural and farm based horticultural activities like mango plantation and harvesting, cashew plantation and processing are the source of employment.
	(b) Large-scale migration of unskilled labourers to Mumbai and Thane for employment and livelihood and remittance of income to the villages has been manifested in the study village.
5. Jalgaon	(a) Agriculture and horticulture are main activities of the people (about 45%).
	(b) Other sources of occupation are mainly fishery, dairy and milk production and goat rearing.
	(c) Recently due to coming up of some chemical industry in the nearby block, some prefer to work in such industries.
Nagpur 1. Pipara	(a) Basically people in the village are engaged in agriculture and agricultural labourers.
	(b) Dairy and milk production, goat rearing constitutes a bulk source of employment and economic activities of the people.
2. Dhamangaon Gavali	(a) Agriculture and farming activities are the main occupation followed by landless labourers as wage earners.
	(b) Dairy and milk production, goat rearing constitutes a bulk source of employment and economic activities of the people.
3. Telkamptee	(a) Agriculture and farming activities are the main occupation followed by landless labourers as wage earners.
	(b) Dairy and milk production, goat rearing constitutes a bulk source of employment and economic activities of the people.
	(c) There have been major industrial activities in the nearby Taluka Kameshwar headquarters under Maharashtra ndustrial Development area. The initiation of Ispat and other small and ancillary industries having forward and backward linkages provides the scope for employment of the people primarily as unskilled labour and other basic services.
4. Khairi (Pannase)	(a) The occupational structure and employment pattern shows that 26 per cent of population is landless agri cultural labourers, 14 per cent are agricultural labourers, 15 per cent are cultivators, 10 per cent are engaged in petty business, trade and brick-kiln manufacturing etc.
	(b) Dominant farm-based activities are fishery, poultry, horticulture mainly orange cultivation etc.

Source: Village Study Reports, LBSNAA, Government of India, Mussoorie, 2003-2009.

(2) The spectrum of economic activities undertaken by the village people comprises agriculture and agricultural labour, fishery, poultry, horticulture, animal husbandry and dairy activities, brick manufacturing, cottage industries, out-migration for employment in construction sector, sugarcane cutting fields and sugar industries. Seasonal agricultural labour availability, the skewed nature of landholdings and the lack of flexibility in labour markets result in significant involuntary unemployment in rural Maharashtra.

(3) The landless agricultural households in the absence of employment in their native villages and even due to their longing for a higher wages in the distant land of the sugar fields migrate to work as the sugarcane cutters. This task is odious and extremely hard. It takes place near the sugar factories, to which they may travel between 200-800 km. Often, the whole family, including children, is required to move to the work site for 3-5 months, depending on the length of the harvest. The biggest losers in this process are the children, whose education is lost. While older children often take care of their younger siblings, some start working with their parents in sugar farms at the age of eight. In addition to involving difficult working conditions and having detrimental effects on the development of their mind and body, sugarcane cutting is, in fact, not secure.

(4) The patterns of rural poverty and land ownership that have been visible from the village survey papers which reveal that SC and ST households are most likely to be the poorest households in Maharashtra state, and that these households have a lower degree of land ownership and a higher reliance on labour income than other households. This would imply that in the context of underemployment in rural areas, these households would be the most likely to exit from the situation they find themselves in rural areas to greater income earning opportunities in urban areas.

(5) Further, production based on land (and therefore, labour) has undergone tremendous change because of improved technology influenced the agricultural practices. This had a tremendous effect on the landless and small landholders who depended on large landlords in a patronage relationship

(Breman, 1993). Besides, the state's failure to redistribute assets and change in the traditional pattern of agriculture has also contributed to the agricultural productivity and the problems associated with rural labour market in the study villages.

(6) Around 55 per cent of the working population still depends on agriculture for their livelihood in the villages of Maharashtra. This intense dependence on agriculture leads to all types of deprivation especially in the rural areas. A major portion of the rural population is in the vicious cycle of poverty, which force them to find alternative jobs. Economic development in the state has been highly polarized towards metropolitans, as about two-fifths of the Net State Income comes from the Konkan region and one-half of the NSDP by the four urbanized districts—Mumbai, Pune, Thane, and Nagpur. Thus, Maharashtra suffers from acute regional inequality.

(7) Migration as a coping mechanism has been adhered to by most of the villagers in the surveyed villages and conspicuously manifested in three districts, namely Ratnagiri, Ahmednagar and Wardha. However, the study revealed that majority of the members of households in the surveyed villages were without occupation despite the Governmental Interventional Schemes (MGNREGA).

(8) One attribute of the village survey data indicate that there is high degree of reliance of rural households on labour income as a means of livelihood, particularly in the state of Maharashtra with high labour/land ratios.

(9) The village study demonstrated that there has been employment potentiality in the field of horticulture/food processing activities in the villages of Ratnagiri and Nagpur districts.

(10) The rural women in some of the study villages can be actively involved through Self-Help Group (SHG) in different home-based industries like different types of handicrafts products, firework industries, bidi making, brick industry, construction industry, electronics industry, spice industries etc.

(11) There is a need for rural occupational diversification which can be implemented through the development of non-

agricultural/non-farm activities. To facilitate this process, several human resources related parametres like education and skill development of rural workers, credit availability for non-farm activities have to be encouraged.

(12) Though the rural villages in Akola, Ratnagiri, Nagpur, and Nashik have distinct advantages in agro-processing, many large-scale processing units have not emerged in these villages. The organized growth of the processing industry also requires priority on post-harvest infrastructures.

(13) The scope for increasing private participation in the development of post-harvest infrastructure such as warehouses, cold storage facilities and transport need to be explored.

(14) In order to remove some of the bottlenecks, contract farming is being practiced in some of the villages of Maharashtra having the facilities of assured irrigation, but for the greater success of contract farming among other things necessitate the promotion of formal relations between growers and industry.

(15) The construction and services sector including tourism, hotel industry, transport and communication and health are the sub-sectors having high potential to generate employment for rural BPL families. The increased disposable rural income, although distributed unevenly, is generating demand for various personal services such as health, recreation, education, travel etc. The textiles and leather, the traditional manufacturing sectors are projected to generate employment for about four lakh rural BPL youth in India, including rural Maharashtra.

(16) National Skill Development Mission (NSDM) envisages to provide 50 crore skilled and productive manpower by 2022. On a very lower side it can be easily estimated that about 5 per cent of total skilled manpower available in India would be from rural BPL households mainly with the initiatives of Ministry of Rural Development and NSDM. It means that approximately 2.5 crore rural BPL youth would be trained in placement based skill development activities by 2022 and will be able to earn a decent income. It can be safely presumed

that by 2015 approximately at least 1.7 crore skilled rural BPL youths would be absorbed in various sectors in India including Maharashtra.

(17) In the rural villages of Maharashtra, there is a need for the establishment of small-scale processing units involving the latest technology to augment non-farm employment, productivity, establishing linkages with the farm sector and finally ensuring avenues of employment to the rural mass.

SMALL AND MARGINAL FARMERS' INCOME

The Situation Assessment Survey of Farmers, 2003 (SAS) conducted by NSSO (59th round) indicates that the monthly per capita income accruing to a farmer household is very low as worked out by Srijit Mishra, IGIDR, Mumbai (September 2007). The near landless (0-0.099 ha.) household, marginal farmers (0.1-1.0 ha.) and small farmers (1.001-2.0 ha.) constitute 9.9 per cent, 55.6 per cent and 18.1 per cent of farmer household respectively. The average family size of the near landless, marginal and small farmers is 5.0, 5.2 and 5.7 respectively. The income of these categories of households has been estimated on the basis of return on *rabi/kharif* crop per annum, return from farm animals and non-farm activity. The monthly income is estimated at Rs. 533 per household in case of near landless households, Rs. 804 for marginal farmers and Rs.1449 in case of small farmer's households in 2002-03. These categories of farmers constitute a significant segment of the rural poor population and thus there is a need to supplement their income through various employment generating/non-farm employment programmes.

The rural BPL households have not a single source of income rather they have to work hard to obtain multiple sources of income. This includes income from wages, cultivation, animal husbandry, non-farm activity etc. A large number of small and marginal farmers, especially in rain-fed areas, falls under the BPL category. The households of farmers can be broadly categorized into nearly landless, marginal, small farmers, semi-medium, medium and large farmers according to size of their landholdings. The income from agriculture (*Rabi* and *Kharif*) to each of these categories of farmers is given in Table 2.15.

Table 2.15: Returns to Cultivation for farmer household, 2002-03

Land-size	*Proportion of farmers HH%*	*Returns from Kharif per annum Rs.*	*Returns from Rabi per annum Rs*	*Total Returns per annum Rs.*	*Family size*
Nearly Landless (<0.099 ha)	9.9	367	462	829	5.0
Marginal (0.1-1 ha)	55.6	3243	2667	5910	5.2
Small (1-2 ha)	18.1	8098	5922	14020	5.7
Semi-Medium (2-4 ha)	10.6	13880	10596	24476	6.2
Medium (4-10 ha)	4.8	22841	20940	43781	6.9
Large (>10 ha)	0.9	33494	34600	68094	7.5

Source: "Farmers, Suicides and Agrarian Crises in India" is there a Way Out? by Srijit Mishra, IGIDR, Mumbai (September 2007), 67th Annual Conference of the Indian Society of Agricultural Economics.

PANCHAYATI RAJ SYSTEM

Both the Governments of India as well as Maharashtra have recognized the need for training of the Panchayat members for capacity-building on participatory local development. Preparing the panchayat members, especially the women among them, for their new roles as local decision-makers, calls for education and training on a massive scale, for which appropriate tailor made training content, methods and tools are needed.

As a first step, there is a need to provide education and training to impart self-confidence to those who have been socially marginalized on caste, ethnic and gender considerations. At the same time, it is necessary to change the attitudes of the socially powerful towards full acceptance of grassroots participation in planning and management of local level development.

A major area of training for Panchayat members is awareness and capacity-building for mobilization and sustainable management of social, physical and financial resources in order to improve the livelihoods of the rural poor who, according to latest official government estimates, make up about 19 per cent of the country's 1.21 billion people. Panchayat members must also be empowered to participate in the planning and implementation of poverty reduction policies/programmes and activities initiated by State and Central Government.

UNICRF with the obligation to promote sustainable development has embarked on activities to strengthen local institutional capacities for improving the status of the poor emphasizing on women and child care. Maharashtra is to improve grassroots participation in decision-making and delivery of support services through decentralization and good district and local governance.

Panchayati Raj is a system of local self-government where in the people takes upon themselves the responsibility for development. It is also a system of institutional arrangement for achieving rural development through people's initiative and participation.

Panchayati Raj involves a three-tier structure of democratic institutions at district, block and village levels, namely Zilla Parishad, Panchayat Samiti and Gram Panchayats respectively. These institutions are considered as training ground for democracy and gives political education to the masses. These institutions were established in 1959 based on the philosophy of decentralization and Gram Swarajya. Rural development plans and programmes are implemented at this level so that fruits of development can accrue to the community directly. Loopholes that devoted in the working of Panchayati Raj institutions can be identified as:

(i) Election not being held on a regular basis.

(ii) Lack of adequate transfer of powers and resources to Panchayati Raj Institutions.

(iii) Lack of Panchayati Raj bodies to generate their own resources such as tax on sale of land.

(iv) Non-representation of women and weaker sections in the elected bodies.

The 73rd and 74th Constitutional Amendments have been made to remove many weaknesses. It has certain features which are binding on the State legislature:

I. Constitutional Status to Panchayati Raj Institutions.

II. Reservation of seats for weaker sections of Society.

III. Election of Panchayats every five years at all levels.

IV. Finance Commission to be set-up by state governments to devolve funds and suggest ways of financing Panchayati Raj Institutions.

V. Election Commission at State Level to conduct Panchayati Raj Elections.

The concept of decentralization has rapidly occupied an important place in international discourse on local governance over the past few decades. This concept has different attributes, including political, economic, administrative and fiscal decentralisation. Yet, in the Indian context, the political decentralisation has been at the core of rural developmental governance. The 73rd Amendment has provided the necessary pace and constitutional backing for the process of devolution of powers to Panchayati Raj Institutions, especially the Gram Panchayat.

Thus participation became a right, and Gram Sabha an accessible forum for citizens to make known their opinions in the process of decision-making at a local level. However, despite the 73rd Amendment, practicing its provisions and enjoying rights of participation has a decade-long trajectory of impediments at the levels of policy and implementation. This has many complex reasons, rooted as they are in various socio-political realities at the policy as well as at the grassroots level. One such reason (at the grassroots level) has been the absence of elaborate and robust 'governance systems' to steer village level decision-making. However, the voluntary sector has increasingly stressed upon the need to encourage and facilitate the practice of local governance based on the principles of 73rd Amendment.

Participation it guaranteed to women and marginal communities by making reservations legal and also by according highest status as a decision-making body to the Gram Sabha (GS). Thus, this Act created conditions conducive to greater decentralization whereby Panchayati Raj Institutions (PRIs) have been bestowed with the responsibility of the village development. To put it simply, the PRIs now have the authority to take decisions, make plans regarding development (mainly pertaining to economic development and social justice) of the village and implement them.

In the post-2000 period, in continuation with the decentralization policy, various government programmes and schemes like Hariyali guidelines for watershed development (2003), Jalswarajya (drinking water and sanitation) project in Maharashtra, National Rural Water Supply Programme (Rajiv Gandhi National Drinking Water Mission, 2008), National Rural Employment Guarantee Act, 2005 and a number of water conservation and sanitation programmes have accorded a key role to the Gram Panchayat. These programmes emphasize on building the capacities of village level committees to plan, implement, operate and maintain various facilities and development activities through a participatory process of informed decision-making and collective action within the ambit of the Gram Sabha and Gram Panchayat. Thus, the Gram Sabha and the Gram Panchayat are in a crucial and a strategic position to determine the development of a village.

Maharashtra pioneered the Village Education Committees much before the Central Government made it mandatory under different schemes. In fact, grassroots level planning and monitoring units in Maharashtra have been in place long before SSA came into existence (SSA Joint Review Committee Report). The majority of the government-funded schools in the state are under the management of Zilla Parishads. The Sarpanch of the Gram Panchayat is the head of the VEC and the other members are community leaders, social activists, local functionaries and the head teacher of the school. Mother-Teacher Associations (MTAs) and Parents-Teachers Association (PTAs) have been constituted and are at the village level.

Maharashtra, one of the leading developed states in India paradoxically faces severe problems in ensuring safe and potable drinking water supply and access in rural areas. Statistics say that out of total number of 86,681 habitations in Maharashtra; near about 40 per cent habitations do not have the capacities to ensure the water supply as per the national norm of 40 LPCD (litres per capita per day) for rural areas. Even of those 60 per cent habitations (nearly 62000) many habitations are slipping back to the original status (being unsustainable), which were tackled earlier by implementing various schemes spending large funds in Maharashtra, the Jalswarajya is the only project which has provided Gram Sabha a prime role in the village level decision-making. The conduct of business regulations (Jalswarajya Project Implementation Plan 2003, hereafter mentioned as PIP) for the Gram Panchayat/PWSC includes a revolutionary clause for the Gram Sabha, which is "all decisions regarding the project will be "prerogative" to the Gram Sabha". This vests supreme powers of the Gram Sabha regarding the village level decision-making about the project (Appraisal Document PAD, Jalswarajya 2002).

The Maharashtra State Women's Policy of 2001 has identified certain areas as relevant and basic to the development of women. Some of the important areas in the context of the villages are:

- One-third representation for women in all cooperative, aided and non-aided institutions;
- Fifty per cent of government funded agriculture related trainees to be women;
- Women to have decisive role in water supply management;
- Retrospective effect to government orders regarding joint ownership in name of husband and wife on all house plots and flats allotted by government;
- Legislation to be introduced for ownership rights for wife in house property acquired by husband;
- Village Mahila Sabha to be held the day before the Gram Sabha, for active participation by women in village activities;
- Strict implementation of rules regarding closure of country liquor shops on demand by 50 per cent of women in an area; and
- Special efforts to increase female literacy (Website of Maharashtra State Commission for Women).

Thus, an optimal utilization of various opportunities provided by the government for women's development has to be made.

PANCHAYATI RAJ SYSTEM IN RURAL MAHARASHTRA

In an attempt to make a critical analysis of Panchayati Raj System in Ajinpur village of Jalgaon district (Maharashtra state), Sampada Mehta, IAS, 2008 batch, remarks that "women members were not found to be very vocal and would speak in the meeting only when prompted by the male colleagues."

Financial position of the Panchayat is not up to the mark. People refuse to pay taxes in the name of GP's failure to provide the basic civic amenities like road, drainage, water and light. GP also does not take strict action for the recovery due owing to political interest. Accounts are maintained but not properly audited. Serious allegations of embezzlement of development funds by the Sarpanch in collusion with the Gram Sevek are noticed.

Commenting on Gram Panchayati System in Randivevadi village of Solapur district Tukaram Haribhau Mundhe, IAS, 2005 batch mentions, "The Sarpanch belongs to the OBC caste. The women members of the Panchayat are just nominal members. In fact, it is their husbands who run the show. In most of the panchayat meetings the husbands are present and the real Panchayat member is absent. The Gram Sabha meetings are seldom held in reality. They are most of the times held on paper."

On Kawatha Village (Akola) Gram Panchayat, Rubal Gupta, IAS, 2008 batch, states "Meetings of the Gram Sabha are conveyed to ensure the development of the people through their participation and mutual cooperation. The annual budget and the development schemes for the village are placed before the Gram Sabha for consideration and approval. The Sarpanch and his assistants answer the questions put by the people. The different problems and difficulties of the people are also discussed in the Gram Sabha."

Naval Kishore Ram, IAS, 2008 batch, remarks, "The Gram Panchayat of Bhopara village (Nanded) there was 7 members including the Sarpanch. All members except two from the general category are from the backward community. The GP has played a remarkable role in the implementation of IAY and total sanitation programme. The fund given under Twelfth Finance Commission could not be utilized because of lack of planning and implementation of Swajaldhara (for drinking water)."

Ashwini M. Joshi, IAS, 2006 batch, observes on the functioning of GP in Telkamptee village (Nagpur), "The people in the village are well aware of the decisions taken by the Panchayat and take keen interest in its functioning and actively participate in the Gram Sabha meetings. The Gram Panchayat works through various committees like water supply, works related, financial committee, health, education and general. These committee meet regularly and take stock of situation". The GP approves the list of BPL families, and through GP all works are executed.

Rahul Ranjan Mahiwal, IAS, 2005 batch, pointed out the noteworthy activities of Maldoli village (Ratnagiri). "Gram Panchayat took commendable efforts in the area of sanitation. Now, all the households in the village are having toilets either individually or community based. Gram Panchayat motivated the people to construct toilets and construct community toilet as well (40 seat capacity). Community toilets are also used innovatively each toilet is allotted to particular 3-4 families and the responsibility of its maintenance rests with them. The village is 100 per cent open defecation free. This village has been awarded "Nirmal Gram Puraskar" from the Central Government."

Examining the ground sordid reality of Dhanora village (Wardha) Gunjan Kinnu, IAS, 2004 batch, remarks, "Though the Gram Sabhas are held on time, i.e. 6 times in a year, the attendance is low and it is difficult to meet the quorum requirement. The scenario only changes when selections of beneficiaries for some schemes are done. At the same time one finds villagers aware of what is going on in the Gram Panchayat and now-a-days the number of applications filed under Right to Information Act is on the rise. The funds to be spent by the GP are generally deposited in the joint accounts of the Gram Panchayat. There is lots of functionalism within the village that hinders the optimal selection of both beneficiaries and works to be taken up under developmental plans. Further, most of the Gram Panchayat members are either themselves contractor or have someone in their families and friends as contractors to whom they want to promote at the cost of public money."

Rucheh Jaivansh, IAS, 2009 batch, while making his study in village Katil Chak has remarked, "The village Katil Chak is an offshoot of a bigger village name Katil located in the Gadchiroli district of Maharashtra. Economy is mainly agricultural and farmers are used to grow single crop. Besides, they are greatly dependent on Tendu leave plucking activity. There is not much forest based economy in the village but they use the minor forest produce, i.e. honey, wood, bamboo etc. for their household purposes. Most of the residents are Dhivar, Kewat and Mahar castes. Community belonging to Mahar caste has 42 per cent of total population of the village. Around 65 per cent houses are single roomed and 90 per cent of houses are electrified, but less than 50 per cent households can afford to avail electricity connections. There are street lights in the village both electric as well as Solar based. Most of the villagers do not have gas connection and they use forest wood for cooking purposes.

Katil Chak does not have independent GP, but comes under main Katil village. The attendance in the Gram Sabha though not good, but seems to be active as job cards are used, the allegation of corruption is rampant, there are disputes in the selection of IAY beneficiaries and maintenance of job cards under MGNREGS."

Notwithstanding some of the problems associated with the effective implementation as well as the success of Panchayati Raj in Maharashtra, one has to reckon with the fact that Maharashtra has secured the top position in the country for effective implementation of Panchayati Raj System in rural areas. The State stood ahead of others in its execution of Central schemes such as Prime Minister's Gram Sadak Yojana, empowerment of women in pachayats, Mahatma Gandhi National Employment Guarantee Scheme etc. Moreover, the State was amongst the first to implement 33 per cent reservation for women in civic body elections.

POVERTY ALLEVIATION PROGRAMME/GOVERNMENT INTERVENTION PROGRAMME FOR RURAL POOR

The Department of Rural Development is implementing a number of programmes in rural areas through the State Governments for poverty reduction, employment generation, rural infrastructure, habitant development, and provision of basic minimum services.

Indira Awas Yojana, drinking water and sanltation facilities, old age pension schemes, Rashtriya Swasthya Bima Yojana and other welfare schemes in operation are expected to improve the living conditions of the rural poor and thereby enhance their capacity to work and thus increase income.

Besides, rural poor focused approach of the Ministry of Rural Development, other Central Ministries/Departments and State Governments are implementing numerous schemes as well for the benefit of rural people including BPL families. Among these, programmes implemented by the Office of DCHL/HC), Ministry of Textiles, Department of AHD&F, Department of Women and Child Development, M/O Social Justice and Empowerment, HRD, Agriculture, Tribal Affairs, etc. have direct bearing on the rural people directly and indirectly benefiting and adding to the income of the rural BPL families.

Keeping in view the fact that rural roads are vital to economic growth and measures for poverty alleviation in the village, government has launched a 100 per cent centrally sponsored scheme called the Pradhan Mantri Gram Sadak Yojana (PMGSY). The Programme seeks to provide connectivity to all unconnected habitations in the rural areas with a population of more than 500 persons through good all-weather roads by the end of the Tenth Five Year Plan period.

Over 11 Plan periods there have been some cumulative gains in a few sectors. In rural areas, seven major flagship programmes are being administered, with less overall coordination between them than is looked for—a contrast against the ease with which the Central Government's major ministries collaborate on advancing the cause of the urban elite—but which nonetheless have given us indication that their combined impact has improved the conditions of some.

The seven programmes are: the Mahatma Gandhi National Rural Employment Guarantee Act (MGNREGA), the National Rural Livelihood Mission (NRLM), Indira Awas Yojana (IAY), the National Rural Drinking Water Programme (NRDWP) and Total Sanitation Campaign (TSP), the Integrated Watershed Development Programme (IWDP), Pradhan Mantri Grameen Sadak Yojana (PMGSY), and rural electrification which includes separation of agricultural feeders and includes also the Rajiv Gandhi Grameen Vidyutikaran Yojana (RGGVY).

The Government of India has time and again claimed that the Eleventh Five Year Plan (2007-12) has sought to raise the share of public expenditure on health (both Central and the States) from less than 1 per cent of GDP in 2006-07 to 2 per cent and then 3 per cent. For this, the National Rural Health Mission (launched in 2005) was proposed to strengthen healthcare infrastructure in rural areas, provide more sub-centres, better staff and equip primary health and community health centies. The Plan targets relating to infant mortality rate, maternal mortality rate, total fertility rate, under-nutrition among children, anaemia among women and girls, provision of clean drinking water for all, and raising child gender ratio for the age-group of 0-6.

RURAL POVERTY IN MAHARASHTRA

It has been considered one of the richest states in India in terms of per capita income for its impressive economic development even though the incidence of poverty in the state remains close to the national average. The Economic Survey of Maharashtra 2007-08 lists

31.7 million people, or 30.7 per cent of the total population, as living below the poverty line (BPL). Going by the National Sample Survey held between July 2004 and June 2005, the latest estimates of poverty prepared by the Planning Commission have exhibited poverty levels declining from 36.9 per cent in 1993-94 to 30.7 per cent in 2004-05. However, in absolute number, the BPL population has grown by 1.2 million during the intervening period. The State's economy grew at a quicker pace than the all-India average during 1980-81 to 1992-93, but it made a slight decline during 1993-94 to 2003-04 due to poorer performance of agriculture and industry. Agriculture's contribution to GSDP has come down to 12 per cent in 2002-03, but more than 50 per cent of total workers are still engaged in this sector (Mishra and Panda, 2005).

Table 2.16 depicts the district-wise percentage of rural households below official poverty line. The district Nandurbar has the highest percentage of poverty households (72%) followed by Gondiya (57.29%), Gadchiroli (54.69%), Dhule (53.65%), Bhandara (51.20%) and Amravati (49.57%).

DISTRICT INCOME

Inter-regional inequality within Maharashtra has been a theme of concern since decades. As early as 1984, a fact-finding committee under the chairmanship of V.M. Dandekar had attempted to quantify the regional imbalance in Maharashtra.

Focusing on Poverty alleviation programmes of Katil Chak village of Gadchiroli district Mr. Rucheh Jaivansh, IAS, 2009 batch, has presented the following illustrations on two important development programmes of the Government.

STATUS OF INDIRA AWAS YOJANA (IAY)

It well known that Indira Awas Yojana has been taken up independently since first January 1996 in order to meet the housing needs of the rural poor. The Indira Awas Yojana (IAY) is a flagship scheme of the Ministry of Rural Development to provide houses to the poor in the rural areas. Housing is one of the basic necessities for economic security and social recognition of the rural poor. Thus, the objective of the Indira Awas Yojana is primarily to help construction/

Table 2.16: District-wise Percentage of Rural Households below Official Poverty Line

Sl. No.	*Districts*	*Percentage of Rural Households below poverty line*
1.	Nandurbar	72.00
2.	Gondiya	57.29
3.	Gadchiroli	54.69
4.	Dhule	53.65
5.	Bhandara	51.20
6.	Amravati	49.57
7.	Chandrapur	47.66
8.	Akola	47.47
9.	Washim	47.33
10.	Yavatmal	46.00
11.	Thane	45.00
12.	Buldhana	44.47
13.	Jalgaon	43.62
14.	Wardha	41.00
15.	Nashik	40.58
16.	Sindhudurg	39.08
17.	Jalna	38.35
18.	Nagpur	37.03
19.	Aurangabad	35.46
20.	Ratnagiri	34.67
21.	Hingoli	34.53
22.	Nanded	33.66
23.	Parbhani	33.26
24.	Osmanabad	32.82
25.	Raigad	30.21
26.	Latur	29.81
27.	Solapur	29.31
28.	Beed	26.84
29.	Pune	24.90
30.	Ahmadnagar	23.84
31.	Kolhapur	17.57
32.	Sangli	16.59
33.	Satara	15.97

***Note*:** Total Urban Area of Mumbai city and Mumbai Suburban are not included.

Source: District Socio-Economic Reviews, Government of Maharashtra (2009 and 2010).

upgradation of dwelling units of members of Scheduled Castes/ Scheduled Tribes, freed bonded labourers and other below the poverty line non-SC/ST rural households by providing them a lump-sum financial assistance. The Indira Awas Yojana is a centrally sponsored scheme funded on cost-sharing basis between the Government on India and the State Government in the ratio of 75:25.

The procedure of the allotment is such that block-wise and panchayat-wise targets are decided at the level of District Rural Development Agency (as per target for the district) and such targets are given category-wise. In addition, panchayat-wise waiting lists are prepared (through software-mixing of BPL waiting list) and these are approved by 'Gram Sabha'. The decided amount, i.e. Rs. 68,500 is given in three installments (*via.* panchayat samiti office) to the beneficiaries in the waiting list as according to the targets and funds allotted for a particular year. The first installment of Rs. 25,000 is released for initiating construction, after completion of phase-1, the next installment of Rs. 25,000 is given. The remaining balance amount/final installment of Rs. 18,500 is released after the construction is over. The construction area must be to a minimum of 250 squre feet. To release the final installment of Rs.18,500 payments, the certificate of the sarpanch and the Gram Sevak is mandatory. The beneficiary has also to construct a toilet, which is also compulsory.

IMPLEMENTATION AND CHALLENGES OF IAY

The experience of the Katli Chak village study highlighted the loopholes and difficulties at every stage of IAY implementation. The benefit takes a long time to reach the beneficiaries in cases where it does reach and in other cases, the benefit does not percolate down at all and the funds are siphoned off.

First and foremost, the problem is that of BPL categorization where many undeserving people enter the scenario. Then, the beneficiaries are not catered as per the priority waiting list and jumps can be easily noticed due to various reasons cited-for example, beneficiary is out-of-station, beneficiary does not have land to build the house etc. However, many a times, such reasons are not true.

Then many of the beneficiaries are uneducated and they are not aware of the allotment procedure, therefore, many intermediaries including public representatives exploit them and extract money in return for the false promises of getting them IAY benefit. Other problem is that the banks and post office branches are extremely reluctant in opening up the accounts in a transparent manner. Also, beneficiaries, who finally are able to cross all these hurdles may not actually get the money as there many cases, where the thumb impression of the beneficiaries are taken on the withdrawal forms and the money is taken out of their accounts without their knowledge.

Another issue is that the money which is given finds its way towards other consumptive needs and physical progress (i.e. actual house construction) is extremely poor in case of Indira Awas Yojana. Survey of 5 HHs having IAY clearly revealed various bottlenecks affecting service delivery of IAY at village level. All the households except one had paid 'commission' (bribe) to the middlemen, banker or block official.

SWARNAJAYANTI GRAM SWAROZGAR YOJANA (SGSY) STATUS

The objective of Swarnajayanti Gram Swarozgar Yojana (SGSY) is to bring the assisted poor families (*swarozgaries*) above the poverty line by ensuring appreciable sustained level of income over a period of time. The objective is to be achieved by *inter alia*, organising the rural poor into Self-Help Groups (SHGs) through the process of social mobilization, their training and capacity-building and provision of income generating assets.

The SHG approach helps the poor to build their self-confidence through community action and interactions in group meetings and collective decision-making enable them to identify and prioritize needs and resources. This process would ultimately lead to the strengthening and socio-economic empowerment of the rural poor as well as improve their collective bargaining power. SGSY lays stress on the cluster approach. This implies that instead of funding diverse activities, each block should concentrate on a few select activities (key activities) and attend to all aspects of these activities, so that, the *swarozgaries* can draw sustainable incomes from their investment.

These key activities should preferably be taken up in clusters so that the monitoring, but the Swarnjayanti Gram Swarozgar Yojana (SGSY) is to bring the assisted poor families (*swarozgaries*) above the poverty Line by ensuring appreciable sustained level of income over a period of time. This objective is to be achieved by *inter alia* organising the rural poor in to Self-Help Groups (SHGs) through the process of social mobilization, their training and capacity-building and provision of income generating assets. The SHG approach helps the poor to build their self-confidence through community action.

There are various aspects of SGSY various stages of evolution of SHGs include formation, group stabilization, micro-credit; micro-enterprise establishment etc. And all these stages involve grading at various levels and linkages with the banks according to the performance indicators.

The role of NGOs, community based organizations (CBOs), community coordinators, facilitators and animators is very important is this regard as the group formation and stabilization is not a spontaneous process. Capacity-building and training of the self-help groups (SHG) is also an important dimension and includes varied levels from the initial activities like book-keeping to the finally taken up economic activities.

In this context, there are around 385 Self-Help Group (SHG) being catered to by around 12 NGO/CBOs/Animators, where key identified activities include dairy, fishery, vegtable growing, medicinal plant cultivation, stitching etc. and there are 4 bank branches (Grameen bank, UCO bank) catering to the credit needs of these group. In addition, field extension officers do the overall monitoring.

Rucheh Jaivansh, IAS, 2009 batch, has remarked, "Though these groups have resulted in overall upliftment of the members and have also led to their economic as well as social empowerment, however, main problems are encountered include apathy of the banks, lack of will on the part of the facilitators, poor repayment capacity in few cases, internal disputes of the group, dying groups and lack of constant monitoring."

In order to attain the minimum desired level of income, approximately, the annual support of Rs. 10,000 or more would be required to the BPL household. At present, in India about 65 per cent of SHGs are involved in the primary sector engaged in the activities of dairy, poultry, fishery and other agricultural allied activities for their livelihood.

The coverage of BPL households under credit linked micro-enterprises and placement based skill development programme will enable them to break the vicious circle of poverty. In this direction, universalization of SHGs and up-scaling the job opportunities for rural BPL youth through skill development need to be accorded a priority in the poverty alleviation strategic framework. Thus, the Mission Mode approach to SGSY intends to provide additional income to the rural BPL households through self-employment and placement based skill development in a time bound manner.

Since the unorganized workers account for about 93 per cent of the total workforce and over the years there is a steady growth in it in India. It is advocated that India had a long tradition of informal social security and social assistance system directed particularly towards the more vulnerable sections of the society, but underwent steady and inevtable erosion. The social security initiatives of the Centre, State and NGOs implemented during the past indicated that the needs are much more than the supports provided and the efforts must be targeted and vast enough to cover the growing unorganized workers.

It is argued that the major security needs of the unorganized workers are food security, nutritional security, health security, housing security, employment security, income security, life and accident security, and old age security. In sum, the study calls for a comprehensive, universal and integrated social security system for the unorganised workers in India.

The ongoing debate over poverty in India—its extent, trends, causes, and cures—is complex and often controversial. The analysis is important in view of the fact that India faces considerable challenges in moving to the next generation of reforms, sustain growth, and expand the benefits of rapid growth across sectors, regions, and people and finally removal of poverty.

On the basis of rural household as a unit, we need to focus on poverty eradication strategy. The rural poor primarily comprise small and marginal farmers, especially in rain-fed areas, landless labourers, fisher-folk, herders, and women-headed households. Households below poverty line subsist on multiple sources of income. The current poverty line is of the order of Rs. 22,000 per annum for a household of five members.

The additional fund requirement over the next seven-year period can be met through a combination of additional budgetary support to the restructured SGSY, better coordination with employment generation and social security schemes of other Ministries, project support from multi-lateral funding agencies, enhanced credit mobilization, National Skill Development Corporation/Fund and Public-Private Partnerships.

In the light of the above-discussion it is concluded that:

1. In the context of Maharashtra, through Zilla Parisad and under it, Block Samiti and Gram Panchayat, all poverty alleviation schemes are implemented in the villages. Therefore, Panchayati Raj System and Rural Development are inter-related. Indira Awas Yojana, SGRY, MGNREGA are some of the poverty amelioration schemes being implemented in the villages.
2. Besides ensuring the availability of funds, strong and efficient governance structure and other factors as mentioned below are essential to implement the programmes in a time bound manner to realize their visible impact:
   (a) Increasing the awareness of programmes and access of rural poor to avail the benefits;
   (b) Change in vision/outlook of rural poor;
   (c) Social mobilization for collective action and economies of scale;
   (d) Replication of successful experiments on mass scale;
   (e) Introduction of appropriate technologies and involvement of experts;
   (f) Removing the design defects of various schemes and programmes based on earlier experiences;
   (g) Availability of timely and adequate credit at low cost;
   (h) Emphasis on strengthening forward and backward linkages;
   (i) Setting-up of dedicated, motivated and professional implementation structure;
   (j) Proper targeting through suitable poverty mapping mechanism;
   (k) Transparency and accountability of implementing structure; and
   (l) Coordination with other ministries and convergence and coordination of their programmes.
3. Though various programmes have been put in place from time-to-time to improve the socio-economic condition and

to strengthen the livelihood system of rural poor to enable them to cross the poverty line, but still in India, 28 per cent of rural population is living below the poverty line. It has been realized that only time-bound outcome based focused approach by following well established strategic framework and dedicated machinery for implementation are prerequisites to tackle the poverty issue within stipulated time period.

4. Since the poor households have multiple sources of income, the core poverty reduction strategy has to ensure that each rural BPL household is provided with a combination of: (i) self-employment, (ii) skill development and placement, (iii) wage employment, and (iv) pension so that combination of them would be able to provide adequate income to rise above the poverty line.
5. The proposed strategy should attach priority in improving access to natural resources (land water, forest), physical (road, power, storage, communication), social (education, health, drinking water etc.) and financial infrastructure.
6. The people centric strategic framework with emphasis on social mobilization, productive and remunerative work, people's participation in choice of work and occupation, social security network to mitigate risk and financial inclusion along with dedicated motivated professional machinery is necessary to tackle the poverty in a time bound manner.
7. Besides, macro-economic policies (monetary, fiscal, trade) have to be pro-poor through emphasis on labour intensive approach to the growth process. These issues have intra-ministerial implications and thus need comprehensive integrated approach through convergence and coordination.
8. Notwithstanding a plethora of governmental intervention schemes for the rural people and poor, the benefits disproportionately percolate in the villages. There exists the problem of regional disparities and critical gaps in the health care delivery system, of infant mortality, obstetric care, maternal and child health, of '*dais*' and *anganwadis*, medical termination of pregnancy, and the desperate need for better staffed primary health centres.

9. As has been observed that what over amount is allocated for employment programme or rural development with a view to alleviating the poverty could not get success due to several factors. These are the whole amount is not properly spent; there are leakages and misappropriation of funds at different stages and only 20 per cent of the funds percolating to the grassroots level. These factors have led to disparity in the distribution of income and wealth, black money and poverty remained as an unsolvable problem. When the invisible amount is not invested the expected employment is not created and therefore, the income for the poor community is not generated. As such, the poor remains poor despite plans and programmes are envisaged.
10. It is paradoxical that the benefits of economic growth have not percolated to the poorer sections in spite of the high growth rate attained by the Indian economy in the recent years. The fundamental objectives of planning such as reduction in poverty, unemployment and regional disparity instead of being mitigated have been accentuated over the periods. The poorer sections have been deprived of growth which demonstrates that equity aspect have been undermined at the cost of economic growth.
11. It has been found out that the poverty alleviation programmes in India are confined to a set of targeted intervention and could not substantially affect poverty. Growth has not penetrated so as to ameliorate the socio-economic conditions of the poor tribes, scheduled castes, agricultural labourers, wage earners and other depressed sections of the society. The incidence of poverty is more concentrated among these groups.
12. But, there are also cases relating to the problems of proper implementation and leakages/misappropriation of funds by the government officials and panchayati functionaries. Therefore, the cancer of corruption needs to be combated through stringent action. If required, we have to formulate proper legislation as well as speedy implementation of such provisions.

Table 2.17 focuses the poverty ratio as well as the district-wise income in the state, estimated for various NSSO regions in

Table 2.17: Per capita income across the districts of Maharashtra

Divisions	*Districts*	*PCNDDP (1993-04 Prices)*	
		Value 2003-04	*Avg. Annual Growth 2000-01 to 2003-04*
Amravati (Western Vidarbha)	Akola	11235	7.2
	Amaravati	11616	4.2
	Buldhana	9644	7.5
	Washim	11035	7.2
	Yavatmal	10474	3.2
	Total	10770	5.3
Aurangabad (Marathwada)	Aurangabad	11976	-0.1
	Beed	9418	-0.6
	Hingoli	10593	8.8
	Jalna	8714	3.1
	Latur	8963	2.9
	Nanded	9220	7.1
	Osmanabad	8134	-3.4
	Parbhani	9713	4.1
	Total	9713	2.3
Konkan Excluding Mumbai	Raigad	18132	3.2
	Ratnagiri	14064	11.2
	Sindhudurg	15812	7.9
	Thane	18723	2.8
	Total	17867	4.0
Mumbai	Mumbai	35483	6.9
Nagpur (Eastern Vidarbha)	Bhandara	11859	7.8
	Chandrapur	13792	6.1
	Gadchiroli	7577	9.6
	Gondia	10051	3.8
	Nagpur	18996	6.3
	Wardha	13379	6.2
	Total	12212	6.5
Nashik (Dhule, Jalgaon and Nandurbar are known as Khandesh)	Ahmednagar	11602	3.4
	Dhule	10360	8.3
	Jalgaon	12677	5.5
	Nandurbar	9761	10.7
	Nashik	14413	4.8
	Total	12470	5.8
Pune (Western Maharashtra)	Kolhapur	16832	3.3
	Pune	20424	2.7
	Sangli	14861	0.5
	Satara	13723	4.0
	Solapur	11639	1.4
	Total	16484	2.6
Maharashtra State		16479	4.8
Maharashtra except Mumbai		13818	4.1

Source: *Economic Survey of Maharashtra*, 2004-05.

Maharashtra. It should be noted that the estimation of district income has started in recent years and such estimates should be considered tentative. Per capita net district domestic product (PCNDDP) for 2002-03 on 1993-94 prices indicates that the districts of Kolhapur, Mumbai (including Mumbai sub-urban), Nagpur, Pune, Raigad and Thane have an income greater than the state's average of Rs.16,479. In all these districts, except Raigad, 60 per cent of the population is urban. Districts of Nashik, Ratnagiri, Sangli and Sindhudurg have PCNDDP that is above an average calculated after excluding Mumbai. None of the districts of Amravati and Aurangabad division have PCNDDP that is greater than the state's average even after excluding Mumbai and urban areas together, the proportion of poor at 13 per cent was the least in the Coastal Region (Konkan division that includes Mumbai and its sub-urban areas) of Maharashtra in 1999-2000. In the Eastern Region (the eastern Vidarbha division after excluding Nagpur and Wardha districts) and the Inland Eastern Region (western Vidarbha division and Nagpur and Wardha districts of eastern Vidarbha), it is as high as 40 per cent, i.e. three times that of the Coastal Region (Mishra and Panda, 2005).

SOCIAL INCLUSION AND THE MOBILIZATION OF THE POOR

Social exclusion is a complex and multi-dimensional process. It involves the lack of or denial of resources, rights, goods and services, and the inability to participate in the normal relationships and activities available to the majority of people in society, whether in economic, social, cultural or political arenas. It affects both the quality of life of individuals and the equity and cohesion of society as a whole. Social exclusion describes a situation where certain groups within a society are systematically disadvantaged because they are discriminated against. Such groups are often differentiated by race, ethnicity, age or gender. Social exclusion exists to some degree in all societies, and can occur across a number of dimensions: economic, social, political and cultural.

The policy of economic empowerment is expected to enhance the capacities of discriminated groups to take advantage of the ongoing social and economic progress. Improved access to income-earning assets will improve the capacities of the discriminated groups and enable them to partake in business activities. Educational and skill development is expected to increase employability and enable them to access jobs in the private and public sectors.

Even if they gain access to incoming earning assets, education and skill through empowerment measures, but due to the practice of discrimination in various market particularly the labour market and non-market transition they may fail to get due share and participation in ownership of assets, employment, social needs like education, health, housing and other. In the absence of equal opportunity policies in the form of reservation, and similar measures, the excluded and the marginalized groups may continue to face denial. It is precisely for this reason that equal opportunity polices as complementary to the policy of general economic empowerment (pro-poor polices) are developed in the form of reservation policy and similar policies in many countries to ensure fair share to discriminated groups.

Faced with social ignorance, anger, deprivation and inhuman treatment inherent in the system, the disadvantaged SC and ST people face the poverty condition. In the absence of sources of livelihood, these groups are likely to adopt the strategy of distress migration.

Poverty and social exclusion are inter-related in India. Social exclusion has its roots in India's historical divisions along lines of caste, tribe, and the excluded sex, that is, women. These inequalities are structural in nature and have kept entire groups trapped, incapable to take advantage of opportunities that economic growth offers. Culturally rooted systems perpetuate inequality and culture of poverty that afflicts disadvantaged groups, it is these inequality traps that prevent such groups from breaking out. Exclusion can be explained by inequalities in opportunities, access to markets, and in voice and agency.

The ongoing debate over poverty in India—its extent, trends, causes, and cures—is complex and often controversial. In recent decades, because difficult measurement issues have arisen, a disproportionate amount of attention has been devoted to assessments of the extent of poverty and the rate of poverty decline. The analysis is significant in light of the fact that India faces considerable challenges in moving to the next generation of reforms, sustain growth, and expand the benefits of rapid growth across sectors, regions, and people.

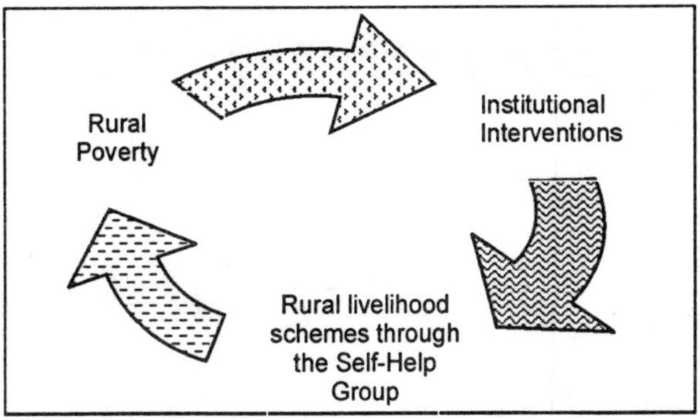

Fig. 2.1: Means of poverty alleviation

In the light of above illustration, we need to develop a mechanism of enhancing the income of the rural poor through Self-Help Group (SHG) initiatives, which is a group approach to share the benefits among the stake-holders.

The SHG approach is all about rebuilding strong and homogenous communities thereby bringing people together and empowering them. The delivery of micro-finance services has been largely through the formation of self-help groups (SHG) or linking of such groups with Panchayati Raj System or established institutional lenders such as banks and micro-finance institutes.

The only way to lower the risk that the rural poor face would be to reduce their vulnerability through the use of micro-finance to engage positively incapacity-building. The phenomenal growth of Indian micro-finance sector and its potential for further expansion attracts everyone in terms of product deepening, diversification and expansion of geographical spread. The Self-Help Group-Bank Linkage Programme (SBLP), pioneered by NABARD in 1992, has emerged as the largest and the fastest growing community based micro-finance programme in the world. The Microfinance Institutions (MFIs) too have emerged as strong players in supplementing the role of formal financial institutions in providing micro-finance services to the poor. However, despite various policy interventions aimed at upscaling the efforts to bring in the excluded families, particularly the weak and vulnerable members of society including those who live on the fringe of forests, tribes etc., within its fold, financial exclusion continues to deprive millions of people living below a

Table 2.18: District-wise progress in credit linkage of SHGs 2007-08 and 2009-10 in Maharashtra

Districts	2007-08						2009-10					
	Commercial Banks	Bank loan Disbursed (Rs.Lakhs)	RRBs	Bank loan Disbursed (Rs.Lakhs)	DCCBs	Bank loan Disbursed (Rs.Lakhs)	Commercial Banks	Bank loan Disbursed (Rs.Lakhs)	RRBs	Bank loan Disbursed (Rs.Lakhs)	DCCBs	Bank loan Disbursed (Rs.Lakhs)
Ahmadnagar	1679	1080.46	N.A.	N.A.	1863	337.78	160	180.87	N.A.	N.A.	1360	604.64
Akola	1120	339.26	944	2.25	368	156.13	436	132.57	417	142	67	9.5
Amaravati	2873	871.87	N.A.	N.A.	107	10.9	946	370.84	7	3.63	105	25.88
Aurangabad	1056	517.57	572	99.74	235	58.12	1615	583.55	1896	986.42	351	144.5
Beed	631	377.93	1434	365.14	131	87.61	844	509.79	407	112.64	117	36.25
Bhandara	1319	346.58	363	110.01	1463	521.91	1575	598.03	485	61.6	923	564.98
Buldhana	1692	614.74	533	0.94	50	13.05	603	205.26	243	61	8	7.9
Chandrapur	2062	461.62	607	172.85	5260	726.38	599	341.41	539	276.01	1142	213.27
Dhule	1095	178.75	0	0	120	17.04	516	70.46	N.A.	N.A.	172	24.38
Gadchiroli	424	172.97	432	131.45	560	57.59	74	42.25	346	143.56	777	165.53
Gondia	568	218.45	514	157	259	64.35	229	93.4	314	96.97	496	99.75
Hingoli	334	194.55	701	175.88	240	35.05	239	195.24	285	105.88	213	37.83
Jalgoan	970	535.36	N.A.	N.A.	229	112.33	1307	194.37	N.A.	N.A.	164	47.38
Jalana	284	53.8	631	145.73	191	41.26	N.A.	N.A.	1059	380.54	201	48.21
Kolhapur	1409	303.68	N.A.	N.A.	4567	363.42	1569	812.6	N.A.	N.A.	3682	250.4
Latur	729	429.84	1813	437.96	1080	69.58	N.A.	N.A.	524	214.22	515	160
Nagpur	2853	964.53	0	0	563	69.03	N.A.	N.A.	N.A.	N.A.	842	222.77
Nanded	1589	498.88	1759	456.8	33	2.01	355	254.88	434	233.25	1	0.34
Nandurbar	623	101.13	N.A.	N.A.	108	1090	347	57.9	N.A.	N.A.	135	19.15

(Contd.)

Districts	2007-08						2009-10					
	Commercial Banks	Bank loan Disbursed (Rs.Lakhs)	RRBs	Bank loan Disbursed (Rs.Lakhs)	DCCBs	Bank loan Disbursed (Rs.Lakhs	Commercial Banks	Bank loan Disbursed (Rs.Lakhs	RRBs	Bank loan Disbursed (Rs.Lakhs	DCCBs	Bank loan Disbursed (Rs.Lakhs
Nashik	1533	482.9	N.A.	N.A.	31	13.06	N.A.	N.A.	N.A.	N.A.	381	550
Parbhani	869	472.51	440	110.79	153	29.77	411	171.5	867	318.5	209	58.82
Pune	7008	3220.19	N.A.	N.A.	2923	371.41	N.A.	N.A.	N.A.	N.A.	2639	1479.77
Raigad	1177	442.04	N.A.	N.A.	511	96.64	339	117.65	N.A.	N.A.	653	183.85
Ratnagiri	188	99.29	75	29.66	244	19.9	1124	403.23	319	146.52	488	248.5
Sangli	994	319.42	N.A.	N.A.	4735	489.76	491	120.28	N.A.	N.A.	2401	340.58
Satara	1996	772.49	N.A.	N.A.	2525	182.9	732	349.86	N.A.	N.A.	1413	183.02
Sindhudurg	309	76.94	101	34.63	554	86.3	N.A.	N.A.	N.A.	N.A.	265	73.89
Solapur	2080	335.28	286	203.58	280	38.27	609	514.09	49	80.12	177	63.24
Thane	720	343.09	70	16.1	1001	129.78	636	244.85	214	50.95	1187	102.87
Osmanabad	759	151.36	998	252.51	249	24.34	N.A.	N.A.	N.A.	N.A.	51	11.9
Wardha	1234	543.5	N.A.	N.A.	322	35.21	1278	749.8	60	15	316	38.49
Washim	1077	303.77	733	1.49	330	150.76	475	105.04	229	55	128	4.23
Yawatmal	5625	1347.55	846	99.77	2304	203.92	832	558.89	595	97.19	1716	257.69
Total	**48879**	**17172.3**	**13852**	**3004.28**	**33589**	**5705.56**	**18341**	**7978.61**	**9289**	**3581**	**23295**	**6279.51**

Note: N.A. = Not Available

Source: Statistical Statement on SHG-Bank Linkage Programme, NABARD, Pune, 2007-08, pp.3-7, 2009-10, pp.3-7.

Table 2.19: District-wise Numbers of SHGs and Bank Loan Disbursement

Sl. No.	Districts	No. of SHGs and Bank loan					
		No. of SHGs 2007-08	Bank loan Disbursed (Rs.Lakhs) 2007-08	No. of SHGs 2010-11	Bank loan Disbursed (Rs.Lakhs) 2010-11	Percentage growth in No. of SHGs (2007-08 to 2010-11)	Percentage growth in bank loan disbursed (2007-08 to 2010-11)
1.	Ahmednagar	3542	1418.24	5367	1814.76	51.52	27.96
2.	Akola	2452	497.64	3823	1252.34	55.91	151.66
3.	Amaravati	2980	882.77	5339	3751.18	79.16	324.93
4.	Aurangabad	1914	739.43	9887	7410.96	416.56	902.25
5.	Beed	2196	830.68	4245	2529.19	93.31	204.47
6.	Bhandhara	3145	978.50	8686	6422.14	176.18	556.32
7.	Buldhana	2275	628.73	4498	4185.67	97.71	565.73
8.	Chandrapur	7929	1360.85	12696	5559.45	60.12	308.53
9.	Dhule	1215	195.79	2131	702.70	75.39	258.90
10.	Gadchiroli	1416	362.01	3483	1992.13	145.97	450.30
11.	Gondia	1341	439.80	2695	1163.93	100.97	164.65
12.	Hingoli	1275	405.48	2698	1991.24	111.61	391.08
13.	Jalgoan	1482	726.77	4079	2448.26	175.24	236.87
14.	Jalana	1106	240.79	2806	1113.11	153.71	362.27
15.	Kolhapur	5976	667.10	12051	1735.42	101.66	160.14
16.	Latur	3622	964.38	5365	2137.38	48.12	121.63
17.	Nagpur	3568	1086.76	4684	1447.34	31.28	33.18
18.	Nanded	3390	959.49	4460	1651.41	31.56	72.11
19.	Nandurbar	731	112.03	1470	782.82	101.09	598.76
20.	Nashik	1564	495.96	4488	3189.13	186.96	543.02
21.	Parbhani	1462	613.07	3865	2799.27	164.36	356.60
22.	Pune	11754	1423.11	15545	3773.12	32.25	165.13
23.	Raigad	1688	538.68	3405	1577.90	101.72	192.92
24.	Ratnagiri	507	148.85	2714	653.36	435.31	338.94
25.	Sangli	5774	824.33	10300	3131.90	78.39	279.93
26.	Satara	5091	1023.79	7946	2154.65	56.08	110.46
27.	Sindhudurg	964	197.87	1671	1155.30	73.34	483.87
28.	Solapur	3941	830.23	5014	1269.23	27.23	52.88
29.	Thane	1791	488.97	5275	2492.58	194.53	409.76
30.	Osmanabad	2006	428.23	2089	476.13	4.14	11.19
31.	Wardha	1557	578.81	4626	2793.91	197.11	382.70
32.	Washim	2140	456.02	3445	1150.32	60.98	152.25
33.	Yawatmal	8775	1651.24	14261	6499.43	62.52	293.61
	Total	**100569**	**23196.40**	**185107**	**83207.66**	**84.06**	**258.71**

Note: Data compiled.

Source: *Statistical Statement on SHG Bank Linkage Programme*, NABARD, Pune, 2007-08, p. 4, 2010-11, p. 2.

sustainable level of income. The comparatively disadvantageous groups like various tribal communities and other vulnerable poor people struggling to have assured means for livelihood need to be addressed.

However, in spite of best efforts of the Rural Financial Institutions (RFIs) and the MFI sector, the magnitude of financial exclusion is truly staggering. Further, one of the key challenges facing the policy makers today is how to make the growth process more inclusive.

Table 2.18 depicts the district-wise progress in credit linkage of SHGs Maharashtra during the period 2007-08 and 2009-10.

Table 2.19 presents the district wise numbers of SHGs and bank loan disbursement in Maharashtra during the period 2007-08 and 2010-11. The data relates to the year 2007-08 and the cumulative figures are shown in the year 2010-11. During the period 2007-08 and 2010-11 there has been highest growth of SHGs in Ratnagiri (435.31%) followed by Aurangabad (416.5%) and Wardha (197.1%). Similarly, in terms of Percentage growth in bank loan disbursed (2007-08 to 2010-11), Aurangabad has recorded the highest growth of 902.2 per cent followed by Nadurbar (598.7%) and Bhandhara (556.3%).

CONCLUSION

To conclude, Maharashtra is economically among the most developed states in the country. The state's economy grew faster than the national average in the 1980s, but has slowed down to a bit lower than the national level growth since the early 1990s. While the slow down period coincides with the post-liberalization phase, we have not attempted to empirically examine whether such a slowdown is a consequence of the liberalization process itself. *A priori*, one can raise points both in favour and against such an argument. The economy is witnessing considerable structural change and might be passing through a transition phase. Anyway, the magnitude of the slowdown is not large and the state's economy continues to grow at an average rate of above 5 per cent per annum.

Maharashtra, with a geographical area of 3,07,713 sq-km., consisting 34 districts is the third largest state in India. As per the Census of 2001, the state has a total population of 96.8 million, that is, 9.42 per cent of India's total population.

Historically known for its industrialization, the state of Maharashtra has achieved higher economic growth as compared to many other Indian states. The state ranks fourth in terms of per capita income and second in terms of industrial growth during the year 2007-08. Since its formation in 1960, the state per capita NSDP grew at 4.73 per cent till 1999-00 and after that the rate has slightly declined to 2.43 per cent. A paradoxical feature of high economic growth of India in general and Maharashtra in particular, is the low level of structural transformation in terms of employment.

Around 55 per cent of the working population still depends on agriculture for their livelihood. This intense dependence on agriculture leads to all types of deprivation especially in the rural areas.

Maharashtra has secured the top position in the country for effective implementation of Panchayati Raj System in rural areas. The state stood ahead of others in its execution of Central schemes such as Prime Minister's Gram Sadak Yojana, Empowerment of Women in Pachayats, and Mahatma Gandhi National Employment Guarantee Scheme.

The state was amongst the first to implement 33 per cent reservation for women in civic body elections.

Maharashtra does not have comparative advantage in agriculture as compared to the other states due to soil and climate conditions. About a third of the state falls under the rain shadow area and the gross irrigated area in the state constitutes only 17 per cent as compared to 41 per cent for India as a whole. Yields for several crops are law and agricultural growth rate as a result has not kept pace with the population growth rate since early1990s. While agriculture now accounts for 12 per cent of GSDP, about 55 per cent of the total workers are engaged in this sector. Responding to its comparative advantage, the cropping pattern has been shifting from cereals to non-cereals cash crops. Sugarcane and horticulture were the major driving forces of agricultural income growth during the 1980s and 1990s. The benefits of growth have, however, not spread equally across social groups or regions, which partly explains the prevalence of high poverty in rural areas compared to other states with similar mean incomes.

Despite these developments, rural poverty in the state has declined due to a variety of factors like some reduction in the proportion of population dependent on agriculture, public employment prorammes and growth of non-farm income. There is need for more systematic data and analysis to conclusively comment on these factors. The absolute level of per capita income for Maharashtra has been considerably higher than that at the all-India level whereas the proportion of poor has continued to be near the all-India average. Possible reductions in share of the poor have not been neutralized by growth in income. At an aggregate level, the literacy rate of Maharashtra, infant mortality rate and per capita income is better than the all-India average.

Even though its per capita industrial production continues to remain high, Maharashtra's contribution to the total industrial income of the nation has fallen during the last decade. Shifts in the industrial production structure away from textiles and towards petroleum and chemicals in the 1990s meant that the share of wages in industrial value added have been coming down.

Similarly, newly emerging industries like information technology, enabled services and bio-technology which have picked up considerably in recent years will mostly generate skilled and semi-skilled jobs in urban areas. Their impact on reducing poverty will mostly be felt indirectly.

REFERENCES

Breman, J. (1993), *Beyond Patronage and Exploitation: Changing Agrarian Relations in South Gujarat,* Oxford University Press, New Delhi.

Centre for Science and Environment: NREGA Implementation Status, January 2008 update:http://www.cseindia.org/programme/nrml/update_january08.htm#NREGA. NREGA facts from The Union Rural Development Ministry.

Cohen, John M. and Norman T. Uphoff (1980): "Participation's place in rural development: Seeking clarity through specificity", *World Development*, 8(3), pp. 215-235.

Comptroller & Auditor General of India, (2007): Performance audit of implementation of National Rural Employment Guarantee Act, 2005 (NREGA).

Datt, Ruddar (2008) Dismal Experience of NREGA: Lessons for the Future, *Mainstream*, Vol. XLVI, No. 17, Monday, 14 April.

District Socio-Economic Reviews, Government of Maharashtra (2009 and 2010).

Government of Maharashtra, *Statistical Statement on SHG Bank Linkage Programme*, NABARD, Pune, 2007-08.

Government of Maharashtra, *Economic Survey of Maharashtra*, 2004-05.

Government of Maharashtra, *Handbook of Basic Statistics of Maharashtra State* 2007.

Government of Maharashtra, *Statistical Abstract of Maharashtra State* 2000-01.

IGIDR (2005) in *State of Environment Report: Maharashtra (Final Draft)*, Mumbai.

In Financing Human Development - VIII, National Institute of Public Finance and Policy, New Delhi.

Kanbur (2005) *The National Rural Employment Guarantee Act of India, 2005*, processed, Department of Applied Economics and Management, Cornell University, Ithaca.

Krishna, Anirudh (2001), "Moving From the Stock of Social Capital to the Flow of Benefits: The Role of Agency", *World Development*, 29 (6), pp. 925-43.

Laxman, Nirmala, (2006) "Employment Guarantee—Sings of Transformation" *The Hindu*, Thursday, May 11 Basu, Arnabk, Nancy H. Chau and Ravi.

Murgai, R. and Ravallion, M. (2005), Employment Guarantee in Rural: What would it cost and how much will it reduce poverty, *Economic and Political Weekly*, 40 (31), pp. 3450-3455.

NSS Report No. 452, January-June 1998.

NSS Report No. 500, and S. Subramanian and D. Jayaraj (2006).

Panda, M. and S. Mishra, (2005), "Poverty Reduction Strategy as Implementation of the Right to Development", Report Submitted to Centre for Development Studies and Human Rights, New Delhi.

Planning Commission (2007), *Agricultural Strategy for the Eleventh Plan: Concerns and Way Ahead*, Yojana Bhavan, New Delhi.

Rangarajan, C. (2005), "Agricultural Credit: Reaching the Marginalized Farmers", *Lecture delivered at the Bankers Conference* (BANCON) 2005, Kolkata, 12 November.

Scandizzo, P., Gaiha, R., and Imai, K. (2007), "Does the Employment Guarantee Scheme stabilize the incomes of households in rural India?";

Paper provided by Economics, The University of Manchester in its series The School of Economics Discussion Paper Series, Number 0706.

Shariff, A. (2008). "Access and use of India's "National Rural Employment Guarantee Scheme": An Empirical Assessment" (mimeo) by Abusaleh Shariff, IFPRI, New Delhi.

Shepherd, Andrew (1998) "Sustainable Rural Development," Palgrave McMillan.

Special Group on Targeting Ten Million Employment Opportunities per year (Dr. S.P. Gupta), Planning Commission, GoI; FICCI Estimate of Manpower, July 2007.

Sridhar, V. (2005) "Empowering the Rural Poor", *Frontline*, volume 22, issue 19, September 10-23, viewed 13th October, 2006.

Srijit Mishra and Manoj Panda (2005), *Growth and Poverty in Maharashtra*, Indira Gandhi Institute of Development Research, Mumbai.

Statistical Statement on SHG Bank Linkage Programme, NABARD, Pune, 2009-10.

Statistical Statement on SHG Bank Linkage Programme, NABARD, Pune, 2010-11.

Von Braun J. and U. Grote (2002), "Does decentralization serve the poor", IMF, Conference on fiscal decentralization, pp. 20-21, Washington DC.

3

Socio-Economic Conditions in Rural Karnataka

TAMANNA MAQBOOL SHAH

Karnataka—*The Royal Grandeur* and the *Oriental Glory*—rightly been termed as *'The Land of Plenty'* lies in the western edge of the Deccan Plateau. The state has been ruled and shaped under the reigns of many dynasties including the Mayuras, Satavahanas, Gangas, Chalukyas and the Vijayanagar Kings. The individual dynasties and the rulers have uniquely offered distinctive arts, architecture, history and culture to the state. This land of fragrance has all the ingredients of a great holiday and tourist attractions—the relaxed length of Arabian sea coastline, majestic Deccan rock to thick lush tropical forests, an incredible variety of rare species of flora and fauna, and a rich culture and heritage. Geographically, Karnataka is located on the south-western part of South India and is rich in natural resources. The Western Ghats that run across the state is a rich source of forest reserves. Above all, it has rich cultural tradition and *puranic* legends of historical importance.

HISTORY OF KARNATAKA

Karnataka is a state of diverse cultures, languages and religions. The economic and social conditions prevalent within the state are much the same as the whole country. It is located between the latitudes 11°.31′and 18°.45′North and the longitudes 74°.12′and 78°.40′East, Karnataka is the ninth most populated state. To its north it borders the states of Maharashtra and Goa; to the east it has Andhra Pradesh; Tamil Nadu and Kerala to the south, while the Arabian Sea forms the western boundary.

Karnataka became a state of the Union of India on November 1, 1956 as a result of the merger of five territories where Kannada was the language of the people. The four districts of the erstwhile Bombay state, three districts of the erstwhile princely state of Hyderabad, two districts and one taluk of the former Madras state, the former Part C state of Coorg (now known as Kodagu), and nine districts of the former princely state of Mysore together formed the state of Karnataka (Planning Commission). Initially Karnataka came to be known as 'Mysore', but subsequently, in 1973, it was renamed 'Karnataka', thereby fulfiling a longstanding demand of the people of the state. For administrative purposes, the state is divided into 27 revenue districts. Bangalore urban district was created in 1986 and, subsequently, in 1997-98, another restructuring led to the creation of Udupi (from Dakshina Kannada), Chamarajnagar (from Mysore), Koppal (from Raichur), Bagalkot (from Bijapur), Gadag and Haveri (from Dharwad) and Davangere (from Chitradurga, Shimoga and Bellary). There were four revenue divisions—Bangalore, Mysore, Belgaum and Gulbarga—which were abolished in 2003 as part of an ongoing process of administrative reforms.

Post-Independence, constant efforts have been made to unify Karnataka. The movement for Unification had been launched together with the movement for freedom in Karnataka. Karnataka came under five administrations in 1947, viz. (1) Bombay, (2) Madras, (3) Kodagu, (4) Mysore, and (5) Hyderabad states (instead of 20). Around 15 minor princely states were merged with neighbouring districts soon after Independence. At the time of its merger, Jamkhandi state had B.D. Jatti as its Chief Minister. At the same the legislatures of Mumbai and Madras States accepted the resolution for the creation of linguistic provinces in 1947. In 1953, the Akhanda Karnataka Rajya Nirmana Parishat launched a major

Sathyagraha and more than 5,000 people courted arrest. Leaders like Jinaraja Hedge, Channappa wali, Chinmayaswamy Omkarmath were its members. Finally, in December 1953, the Fazl Ali Commission was appointed and as per the recommendations of this Commission, linguistically united Mysore State (Karnataka) came into existence on the 1st November, 1956 and S. Nijalingappa became its Chief Minister. Later, during D. Devaraj Urs's regime, the state was named 'Karnataka', a long cherished aspiration of the Kannadigas in 1973.

DEMOGRAPHY OF KARNATAKA

Karnataka, with 30 districts, is the 8th largest state (area-wise) and 9th largest in terms of population. Table 3.1 below, prepared as per the Census 2011 data, illustrates key demographic indicators of the state.

Table 3.1: Geographic and Demographic Indicators—Karnataka

Sl. No.	*Indicators*	*Year*	*Unit*	*Karnataka*	*India*
1.	Geographical Area	2011	Lakh Sq. Km	1.91	32.87
2.	Population	2011	Crore	6.11	121.02
3.	Decadal Growth Rate	2011	Percentage	15.67	17.64
4.	Density of Population	2011	Population/Sq. Km.	319	382
5.	Urban to Total Population	2011	Percentage	38.57	31.16
6.	Sex Ratio	2011	Females/1000 Males	968	940
7.	Literacy Rate (LR)	2011	Percentage	75.60	74.04
8.	Birth Rate	2011	Per 1000 Mid-year Pop.	18.8	21.80
9.	Death Rate	2011	Per 1000 Mid-year Pop.	7.1	7.1

Source: *Census* 2011.

ECONOMIC OVERVIEW OF KARNATAKA

The share of primary, secondary and tertiary sectors in the State's economy stood at 17.20 per cent, 26.50 per cent and 56.30 per cent respectively in 2011-12. The average NSDP growth rate between 2004-05 and 2011-12 was 14.7 per cent. Table 3.2 below shows key economic indicators of the economy of Karnataka. The share of primary, secondary and tertiary sectors stood at 17.20 per cent, 26.50

per cent and 56.30 per cent respectively in 2011-12. The average NSDP growth rate between 2004-05 and 2011-12 was 14.7 per cent.

Table 3.2: Economic Overview of Karnataka

Particular	*Unit*	*2010-11*	*2011-12 Q.E*	*2012-13 A.E*
Gross State Domestic Product (GSDP)	Rs. Crores			
Constant (2004-05)	Prices	271,485	286,410	303,444
Current Prices		406,470	463,243	527,492
Economic Growth Rate as per GSDP	Per cent			
Constant Prices		9.7	5.5	5.9
Current Prices		20.4	14.0	13.9
Per Capita Income				
Constant Prices	Rs.	68,695	77,491	87,359
Current Prices		45,882	47,911	50,254

Q.E—Quick Estimates, A.E—Advance Estimates.

Source: *Economic Survey* 2011-12/2012-13.

INFRASTRUCTURE

- *Roads:* There is about 231,997 km (2012-13) of road network in the state of Karnataka.
- *Railways:* As of March 2011, the state had railway network of 3,073 km.
- *Airports:* Karnataka has 5 domestic airports located at Bengaluru, Mangalore, Hubli, Mysore and Belgaum. Only two airports, namely, Bengaluru and Mangalore operate the International flights.
- *Ports:* There are 11 ports in Karnataka, of which new Mangalore is a major port.
- *Power:* As of January 2013, the state had a power generation installed capacity of 13,596.28 MW which consisted of 7279.56 MW of state share, 4720.63 MW of private share and 1596.09 MW of Central share (foodprocessingindia.co.in).

Agriculture

During 2012-13, the total production of foodgrains (cereals and pulses) in Karnataka was around 125 lakh MT. Table 3.3 below presents the production figures for the agri-crops of Karnataka (http://www.agricoop.nic.in):

Table 3.3: Total Production of Foodgrains in Karnataka

Crop/Group	*Unit*	*2012-13 A.E*	*2011-12*
Cereals	Lakh MT	111.64	108.22
Pulses	Lakh MT	13.36	10.61
Total Foodgrains	**Lakh MT**	**125**	**118.83**

Source: Economic Survey 2011-12/2012-13.

The most prominent commercial crops grown in the state are oilseeds, cotton, sugarcane and tobacco. Table 3.4 below presents figures for the production of these crops over the last two years.

Table 3.4: Total Production of Commercial Crops in Karnataka

(In Lakh MT)

Crop/Group	*2012-13 A.E.*	*2011-12*
Oilseeds	9.50	9.24
Cotton (In Lakh Bales)	10.91	12.79
Sugarcane	303.20	400.33
Tobacco	0.94	1.06

Source: Economic Survey 2011-12/2012-13.

Horticulture

During 2010-11 the production of horticulture crops stood at 152.13 lakh MT. Karnataka is one of the largest producer of coffee and cocoa in the country. It is the second largest producer of flowers and grapes, third largest in production of plantation crops, fourth largest in the production of spices and fifth largest in fruits production (http://www.nhb.gov.in).

Fruits and Vegetables

According to the advance estimates by National Horticulture Board for 2012-13, fruit production in Karnataka is estimated at 67.38 lakh MT. Further the advance estimates for the year 2012-13 indicate that the production of vegetables in Karnataka is around 79.56 lakh MT.

Agro-Marketing Infrastructure in Karnataka

- The key features of the functional **APMC Act** in Karnataka include the provisions for setting-up private *mandis*, direct procurement/sale from farmers' fields, contract farming, setting-up and promoting agricultural marketing extension units etc.
- ***Market Yards/APMCs:*** With around 155 notified market areas/APMCs, 353 sub-market yards and 742 other kinds of market yards (seasonal), the state offers great market access to its people.
- ***Status of Logistics and Warehousing Facilities in the State:*** As on February 2012, there were 121 warehouses in operation in Karnataka. These were being operated by the Karnataka State Warehousing Corporation (KSWC). Around 74 per cent of the capacity of these warehouses and storage space is used so far.
- ***Cold Storages:*** The State has around 180 cold storages with a capacity of 4.87 lakh MT.
- ***Abattoirs/Slaughter Houses:*** There are seven licensed slaughter houses in the State. There are no APEDA supported abattoirs in the State as on date.
- ***Mega Food Parks:*** The Ministry of Food Processing Industries (MoFPI) has sanctioned one Mega Food Park project under its Mega Food Parks Scheme for the state of Karnataka. The project is located in Tumkur and is currently under implementation.
- Apart from MoFPI's Mega Food Parks Scheme, the State Government also has a Food Parks Scheme under which food parks are being established in six districts including Bangalore (Rural), Tumkur, Shimoga, Davangere, Bijapur and Belgaum. The State Government is also planning to

set-up a spice park at Byadagi in Haveri district (foodprocessingindia.co.in).

- ***Cold Chain Projects:*** Three cold chains have been sanctioned by MoFPI under its *"Scheme for Cold Chain, Value Addition and Preservation Infrastructure"*.

NATURE AND SCOPE OF STUDY

This study is an attempt to bring out the socio-economic conditions prevalent in the selected districts of Karnataka. While the overview of the state and the districts is largely based on secondary data derived from standard state publications, journals, and the Census of India. The village level study is primarily drawn from the Socio-economic studies conducted by the I.A.S. probationers as part of their assignments for the District Training.

While the secondary data collected from various sources provides an insight into the state and its various developmental strategies for different sectors, the main focus of the chapter lies on the village level observations of the probationers. The chapter, therefore, preserves the information provided by the probationers as well as acknowledges the quality of their findings and provides for unedited excerpts from their studies. Village information, case studies and suggestions from probationers is presented at appropriate places. At the end of each excerpt, the surname of the probationer, and the year of joining are mentioned. A list of studies conducted by the probationers is presented in Table 3.5.

OBJECTIVES OF THE STUDY

(a) To understand the social, economic, cultural and geographical features of the village, which affect the quality of life of the rural people.

(b) Sensitization towards the problems faced by the people through proper recording of qualitative information of the villagers.

(c) To make an appraisal of the implementation of the poverty alleviation programmes in the village.

(d) To make an appraisal of the implementation of the Land Reform measures in the village.

Table 3.5: Socio-economic Surveys of IAS Probationers of the Karnataka Cadre

Divisions	*Villages*	*Probationer*	*Batch*
GULBARGA			
	Bhim Nagar	Pallavi Akurathi	2009
	Saidapur	Ujjwal Kumar Ghosh	2010
	Srinivasa Sardagi	Randeep D.	2006
DHARWAD			
	Managundi	Sameer Shukla	2005
MYSORE			
	Jayapura	Deepa Cholan	2008
	Hittuvalli	Pooja Kulkarni	2003
	Maidanahally	Shamla Ahammed	2002
	Gujjegowdanapura	Priyanka Mary Francis	2009
HASSAN			
	Jayapura	D.K. Ravi	2011
	Bhuvanhalli	P. Rajendra Cholan	2008
KOLAR			
	Shettykottanuru	Vipul Bansal	2005
DAKSHIN KANNADA			
	Nadugodu	Thrilok Chandra	2007
	Kadandale	Gurneet Tej	2006
	Balthilla	Rohini Dasari	2009
SHIMOGA			
	Shimoga	Anurag Tewari	2007
		Venkatesh M.V.	2009
MANDYA			
	Ummadahalli	S. Sasikanth Senthil	2009
BELGAUM			
	Bailwad	K.P. Mohan Raj	2007
	Sultanpur	P.C. Jaffer	2003
	Kakati	Bagadi Gautham	2009
	Mutaga	Dipti Mehendale	2008
BELLARY			
	Mincheri	K.G. Jagadeesh	2005
	Gududur	V. Anbukkumar	2004

(e) To facilitate the understanding of factors which cast crucial influence upon administrative planning and decision-making.

Since the village level survey was carried out keeping certain developmental aspects in mind, it would be best to look at each of these aspects separately and present data for the different districts for the periods provided. In the following sections we would address each of these issues, look at the national level data available and analyze development in the sample villages. For the sake of understanding and convenience of the readers the sections that follow are numbered as follows:

I. Literacy and Education
II. Health and Sanitation
III. Agriculture
IV. Occupational Patterns
V. Land Reforms
VI. Poverty Alleviation Programme
VII. Panchayati Raj Institutions

METHODOLOGY OF THE STUDY

The Village Visit programme is a very important component of the Foundation Course, where the Officer Trainees are taken out of the confines of the classrooms and are exposed first hand to the realities and complexities of rural life. There can be no doubt that an officer trainee, irrespective of background or the service to which he/she belongs, and his/her perception of the role of the service, requires an organized sensitization to the rural dynamics as an interested participant-observer.

Poverty, inequalities of opportunity, lack of access to various facilities is facts of life in the rural areas. Development of rural areas and alleviation of poverty have been given priority in the plans and policies of independent India. There are a large number of Government sponsored programmes/schemes being implemented in the rural areas for achieving the above objectives. The Officer Trainees are expected to gain a firsthand understanding of these aspects in the course of their stay in the villages. At the same time, the Officer Trainees will no doubt also look for possible silver linings in the scenario of deprivation of initiatives that have succeeded, seeds of change that have been sown, opportunities that have been utilized and interventions, whether governmental or non-governmental that have worked. A conscious effort has been made to send you to villages, with varying levels of development and socio-economic characteristics with the intention of exposing you to a wide range of rural scenarios.

In order to make the study representative in nature, random sampling technique was used. A list of all census villages was prepared along with their population. The names of villages with population less than 300 and more than 3000 were removed as per the required guidelines. A random sample was chosen from the Table of random numbers provided. The sample number being greater than the number of villages, it was divided by the number of villages and the remainder taken as the serial number of the village to be studied. The same random sampling method was followed in the selection of households for the household survey. A list of all the households was drawn habitation-wise and proportionate random sampling was done for each of the habitations.

During the present Village Visit Programme, the probationers used three methodologies to explore and learn the rural realities.

- **Participatory Learning and Action (PLA)**
- **Focus Group Interview (FGI)** to gain deeper understanding of some specific issues like Education, Health, Agriculture and Land Reforms, Functioning of Panchayati Raj Institution, and Poverty and any other issues which the village may throw up. Gender will cut across all these issues.
- **Interview Schedule** followed to collect basic data at village level.

Participatory Learning and Action emphasizes local and indigenous knowledge and encourages local people to make their own appraisal, analysis and plans. Participatory Learning and Action (PLA) is an approach for learning and organizing participation of local communities and groups for interacting with them, understanding them and learning from them.

Participatory Learning Action (PLA) Tools encompass both learning and executing in a participatory manner. Participatory learning takes place by direct contact with people in the village, listening to people to understand rural realities, issues and problems, local knowledge and practices. Therefore, establishing rapport with the villagers to make them comfotable becomes essential. The villagers or the local people should feel free to talk, share their views, and take interest to participate in exercises which are very meaningful to understand the rural realities.

"It comprises a set of principles, a process of communication and a menu of methods for seeking villagers' participation in putting forward their points of view about any issue and enabling them do their own analysis with a view to make use of such learning. It initiates a participatory process and sustains it" (persmin.nic.in). The different principles and tools used in the participatory learning method help organize participation and generate results. Listening and learning through participatory interaction is the most important principle of PLA. The local people are in possession of enormous indigenous knowledge, experience, skills, culture, views and ideas. In addition to these, local people are also able to identify their problems, priorities and preferences. The participatory learning and action (PLA) techniques enable the outsider to learn and collect information about the community by listening and observing.

LIMITATIONS OF THE STUDY

The study presented the following limitations:

(a) The total number of villages covered over the years is fairly small.

(b) The study was conducted in different villages of different districts, further limiting the number of study per village.

(c) The samples are too small for generalization.

(d) It was difficult to ascertain the impact of Governmental intervention and development levels because of the small samples.

(e) Data collected by the probationers also seems to be sketchy and inadequate at places.

(f) An in-depth analysis of all socio-economic aspects seems to be missing.

INTRODUCTION TO THE VILLAGES

The economy of Karnataka has grown manifolds during the Eleventh Five Year Plan. It grew by 8 per cent while the country's economy as per CAGR grew by 7.9 per cent. GDP of the State during 2011-12 was Rs. 2,97,964 crore. The services sector recorded 10.6 per cent growth rate. Karnataka recorded the second highest level of per capita development expenditure during 2010-11, being Rs. 7853 while all State's average was Rs. 6055 Per Capita plan expenditure has been Rs. 6345 (ssakarnataka.gov.in). Literacy rate increased from 66.64 per cent in 2001 to 75.60 per cent in 2011. The following sections provide a brief overview of the districts covered for the study followed by an analysis of the different socio-economic aspects on which data was collected.

Gulbarga District

In ancient times, Gulbarga was popular as ***'Kalburgi'***, which means *'stony land'* in Kannada. Gulbarga became a part of Karnataka after the re-organization of states. Gulbarga is a drought-prone area. The area receives an average rainfall of 777 mm and the normal rainy days are 46 in a year. It is also one of the most backward districts of Karnataka.

Dharwad District

Dharwad is divided into three natural regions, viz., the Malnad, Semi-Malnad and Maidan. Crops like cotton, wheat, *ragi, jowar* and oil-seeds are grown in the prominent black soil in the district and paddy on the red soil. The district is affected by the monsoons since it is located in the tropical region. This also contributes to the district having an agro-based economy. The mineral and forest wealth of the district are unattractive. Manufacturing industry, particularly agro-based industry is the main contributor to the economic growth of the district. Hubli-Dharwad are the two major commercial centres in the district.

Mysore District

Mysore lies in the southern plateau of India. The region may be classified as partly maidan and partly semi-malnad (malnad hilly lands). The climatic conditions of the district are favourable to crops like paddy, *jowar, ragi*, pulses, sugarcane and tobacco. The climate of Mysore district is temperate with little variations in the temperature in different seasons.

Kolar District

According to the 2011 Census, Kolar municipality had a population of 1,38,553. The municipality had a sex-ratio of 978 females per 1,000 males. Effective literacy was 84.02 per cent; male literacy was 87.28 per cent and female literacy was 80.69 per cent. Kannada is the major language, however a significant population speaks Telugu (Census, 2011).

Hassan District

Hassan is located in the south-western part of Karnataka. The district is popular for its enchanting natural scenic beauty and is rich in architectural beauty of the Hoysala dynasty.

Belgaum District

Belgaum ranks second in the state of Karnataka in terms of population and accounts for 7.97 per cent of the state's entire population (Census, 2011). The Sex ratio (females per 1000 males) is now 969 which earlier was 960. The density of population per sq. km. has risen to 356 from 314. The entire district falls in the Krishna river basin. The river Krishna, along with its tributaries Ghataprabha and Malaprabha are perennial and effluent in nature and flow in easterly direction. The drainage density varies from 0.80 to 3.4 km/sq.km.

Mandya District

The land of sugar and rice, Mandya is an important agricultural district of Karnataka. The district has irrigation waters of river Cauvery and Hemavathi which makes the district greener than the rest of Karnataka. Paddy and Sugarcane are the main crops of the irrigated region. *Ragi*, Horse gram are the major crops of dry land agriculture. Agriculture is the main occupation of people in the district.

Shimoga District

A major part of Shimoga district lies in the Malnad region of the Western Ghats. Shimoga city is its administrative centre. As per the 2011 Census data, Shimoga has a population of 17,55,512.

Bellary District

Bellari district takes its name from the word *Belari* which refers to "goddess Durugamma as this goddess had manifested herself in the town". Bellari district is spread from south-west to north-east and is situated on the eastern side of Karnataka state.

Dakshin Kannada District

Dakshin Kannada, also known as **South Kanara**, is a coastal district in Karnataka. Mangalore is the headquarters and the chief city of the district. Dakshin Kannada district has an area of 4,866 square kilometres, and a population density of 430 persons per square kilometre. There are 354 villages in the district (Census, 2011).

I. LITERACY AND EDUCATION

Education is often a starting point to ensure development of a region. It helps achieve the goals of employment, human resource development and bringing about a congenial social and economic environment. This in turn leads to the overall upliftment and progress of the community through efficient use of resources. A successful education policy helps "cultivate knowledge, skill, positive attitude, awareness and sense of responsibility towards rights and duties and imparts inner strength to face oppression, humiliation and inequality" (Ninth Five Year Plan, 1997-2002).

Karnataka has made remarkable achievements in education. It has successfully moved towards universal literacy and achieved literacy just above the national average. The male to female literacy rate differential is high, with 76 per cent male literacy and 57 per cent female literacy. Female literacy is highest in Dakshina Kannada (77.39%) and Bangalore Urban (78.98%), which is far lower than the highest among the states of Kerala, Tamil Nadu and Maharashtra. The rural areas of Karnataka project the highest disparity between male and female literacy rates. Rural female literacy in the State is low. Around 12 districts have female literacy below the national average of 54.16 per cent (Census, 2011). Therefore, "the gender disparity in literacy is declining rather perceptibly and the decline is much more evident in the less economically developed districts of the state" (planningcommission.nic.in).

The Planning Commission reports that over the years, the "number of habitations with primary schools within a distance of one kilometre increased from 84 per cent in 1993 to 88 per cent in 2002. Enrollment in primary education grew at the rate of one per cent for boys and two per cent for girls per annum from 1990-91 to 2003-04. The dropout rate for Classes I to IV came down from a high 31 per cent in 1993-94 to six per cent in 2001-02, but increased thereafter to 11 per cent in 2003-04. For classes I to VIII, the dropout rate declined from 54.59 per cent between 1992 and 2000 to 45.4 per cent in 2003-04."

Currently there is an elaborate high school network operational in the state. The primary schools lack adequate infrastructure, although south Karnataka has better infrastructure. "More than 3 per cent schools do not have teachers and 19 per cent function with single teacher" *(Seventh All-India School Education Survey, Provisional Statistics*, 2002). The percentage of girls' and boys' enrollment in secondary education in the state still shows marked differentials (boys: 6,86,893 and girls: 5,97,244 in 2003-04) despite a steady improvement over the years. The quality of instruction and instructional material will have to improve considerably to ensure better retention of students from 1990-91 to 2002-03, the largest allocation of public education expenditure went to general education, and primary and secondary education within general education, a pattern which reflects the government's priorities. Despite this, the share of primary and secondary education in the state income and in the education budget has been more or less static.

Karnataka has made rapid strides in its literacy level as compared tc many other states of India. However, all the four southern provinces, including Karnataka, have, no doubt, registered higher literacy as compared to All-India rate (65.46). But there are inter-state differences in the achievement levels. For example, Karnataka (75.60%) is behind Kerala (93.91%) and nearer to Tamil Nadu (80.33%) and ahead of Andhra Pradesh (67.66%) (Census 2011). This achievement is obviously the result of the effective steps taken by the State in achieving universal literacy.

However, the 2011 Census has also shown that nearly one quarter of the population, aged 7+ years, still remains illiterate – being not able to read or write in any language. Such a sad situation is a mirror to the fact that the magnitude of low literacy levels is gender-biased also. Data show that about one-third of female population still remains illiterate. This is evident from the data on literacy rates for males and females, as well as by districts. The Census 2011 also shows that the literacy gap has narrowed down over the years, both in Karnataka state as well as at All India levels as far as male and female population is concerned. Over a period of time, both the state and the country have moved more or less at the same pace leading to no remarkable transformation among the needy and deserving sections of the population. This can be seen from the statistics presented in Table 3.6 below:

Table 3.6: Literacy Rates for Karnataka compared to the All India Level, 1951-2011

Year	*Karnataka*			*All-India*		
	Persons	*Male*	*Female*	*Persons*	*Male*	*Female*
1951	20.6	N.A.	N.A.	18.3	27.2	8.9
1961	25.4	36.2	14.2	28.3	40.4	15.4
1971	31.5	41.6	21.0	34.5	46.0	22.0
1981	38.5	48.8	27.7	43.6	56.4	29.8
1991	56.0	67.3	44.3	52.2	64.1	39.3
2001	66.6	76.1	56.9	64.8	75.3	53.7
2011	75.6	82.9	68.1	74.0	82.1	65.5

Note: Literacy rates for 1951, 1961 and 1971 related to population aged five years and above. The rates for the years 1981-2011 related to the population aged seven years and above.

Source: *Census of India*, 2011, Karnataka, Provisional Population Totals; *Census of India*, 2011, India, Provisional Population Totals, Paper 1 of 2011, Series 1).

It is clear from the above Table 3.6 that illiteracy levels were very high in the early years of India's Independence. It is evident that during the decades 1951-61, 1961-71 and 1971-81 was slow as compared to All-India level. However, with various policies and programmes that were implemented, the state gained strength and made surges in its educational profile and registered a growth of literacy during 1981-91. There was an increase of around 17.5 per cent in the literacy level from 38.50 per cent in 1981 to 56.00 per cent in 1991. During same period, the literacy at All-India level could pick up and grew by 9 per cent only. Again, it is astonishing that in the subsequent decades, there has been a reduction in the rate of growth. The situation as regards intra-state disparities is equally tense. Nearly half of the districts in Karnataka are close to or above state's average. Two districts from southern Karnataka (Ramanagaram and Chamarajanagara), two from Mumbai Karnataka (Bagalkot and Bijapur) and five districts from Hyderabad Karnataka area are below state average. The newly formed district of Yadgir stands at the lowest level among all the districts in terms of total literacy rate.

Table 3.7: Literacy Rates by District for Karnataka, 2011

Range	*Name of the District with Literacy Rates* (in Parenthesis)*
80 Per cent and Above (7 Districts)	Dakshina Kannada (88.62), Bangalore (88.48), Udupi (86.29), Uttara Kannada (84.03), Kodagu (82.52), Shimoga (80.50), and Dharwad (80.30)
75-80 Per cent (6 Districts)	Chikkamagalur (79.24), Bangalore Rural (78.29), Haveri (77.60), Davanagere (76.30), Hassan (75.89), and Gadag (75.18)
70-75 Per cent (8 Districts)	Kolar (74.33), Tumkur (74.32), Belgaum (73.94), Chitradurga (73.82), Mysore (72.56), Bidar (71.01), Mandya (70.14), and Chikkaballapura (70.08)
60-70 Per cent (8 Districts)	Bagalkot (69.39), Ramanagaram (69.20), Bellary (67.85), Koppal (67.28), Bijapur (67.20), Gulbarga (65.65), Chamarajanagara (61.12), and Raichur (60.46)
50-60 Per cent (1 District)	Yadgir (52.36)

Note: * Literacy rate is the percentage of literates to population aged 7 years and above.

Source: Census of India, 2011, Karnataka, Provisional Population Totals.

The State has made major changes and progress by providing lower primary schools within 1 km distance to about 98 per cent of the population and higher primary schools within 2 km distance. Access to primary education is no longer an impediment to the goal of universalization. There has been about 25 per cent increase over the past 10-12 years in the number of schools constructed in the State.

Post Independent era, especially since the Sixth Plan and Ninth Plan period onwards, a lot of efforts were made to popularize education by opening of schools in the rural and remote areas. Opportunities for a decent living and livelihood thus became an important aspect and it took precedence over the quality of education. Rural-urban, regional, inter-religious, inter-class disparities in education have continued even after Independence. Despite much progress having been achieved, a lot more still needs to be done, in terms of quantity and quality aspects of such education/literacy.

The country has seen remarkable growth in the literacy rates primarily because of the expansion of elementary education. The Compulsory Elementary Education Act under RTE Act, 2009 has made education free and compulsory for all children of 6-14 years. In 2001, the Government of India launched the *'Education for All'* movement called *'Sarva Shiksha Abhiyan (SSA)'* to universalize and improve the quality of elementary education for all the states and union territories.

Another government programme called the Saakshar Bharat Programme is being implemented in rural areas of 18 districts of Karnataka. In these districts female literacy is less than 50 per cent. In order to improve the literacy rates, Government needs to improve the position in regard to proportion of female teachers. The State Government needs to provide the districts with proper infrastructural facilities for the schools. Women in almost all the sample villages were seen more enthusiastic about getting educated. Education was seen as a factor that increased their self-confidence and helped them face challenges with more confidence.

Insights on Improving Literacy and Education in the Villages by Probationers

The Saidapur village in Gulbarga district boasts of one of the better literacy rates of the region. The male literacy is much higher than female literacy. Literacy rates are higher among the Lingayats than the Kurubas, Kabbaligas and SC/STs. The schools have good facilities with toilets though there is need for more classrooms. Children's attendance varies with the season. The dropout rate is high. Adult literacy classes are timely. However, there is a lack of enthusiasm and participation. The SGSY SHG are very active and majority have become literate. *The different educational societies working in the region need to be mobilized for spreading awareness on education* (Ghosh, O.T., 2010).

As per the 2006-07 survey, Bhim Nagar village in Gulbarga district has 515 male literates which means only 43.27 per cent males are literate. Bhim Nagar has only 304 female literates which means only 24.5 per cent women are literates. The primary school in Bhim Nagar has a total enrollment of 324 students. *The strength of girls in this village is more than the boys.* There are 167 girls and 157 boys enrolled. The classes are well equipped. There are no toilet facilities for the teachers or the children. There is also lack of proper water facilities in the schools. The upper primary school in the village needs two more classrooms. The school has a playground, but no compound wall. There is proportionate representation of students from the various sections of the society. The Mid-Day Meal programme was not functioning for more than six months. The village has opportunities up to Class VIII. There is a need for classes for the adults. It was also evident that Bhim Nagar children had access to schools, but not to proper education (Akurathi, O.T., 2009).

Another village highlighted the need for literacy campaigns should be held on regular basis. Adult literacy centres were missing in most villages (Randeep D., O.T., 2006).

Children enrolled in schools are also made to clean their classrooms. This needs to be checked immediately. Schools lack innovative practices of teaching. There are a lot of reasons that increase the dropout rates. Poverty, migration, child labour, parental apathy, lack of interest in children etc. are some of the reasons (Venkatesh, O.T., 2009).

Yet in another village, the quality of food at the schools is debatable. Devising a method to detect pilferage needs to be done (Tewai, O.T., 2007).

Infrastructure of the schools needs to be improved. Number of teachers in the schools should be increased. Concerted efforts should be made in achieving complete literacy and non-formal education (Jaffer, O.T., 2003).

II. HEALTH AND SANITATION

> *O Varuna Deva,* May water and flora bond us in friendship for ever. —*Rig Veda, Varuniya Samhita,* 6.22

Globally, 2.4 billion people lack access to adequate sanitation and most of them live their lives in poverty (Myles, 2003). While in the developing countries 50 per cent of the population does not live in descent sanitation conditions (World Bank, 2003) "and suffer with diarrhoea, trachoma and schistosomiasi" (WHO and UNICEF, 2000). In order to arrest the growing concerns over the sanitary conditions of the poor, provisions of sanitation were made part of the Millennium Development Goals.

In India, to address the sanitary situation of the poor, the Fifth Five Year Plan put sanitation in the forefront and quoted, "the elimination of abject poverty will not be attained as a corollary to certain acceleration in the rate of growth of the economy alone, but improvements in drinking water and environmental sanitation have direct correlation with levels of living" (Planning Commission). Thus, providing for basic public health facilities is a major aspect of the poverty alleviation programmes put forward by the government.

The Government of India runs a lot of programmes to meet the growing demands of the society. One such programme was the Total Sanitation Campaign, which provides for "latrines plus services such as, provision of latrines, disposal of liquid and solid waste and domestic as well as environmental hygiene" (TSC, 1999). The Total Sanitation Campaign was developed based on the baseline survey, *"On Knowledge, Attitudes and Practices in Rural Water Supply and Sanitation"* conducted by Indian Institute of Mass Communications (1996-97). "According to survey results, 55 per cent of those with private latrines were self-motivated and 51 per cent of the respondents were willing to spend up to Rs.1000 to acquire sanitary toilets" (GoI, 2002).

In Karnataka majority of the people depend on the groundwater as a source for drinking water. In the rural areas of the state, more than 90 per cent of the schemes related to drinking water are based on ground water. Because of the increased dependence on groundwater, it is fast depleting with 34 taluks considered as critical due to over exploitation.

"Availability of safe drinking water is a major problem having environmental repercussions. More than 50 per cent of rural habitations have less than 55 litres per capita of water supply. In the drought prone districts of Bijapur, Bidar, Bagalkot, Chitradurga, Davangere, Tumkur, Koppal, Raichur and Gadag, more than 30 per cent of rural habitations do not have access to 55 litres per capita per day water supply" (Planning Commission).

Box 3.1 : Initiatives of the Government

The Karnataka Groundwater (Regulation for Protection of Sources of Drinking Water) Act, 1999 of the Rural Development and Panchyat Raj Department has come into force from December 2003. This Act prohibits sinking of borewells within 500 metres of public sources of drinking water.

Swajaldhara, a centrally sponsored programme based on community participation to operate drinking water supply schemes has been launched.

Nirmala Grama Yojana is under implementation since 1995 to build household latrines in rural areas. Under this programme, household toilets in the villages would be sanctioned with a maximum financial assistance of Rs. 2000 or 80 per cent of the unit cost.

Swachchha Grama Programme has been initiated to promote total village sanitation and all-round development of villages.

The *Panchasutras* for total village sanitation include:

- Paving of internal roads and streets in the village;
- Construction of efficient sullage and storm water drainage.
- Provision of community compost yards and removal of manure pits from the dwelling areas of the village;
- Provision of smokeless *chullas*/bio-gas for all households.
- Construction of household latrines/group latrines with individual ownership, community latrine complexes, and institutional latrines in schools.

Under the Sub-mission programme launched by the Rajiv Gandhi National Drinking Water Mission, safe drinking water is being provided to villages affected by Fluoride, Nitrate and Brackishness.

National River Conservation Plan is being implemented to prevent pollution in the catchment area of river Cauvery and Bhadra caused by towns situated in the basins.

The State Government has launched on pilot basis, a rural water and sanitation programme called the ***Sampurna Nairmalay Yojana*** to cover Mysore, Dakshina Kannada and Bellary districts.

The Department of Ecology and Environment has directed that drinking water should not be used for non-potable purposes like washing, gardening, servicing of vehicles etc.

Source: Planning Commission.

It is not just the rural areas that face the drinking water shortage, in most of the urban areas similar problems have been reported. Of the 208 urban local bodies under the Karnataka Urban Water Supply and Drainage Board, in 161 urban local bodies (77%) the drinking water supply is inadequate (Planning Commission). "Bellary, Bangalore, Bijapur, Tumkur, Kolar and Chitradurga are considered as hotspots for drinking water supply as they show all the three problems of inadequate water supply, declining groundwater level and poor water quality (http://parisaramahiti.kar.nic.in/hp_water.html). Dharwad has problem of both inadequate water supply and declining groundwater level. Chamarajnagar and Haveri have been listed as hotspots for inadequate water supply and poor water quality" (Reports of the Government of Karnataka).

Insights Presented by Probationers on Improving Health and Sanitation in the Villages

The village shows presence of a sub centre of the Public Health Unit. It is sufficiently stocked with medicines and antibiotics. Power supply is a major problem faced by the staff in the PHU in storing the injections. There are no private health services available to the villagers. The village is also marked by the presence of quacks who promise cures for all ailments. There are no major epidemic outbreaks that the village has faced. The AWW and ANM are properly trained to treat pregnant women (Randeep D., O.T., 2009).

There is an urgent need to reform the Sub-PHC set-up in Shimoga village. Absenteeism needs to be checked (Tewari, O.T., 2007).

There is no PHC in Kakati village. The sub-PHC is also rarely used by the villagers who prefer to use the robust medical infrastructure in Belgaum. As a result dates of MMR and IMR were also not available (Gautham, O.T., 2009).

III. AGRICULTURE AND AGRARIAN RELATIONSHIPS

Topographically, Karnataka is highly suitable for agricultural activities. Agriculture accounts for about 17 per cent of the states GDP. About 60 per cent of the total work force is engaged in agricultural activities and are mostly unskilled manual labour. Economically, Karnataka's economy is dominated by a strong service sector which is expected to grow by 10.6 per cent in 2011-12 (*Census, 2011*). However, Agriculture and allied sectors have shown a negative growth of 2.9 per cent. The Economic Survey of Karnataka for the years 2011-12 suggests that "over the years, the contribution of the agriculture sector to the economy has been declining continuously without a commensurate decline in the workforce deployed in agriculture" (p. 2). Karnataka is particularly paying attention in achieving a balanced growth and development of its agricultural sector. In 2011-12, the Karnataka Government presented a budget for the agricultural sector wherein schemes were presented promoting better usage of land and water. It is also enhancing its capabilities in agricultural research, extension, education and training. As a result of these efforts the state has demonstrated a steady growth in the production of milk, meat and wool and it is expected to increase further.

Climatically, Karnataka has a very pleasant weather. Such weather enables the farmers to cultivate almost all types of cereals, pulses, oilseeds and commercial crops. Out of the 29, 406 villages in Karnataka having an area of about 1,90,49,836 hectares, 1,04,04,107 hectares of land was the net area cultivated in all the three seasons during the year 2009-10. "The state is divided into three major climatic zones, namely, coastal, north interior and south interior. Of these, the coastal zone receives the heaviest rainfall with an average rainfall of about 3,638.5 mm (143 in) per annum, far in excess of the state average of 1,139 mm (45 in)" (Government of Karnataka Reports). Climate of Karnataka falls into three categories: Arid, Semi-arid and humid.

Table 3.8: Season-wise rainfall condition in the State, 2008-09

Season	*Rainfall (in mm)*		*Departure from Normal rainfall (%)*	*Rainfall pattern*
	Normal	*Actual*		
Kharif	839	900	7.3	Normal
Rabi	346	308	-11.0	Normal
Summer	13	24	84.6	Excess
State	**1198**	**1232**	**2.8**	Normal

Source: Rainfall section, DES.

Among the crop groups, cereals account for 49 per cent with a production of 111.92 lakh tonnes, pulses 25 per cent (production of

12.32 lakh tonnes), oilseeds 15 per cent, cotton and sugarcane 5 per cent each and tobacco 1 per cent of gross cropped area (*See* Table 3.9 below). It is also interesting to note that during 2010-11 Karnataka was able to achieve highest foodgrain production of about 139.86 lakh tonnes. Cotton production also touched an all-time high of 12.18 lakh bales during the year 2010-11 (*The Hindu*, 2011). Thereafter, Karnataka also bagged the prestigious *"Krishi Karman Award"* in 2011 for achieving highest production of coarse cereals (78.45 lakh tonnes) during the year 2010-11. Such high yield was possible because of the favourable rainfall received during the months of April to November 2010. But in October 2011, the government had to declare 123 taluks in 24 districts as "Drought Affected Taluks" because of a scarcity of rainfall.

Table 3.9: Area and Production of Major Crops in the State

(Area in lakh hectares, Production in lakh tonnes)

Crop/Group	*2011 – 12***		*2010 – 11**	
	Area	*Production*	*Area*	*Production*
Cereals	50.98	111.92	54.45	124.21
Pulses	23.78	12.32	27.91	15.65
Total Foodgrains	74.76	124.24	82.36	139.86
Oilseeds	14.50	10.01	16.24	12.70
Cotton#	5.23	9.09	5.48	12.18
Sugarcane	4.30	379.91	4.23	396.57
Tobacco	1.04	0.89	1.25	1.34

lakh bales of 170 Kg. lint.

*Final Estimates.

**2011-12 Revised 2nd Advance Estimates of DE&S.

Source: Indiastats.

Land Utilization

About 38,284 sq. km of Karnataka (i.e. 19.96 per cent of the state's geographic area) is covered by forests. The forests are classified as reserved (74.94%), protected (10.27%), unclosed, village and private forests. Therefore, about one-fifth of the State's geographical area is under forest cover. About 7.3 per cent of the total area is land that is used for non-agricultural purposes. 4.1 per cent of the total geographic area was barren and uncultivable land and about 53.5 per cent of the total area was the net sown area in the state.

Holdings

As per the Agricultural Census of 2005-06, the total number of operational holdings in Karnataka is around 75.81 lakhs. The total area of operational holdings is around 123.85 lakh hectares, which is an increase of 0.6 per cent from the 2001 census. Small and marginal holdings together account for 75 per cent of the total holdings and 37 per cent of the total operated area, while semi-medium, medium and large holdings together account for 25 per cent of the total holdings and 63 per cent of the total operated area. The number of small and semi-medium size classes has increased over the years. The number of operational holdings has increased by 5.5 per cent and the area marked an increase of 4.9 per cent under small holdings and 1.5 and 1.1 per cent under semi-medium category. The figures saw a decrease in previous years for the medium size class holdings. The number and area of operational holdings decreased by 2.5 per cent and 3.3 per cent respectively between the two censuses. "The number of marginal size class holdings has increased from 32.52 lakhs in 2000-01 census to 36.55 lakhs in 2005-06 census, by around 12.4 per cent and also the area of operational holdings increased from 14.92 lakh hectares in 2000-01 to 16.51 lakh hectares in 2005-06 by 10.7 per cent" (Agricultural Census 2005-06).

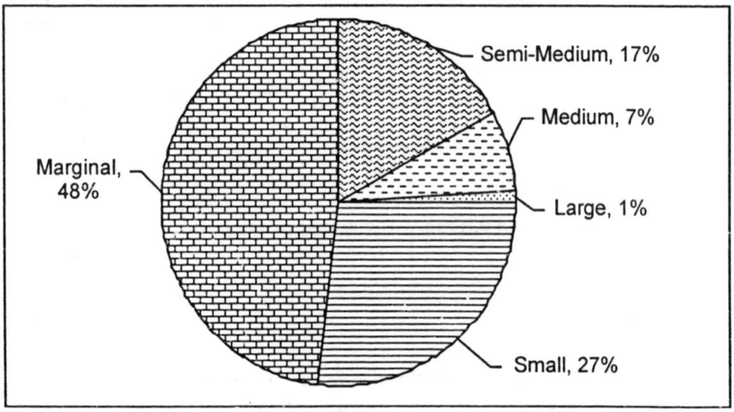

Fig. 3.1: Operational Holdings in Karnataka
Source: *Economic Survey of Karnataka,* 2011-12.

The Planning Board also reported about the shrinking of landholding size. It suggested demographic and market pressures on land. "The average size of landholding is 1.63 ha and the number of holdings having land less than 1.0 ha account for 42 per cent of the total holdings in the State" (Planning Board, 2010). As a result of which a large number of farmers are becoming economically unviable by the day. Also land that was initially used for agricultural purposes is now being used for non-agricultural purposes (Planning Board, 2010). This data is also suggestive of the fact that a large number of farmers in Karnataka, being unskilled labour are also finding it hard to take up other jobs hence creating a surplus for the State. This unskilled labour force is now being directed towards non-agricultural activities, further reducing the number of hands employed in agriculture, giving rise to low productivity and degraded soil health and eventual shrinkage of land under agriculture.

Cropping Patterns

"In 2008-09, the net area cultivated in Karnataka was 1,01,95,088 hectares and area sown more than once was 21,73,357 totaling to 1,23,68,443 as gross cropped area compared to 1,28,92,671 hectares during 2007-08" (*Economic Reports of Karnataka*). The gross cropped area under food crops was 88,57,851 hectares (71.6%) and that of non-food crops was 35,10,592 hectares (28.4%). Area under cereals and minor millet crops increased in Paddy, Jowar and Ragi crops and decreased in other cereals and millets and among pulses. Area under food and non-food crops decreased due to untimely rain and change of crops and the area under food and non-food crops increased due to good demand and price in market and profitability.

Source of Irrigation

Tanks as a traditional and major source of irrigation have faded in importance. The share of tanks has declined to about 6 per cent of the total net irrigated area. Among the other sources of irrigation, tubewells and borewells constitute around 37 per cent.

Insights Presented by Probationers on Improving Agriculture in the Villages

■ *Bhim Nagar Village*

Total cultivable land is around 2,556 acres and 27 guntas. The net sown area adds up to 2,393 acres and 20 guntas and fallow land is around 163 acres and 7 guntas. The entire land is *Kushki* land. The major crops sown by the villagers are togari, *jowar*, and *chana*. Multiple cropping patterns is followed by the farmers and annually only one crop is raised by them. Toor is the *Kharif* crop in the village. Hybrid seeds are sown by many farmers. Only 5 per cent of the farmers use tractors. Bore wells are also common. The daily wages are higher for the males compared to the females (Akurathi, O.T., 2009).

■ *Srinivasa Sardagi Village*

Total cultivable area is around 12731.19 acres and the net sown area is 12731.19 acres. Fallow land totals to 892.17 acres. The major crops sown are *tur*, *jowar*, maize, and sunflower. All land is under ownership cultivation as per records since tenancy is abolished in the state. External labour is employed to work on the land on payment basis annually. This is not brought on record. Monocropping is practiced widely as most of the agriculture is rain-fed. Some fields have bore-wells with pump sets. The fallow lands have lost their nutritive value and require a lot of inputs to make them productive. Watershed work taken up under NREGA has ensured that the water table has risen and erstwhile dry lands have been put to use for agriculture (Randeep, D., O.T., 2009).

■ *Saidapur Village*

Net cultivable land is around 78.28 acres, with land being predominantly fallow. Agriculture is mainly rain-fed. Non-Irrigated Land: 36.92 acres is waste land which is locally called *gochar land*. The use of fertilizers is not extensive. Tractors are used for tilling of land. Livestock and Animal Husbandry in the district are important for the social and economic well being of the farmers. Majority of the workers are cultivators and they work in their own farms. Some of the villagers are also enrolled with MGNREGS where they get Rs.100 per day. The market rate of labour is abysmally low with the female worker getting very less wage (Ghosh, O.T., 2010).

■ *Jayapura Village*

Total landholders in the village are around 732. Villagers are engaged in agriculture, but a majority of them involved in wage labour. Villagers have small plots of poor quality land. They have few economic opportunities and are not able to secure enough income from one activity. As a result most of them are engaged in allied activities like dairy farming. Also the farmers have very little investment in agriculture. The village also has little permanent migration. There is no significant use of technology seen as most landholdings are small and fragmented. The use of high yielding seeds is also limited. Raitha Samparka Kendra provides technical information to the villagers. There is no major initiative for taking up water shed development programme though the village ground water level is low and faces acute water shortage (Cholan, O.T., 2008).

■ *Hittuvalli Village*

Cropping pattern determined by the availability of water and soil characteristics, besides the market pulls and consumption needs. Paddy and sugarcane are the dominant crops since the fields are wet because of the Cauvery Canal. Fertilizers and pesticides are applied in excess. Traditional practice of leaving stagnant water in the fields leads to wastage of water. Farmers follow unscientific practices. Excessive seeding in the same small area which saps the soil of essential nutrients. Excessive use of Urea has led to salinity of soil. Agricultural marketing has benefited the farmers a lot. There is lack of proper agricultural credit availability in the village (Kulkarni, O.T., 2003).

Although the village depends on the vagaries of Cauvery for irrigation purpose, the water intensive crops like paddy still are predominantly sown over a large area. There is a need to shift the crop into less water intensive crop. Some villages are on the road and therefore, have access to bigger markets. Floriculture is one of the alternatives to water intensive crop, palm oil is another viable alternative to water intensive crops. There is a need to popularize more efficient system of irrigation like drip irrigation. Although the initial cost may be high but its efficiency is almost three times more than the traditional system of irrigation prevailing in the dry tracks. There is a need to popularize the use of bio-fertilizers. Cold storages need to be set-up in most of the villages to reduce crops from going bad. More emphasis is needed on better post-harvest processing and value addition on agriculture. Farmers should be encouraged to make better use of the Raitha Mitra Kendras for technological support. Kissan Credit Cards should also be popularized (Kulkarni, O.T., 2003)

In India, Agriculture remains the primary occupation of the people. It is also a major source of employment for majority of the population. As per Census (2011) data, "the proportion of rural workers employed in agriculture (including animal husbandry, forestry and logging and fishing) declined from 84.40 per cent in 1983 to 81.90 per cent in 1993-94 and remained at about the same level thereafter" (*Planning Commission*).

REGIONAL DIMENSIONS OF EMPLOYMENT

"Employment of small and marginal workers has grown at a decennial growth rate of 24.6 per cent between 1991 and 2001, largely contributed to by the growth in the number of marginal workers. The number of main workers increased at a rate of 12 per cent and marginal workers by 161.5 per cent during this period. The growth of employment is highest in Bangalore Urban district (54.8%), followed by Dakshina Kannada (27.8%), Dharwad (27.6%), Koppal (24.9%) and Mysore and Raichur with about 26 per cent each" (*Planning Commission*). These are the districts that have shown remarkable growth in employment compared to the rest of the districts.

Data presented by the Planning Commission also suggests that Bangalore is one place that has offered maximum employment opportunities for the people of Karnataka. The city is seen "supporting a large number of Information Technology based industries, which generate high-end, skill-based employment" (p. 34). "There has been a significant increase in marginal employment in Bangalore as well, mainly due to construction activities. There is a large influx of migrant unskilled labourers to Bangalore resulting in the high growth of marginal workers. Much of this migration has been triggered by low growth and recurrent drought in the State" (*Planning Commission*, p. 78). In spite of the employment generated by the city, it has also created conditions for mass migration from the rural areas to urban areas and put pressure on the urban resources, especially infrastructure.

IV. OCCUPATIONAL PATTERNS

The status of employment of members, its nature and duration, has significant impact on the income level of a household. This in turn determines the level of consumption and the standard of living of the household. The following analysis presents the livelihood conditions of the households. Most of the villages are predominantly agrarian with very few villagers involved in different occupations. In rural areas, possession of land and other assets determine the nature of employment—self/wage and casual as well as permanent. Land is an important production asset. This is unevenly distributed across the households. The studies of occupational patterns give an overview of the economic conditions of the villages.

Occupation-wise analysis of the employment pattern of the households indicates that self-employment is dominant in agriculture. Agriculture is the main sector of the district economy. There is less diversification of employment due to poor resource base of the economy and low level of industrial development. A large proportion of sample households are employed in agriculture either as cultivators or agricultural labourers. The small and marginal farmers combine cultivation with wage employment to get minimum livelihood.

Insights Presented by Probationers on Improving the Non-Farm Sectors in the Villages

(a) Gulbarga

Employment is mainly in dry land agriculture, which is both insecure and less remunerative. Therefore, employment needs to be given top priority, as the present employment does not fetch enough income to the people. The average male wage in agricultural work is Rs.50 per day and employment is available for only 6-7 months in a year. The female wage rate is only Rs.30 per day, and female work participation is 32.91 per cent. A large proportion of them are marginal workers, but their earnings are essential for the survival of the family.

The service sector is growing in the district. There is a need to sustain its growth and increase the participation of these households in this sector through provision of credit, marketing and skills. Entrepreneurship training for the Muslim community may help them to develop small industries and trade. The focus of the plan should be on training and skill development in these specific areas.

A substantial portion of the working population in Hittuvalli village does not find employment throughout the year. Agricultural labour gets employment only for seven months in a year. There is out migration during the summer months especially to Andhra Pradesh during the Mango and Tamarind harvesting season.

Livestock provides a supplemental income for most of the villagers. Poultry is maintained mainly for household consumption (Kulkarni, O.T., 2003).

There is need for immediate attention to take pressure off the land and develop the non-farm sectors. Market surveys should be conducted for sale of non-traditional livestock like Turkey and Rabbit which fetch higher prices than the traditional livestock. The larger hotels in the districts can be approached for probable tie-ups (Kulkarni, O.T., 2003).

V. LAND REFORMS

Land reforms are an expression that has run the risk of acquiring an omnibus meaning, and is seen as a medicine for all rural ills. Land Reforms, for the purpose of this survey are taken to mean the intervention of the state in the prevailing pattern of ownership control and operation of land, both for the purpose of redistribution of ownership and alteration of land relations. Operationally a programme of land reforms would include redistribution of public or private land in order to change the pattern of land distribution and size of holdings, changes in ownership and tenurial rights with or without physical distribution of land, allocation of redistributed land to new owners or farmer working on land, making tenants owners of the land they work on, changing conditions of tenure such as providing security of tenure etc.

The main aim of land reforms is to redistribute land from the rich to the poor. "More broadly, it includes regulation of ownership, operation, leasing, sales, and inheritance of land (indeed, the redistribution of land itself requires legal changes)" (Planning Commission). In India, the agriculture sector faces problems like scarcity of resources, unequal distribution of land, and farmers living below the poverty line. It therefore has received a lot of attention from the government in the form of policies and initiatives. In 1949, the Constitution of India left the adoption and implementation of land and tenancy reforms to State Governments. This created total chaos across the states of the country since implementation of the different government programmes was not uniform across the states.

"Land reform legislation in India consisted of four main categories:

- Abolition of intermediaries who were rent collectors under the pre-Independence land revenue system;
- Tenancy regulation that attempts to improve the contractual terms faced by tenants, including crop shares and security of tenure;
- A ceiling on landholdings with a view to redistributing surplus land to the landless; and
- Attempts to consolidate disparate landholdings" (Kapila, 2009).

A lot of resistance was faced post the above suggestions. Resistance was mainly from the landowners and intermediaries. Landowners resisted the implementation of the reforms by using coercion and political influence. A lot of illegal steps were also taken like the forging of documents, bypassing ceiling, and the shuffling of tenants on different plots of land. Under such circumstances implementing any reform measures becomes a major problem for the government.

Besley and Burgess (2000) have conducted an in-depth study using state-level data for the sixteen major Indian states from 1958 to 1992. They studied the variation across states and over time in land reform legislation to identify the effect of land reform on productivity and poverty. They concluded that the abolition of intermediaries or the imposition of a ceiling on landholdings does not have much effect on either poverty or productivity. But land consolidation has a major impact on the conditions of the poor people. Besley and Burgess argue that "land reforms did not have much effect on the distribution of land and seems to have operated mainly through altering the contractual relations in agriculture" (p. 67).

Another study by Banerjee, Gertler and Ghatak (2002) who studied tenancy reforms in West Bengal argued that, "tenancy reforms improved agricultural productivity". After the launch of Operation Barga, designed to implement and enforce the agricultural tenancy laws in the state which also regulated the rents and security of tenure of the sharecroppers. The operation was able to streamline the terms of contracts and provided for more secure tenures. "Tenancy reform had a direct positive effect on tenants who were directly affected by it, but the indirect effects of this reform on the rural land market as a whole are less clear" (p. 67).

Besley and Burgess (2000) also found that the political influences on the land reforms had a major impact on their implementation. Annother study by Conning and Robinson (2005) investigated the determinants of land reforms. They argue that "the likelihood of reforms increases when land inequality is higher and where peasants have greater political power" (p. 88). Bardhan and Mookherjee (2005) study village-level data from West Bengal and find that land reform activity is highest where left-wing parties hold a larger number of seats in the state legislature and, interestingly, where they faced greater political competition. One can conclude that land reforms in India are largely driven by the political motives of the people in power.

Karnataka Land Reforms Act 1961

The Karnataka Land Reforms Act, 1961, came into force on 2-10-1965. The Act was in execution of the policy of agrarian reforms and was intended to give ownership of the land to the actual lawful tiller and to avoid absentee landlordism. Certain revolutionary amendments were made to the provisions of the Act by Act No. 1/1974, which came into force w.e.f. 1-3-1974. The Land Reforms Act as amended is relevant for the purpose of this case. According to the Land Reforms Act as amended, all agricultural lands which were under cultivation by the tenants as on the appointed date, i.e. as on 1-3-1974 stand vested in the State Government under Section 44 of the Act, Section 45 of the Act provided for registering the tenants as occupants of the agricultural lands of which they were the tenants.

Preamble to the Karnataka Land Reforms Act would show that the said Act has been enacted to have uniform law relating to agrarian. Interpretation has to be in favour of the weaker sections of the society which would achieve the object in terms of the intentment of the legislation. 'Tenant' has been defined to mean an agriculturist who cultivates personally the land he holds on lease from a landlord, and 'Agriculturist' has defined to mean a person who cultivates land personally.

Crop-share is one mode of tenancy in agricultural operation. In ascertaining the status of a person as tenant, the mode of cultivation as shown in the Act becomes very relevant. There are in all, six modes, viz. (i) cultivated by holder himself, (ii) cultivated by hired labourer, (iii) tenant paying cash, (iv) share of crop, (v) fixed quantity of produce, and (vi) proximity of aforesaid forms. It is true that burden of proving tenancy is upon the person who asserts it or who claims it.

Tenancy means relationship of landlord and tenant but in view of the peculiar and special provisions of Section 2 (18) and Section 4, a person in possession may have no relation with the landlord in a given case but he, nevertheless, be called as tenant. The provisions show that a person who is merely in possession, lawfully of course, is also a tenant. Definition of 'tenant' is divided into two parts—one contractual and the other statutory or who can be described for brevity's sake 'deemed tenants'. It could very well be visualized from the aforesaid provisions that "deemed tenant" or a statutory tenant means a person who lawfully cultivates any land belonging to another person if such person is not a member of the owner's family or a servant on wages payable in cash or kind, but not in share or a hired labour cultivating the land under the personal supervision of the owner or any member of the owner's family or a mortgagee in possession. Section 4, therefore, far from defining a statutory tenant, raises a presumption of statutory tenancy in the circumstances provided therein. A presumption can be rebutted by showing not necessarily the exceptions provided in the section itself but by other circumstances also by showing that the person holding the land is not so holding in the capacity of a tenant but in some other position. The concept of "tenant" in the Tenancy Act is founded primarily on "land" and its "cultivation". The process of thinking embodied in Section 4 is primarily based on the "land" and its lawful cultivation and not merely cultivation. The cultivation must have its origin in some lawful act and that is why the section describes and not defines a deemed tenant, as one who is "lawfully cultivating any land belonging to another" that is to say, so cultivating any land in his own right and not on behalf of another.

The expression *"lawfully cultivating"* would mean the same thing as cultivating "on one's own account" and for "one's own profit", in part or in full. The underlying purport and design behind Section 4 is to protect a lawful cultivator actively engaged in the act of raising the crops on the land or its major part though he may not be holding the land on lease in a traditional sense of the terms. The expression "lawfully cultivating" is now very well settled. It cannot exist without the concomitant existence of lawful relationship which can be proved even without the formal proof of a traditional form of lease.

Insights Presented by Probationers on Improving Land Records in the Villages

There is a need to focus on revenue work by the revenue authorities. Authorities in most districts were found to be overburdened with other work and this hampers the revenue work. There should be regular Jamabandi by higher authorities so that the land records are maintained and updated properly by the village accountants. There should be detailed training given to the street level bureaucracy so that they understand the broader picture and develop proper perspective (Mehendale, O.T., 2008).

VI. POVERTY ALLEVIATION PROGRAMMES

Poverty in simple terms is the lack of minimum food and shelter. Poverty is deprivation of the many and affluence for the few. Poverty may, therefore, be conceptualized as the socio-economic phenomenon where the resources available to a society are used to satisfy the wants of the few while many cannot even meet their basic needs. Poverty in India is a complex socio-economic phenomenon. Ahluwalia (1974) argued that poverty is neither a new concept nor has it suddenly appeared. It has been a prevalent problem for a very long time and people are aware of its effects within and outside the country.

World Bank defines poverty as "pronounced deprivation in well-being, and comprises many dimensions. It includes low incomes and the inability to acquire the basic goods and services necessary for survival with dignity. Poverty also encompasses low levels of health and education, poor access to clean water and sanitation, inadequate physical security, lack of voice, and insufficient capacity and opportunity to better one's life" (online report).

Prof. Amartya Sen argues that "poverty is a deprivation of basic capabilities rather than merely low income… enhancement of substantive freedoms, which provide people with capabilities to choose a life they have reason to value should be the main objective and primary means of development" (p. 89).

Karnataka has initiated various poverty alleviation programmers in both rural and urban areas. While these programmers have resulted in a marked decline in the number of the state's poor, much remain to be done to address regional and social variations in poverty. Towards ensuring food security to its citizens, the state operates an extensive food distribution system to provide basic foods with a focus on those who are below the poverty line. The state has also recently completed an elaborate exercise to weed out fake ration cards and to enhance the targeting of the public distribution system. The state has also established institutions to provide affordable housing to the poor. Having attained a reasonable decline in poverty estimates in spite of the 2009 floods, sustaining this growth of reduction of poverty and tackling urban poverty should be the main areas of concern in the forthcoming Plan. In order to sustain the existing growth in the reduction of poverty, proper implementation of different schemes is necessary. Promotion of livelihood opportunities through modernizing agriculture, establishing rural industries, and skill up gradation is considered as effective strategies.

A noteworthy initiative was undertaken by the government of Karnataka to estimate poverty incidence at the district level from pooled 1993-94 NSS 50th round data for the Karnataka Human Development Report (Government of Karnataka, 1999). This paper updates these estimates to 1999-2000 by combining the Central and State samples for Karnataka from the 55th round to examine regional variation in poverty across the State.

Planning Commission reports on the districts of Karnataka show the presence of strong regional disparities. As per a study conducted in 1980-81, Bangalore Urban and Dakshina Kannada were declared the most developed districts (Iyengar and Sudarshan, 1983) with Kodagu, Shimoga, Dharwad and Belgaum following closely behind. Hassan, Tumkur and Bijapur were declared the backward districts. Raichur, Bidar and Gulbarga, emerged as the most backward districts of Karnataka (State Domestic Product, 2001-02). Bangalore emerged as a major contributor of the State income. It contributed around 22 per cent to the State income. Bijapur continued to be the poorest in terms of per capita domestic product. "The pattern of growth over two decades indicates a stratification of districts based on geographic location, with the northern districts consistently performing poorly. This has serious implications for the distribution of poverty across districts" (p. 54).

State Policy Interventions

Over the years the Karnataka Government has floated a lot of policy interventions to alleviate the conditions of the people of the state. These interventions have a focus on reducing the deprivation levels, promoting growth and maintaining equity. "Broadly, the redistributive strategy seeks to reduce poverty by means of the following interventions:

- Promote asset endowment of the poor by programmes such as land reforms and Swarnajayanti Gram Swarozgar Yojana (SGSY);
- Offer direct employment opportunities through programmes like the Sampurna Grameen Rozgar Yojana (SGRY) and Stree Shakti; and
- Promote food security through the public distribution system and subsidized foodgrains" (*Planning Commission*, p. 34).

The above measures have to a certain degree reduced the burden on the poor, but still a lot needs to be achieved. However, the alleviation that one has seen is not uniform across districts. "One major policy emphasis in recent years has been on growth in the rural areas by measures to promote:

(a) Productivity in agriculture and related activities;
(b) Coverage and quality of infrastructure; and
(c) Quality of services and hence, human resources" (*Planning Commission,* p. 56).

Besides the poverty alleviation schemes, the Government of Karnataka has implemented schemes to develop rural infrastructure encompassing rural communications, housing, water supply and sanitation, watershed development and minor irrigation.

Employment Generation and Opportunities

The Government of India has put forward two categories that deal with the schemes for generating employment opportunities in the states. These categories are:

(i) Schemes under Sampurna Grameen Rozgar Yojana (SGRY): These provide wage employment, and

(ii) Schemes under Swarnajayanti Gram Swarozgar Yojana (SGSY), Stree Shakti and Swavalambana: These promot self-employment to the rural poor.

Planning Commission reports put forward the following features and achievements of these programmes in recent years:

- "Various government programmes, including direct wage employment programmes, such as Swarnajayanti Gram Swarozgar Yojana, Sampurna Grameen Rozgar Yojana; and
- Departmental works in irrigation, roads, buildings, command area development etc. generate considerable wage employment, which support the employment needs of the rural sector" (p. 66).

Insights Presented by Probationers for Better Implementation of Policies in the Villages

In most of the villages there is a need to keep a close watch over the involvement of contractors in various schemes meant for providing wage employment to the workers. A strong vigil should be kept over the roll book maintained by the panchayat to check any discrepancy. The funds received during the last two quarters must be retained to execute works during the lean season. The BPL List has to be drawn up with great care, and the officers and members should be made responsible for ineligible persons creeping into the list (Kulkarni, O.T., 2003).

Villagers need to be made more aware of the schemes run by the government so that they can get maximum benefits. There exists improper selection, lack of infrastructure, insufficient funds and poor resource management and lack of motivation. More responsive nature of implementing agency required for effective developmental work. The transparency in selection procedure is required. People should be informed about the implementation of various development schemes along with their benefits. Attention should be paid to monitoring and evaluation of the schemes and interventions. There should be a proper monitoring system, any deviation from the said guidelines should be detected and rectified on the spot. Also there is an overall need for more awareness among the farmers that can be generated by the use of campaigns and governmental efforts. Social audit, transparency and accountability should be ensured in implementing the schemes. This will create a sense of trust among the people and they would start participating in the schemes and hence increase the implementation (D. Cholan, O.T., 2008).

VII. PANCHAYATI RAJ INSTITUTIONS

In the state of Karnataka, local self-governance emerged as early as 1874, with the setting-up of "local fund committees" in every district. These local fund committees were supposed to take up development activities like the construction of roads and other subsidiary works. Attempts were made to make these institutions responsible and more people oriented. Then under the 1959 Act, the government enacted the Panchayati Raj Institutions (PRIs). Such institutions were missing from the local village set-up. They provided a fair platform for the communities to represent themselves and voice their problems. The Act also called for reservations for women, the Scheduled Castes (SCs) and Scheduled Tribes (STs) to the elected bodies. With further deliberations, the Ashok Mehta Committee was set-up in 1978 to look into the problems of the Panchayati Raj Institutions and to further reform it. The Committee sought a more comprehensive role for Panchayati Raj Institutions so that they would "undertake democratic development management under conditions of rapid changes, continuous growth and sustained innovations in all spheres of rural life" (Government of India, 1978, p. 77). Thereafter, the Government of Karnataka enacted a number of Acts like the Karnataka Zilla Parishads, Taluk Panchayat Samitis, Mandal Panchayats and Nyaya Panchayats Act in 1983, in order to establish a new Panchayati Raj structure consisting of mandal panchayats at the village level, taluk panchayat samitis and zilla parishads. "The Act provided for a gram sabha (village assembly) which comprised all eligible voters of a given mandal panchayat, panchayat members and government officers who were expected to use the forum to—

(i) Discuss and review all development problems and programmes of the village;
(ii) Select beneficiaries for beneficiary oriented programmes; and

(iii) Plan for the development of the village economy and its people which included minimum needs, welfare and production oriented activities" (*Planning Commission Report*).

Gram sabhas were popularized as an institution where members of a community could freely voice their opinions and needs. It also made the people in power accoutable for their actions and inactions. Women and the members of the marginal community got a lot of representation in the gram sabha. "People's participation in local government was enabled by holding gram sabhas, which were mandatorily convened twice a year" (*Planning Commission*, p. 79).

The PRIs have their shortcomings which have extensively been reported by many scholars. The greatest shortcoming of the PRIs is that despite the freedom and voice given to the women and backward castes, they were not offered leadership roles such as a Pradhan in the mandal panchayat or Adhyaksha of the zilla parishad. "Members of the dominant communities wrested these positions due to their control of rural society" (Amal Ray and K. Jayalakshmi, October, 1987; A. Aziz, 1994). The financial condition of the PRIs was improved by the introduction of the Jawahar Rozgar Yojana funds, but they did not have financial autonomy since they were way too dependent on State Government grants.

The work that the PRIs undertook was not balanced. They focused on few aspects more than the others. Most of the evaluation and research studies concluded that their focus was primarily on construction, repairs, infrastructure, buildings, roads, and bridges, rather than production oriented (A. Aziz, 1993; A. Aziz, 1994; and Planning Department, Government of Karnataka, 1987).

The PRIs also did not conduct any elections for the elected members. But with the 73rd Amendment to the Constitution of India, Constitutional guarantees were given for PRIs to conduct elections. The state had to elect by conducting elections to the Panchayati Raj (PR) bodies. There was reservation for the weaker sections and women.

"Karnataka is ahead of many states in terms of the powers and functions that have been delegated to PRIs. Under the 1993 Act, the panchayats shall function in accordance with the principle that what is appropriate at a given level should not be done at a higher level. The

29 functions listed in the Eleventh Schedule to the Constitution, and devolved to panchayats were delineated in three separate schedules, each of which was applicable to the gram panchayat (GP), taluk panchayat (TP) and zilla panchayat (ZP) respectively. The functions include preparation of annual plans and annual budgets; preparation of sectorial development schemes to promote agriculture, animal husbandry, rural housing, drinking water, roads and bridges, rural electrification, education, public health, sanitation, women and child development, social welfare, maintenance of community assets, promotion of libraries and so on. More powers and functions were devolved in 2004-05 and in order to remove ambiguity, a detailed activity map was prepared for each of the three panchayat tiers. Certain distortions and ambiguities noticed at the implementation level were sought to be removed by rationalizing or merging schemes. Such rationalization has resulted in the reduction of schemes from 421 to 217. This means that PRIs are now less constrained and straitjacketed by the normal plethora of department schemes, each with a set of inflexible guidelines that clamped a tight hold on expenditure and left little room for innovation or flexibility" (*Planning Commission*, p. 89).

Insights Presented by Probationers on Improving Panchayati Raj Institutions in the Villages

In the gram panchayat meeting the members of women self-help groups (SHG) try and assert themselves. The institution of SHGs strengthens to realize the goal of empowerment of women. Although women get Constitutional reservation in Panchayat body almost all the duties of women members in the panchayat are discharged by their husbands. There is a need to organize women folk to overcome the male psychological hegemony in the society. It is difficult to expect that the villagers will truly identify the poorest of the poor in an egalitarian manner, for there is little difference in the level of poor and the poorest. A family earning Rs. 2000 per month also cannot afford constructing a house by them, so it would obviously not recommend another poorer family for selection as a beneficiary overlooking it. The strengthening of the SHGs would also go a long way in reducing the influence of the usurious money-lenders (Kulkarni, O.T., 2009).

There is need for regular and stringent monitoring of the development schemes like NREGA run by the Government. Skill development for the proper execution of the schemes by the officers in charge is an absolute essential (D. Cholan, O.T., 2008).

There is corruption in the Gram Panchayat in which both political and administrative wings are involved. Corruption starts right from the election to Gram Panchayat. Cash and liquor for votes is an integral part of the campaigning. Improper implementation of MGNREGA has revived the old contractor-political-administrative nexus and has resulted in misappropriation of money in the Gram Panchayats. Action plans need to be prepared in the specific time period (Francis, O.T., 2009).

Pace of development in the villages is very slow or at times lacking. Schemes that are meant for the development of the rural people have not achieved the expected results. There is absolute lack of transparency, biasness, and ignorance is rampant. Due to the lack of a proper monitoring system, disparity in the distribution of funds among the beneficiaries was seen at many places in the surveyed villages. The deserving cases were exploited and deprived of their rights of getting any benefit. Funds of the deserving cases were distributed among the non-deserving who were mostly related to the Sarpanch. Lack of awareness about the benefits of various schemes is a major cause of exploitation among the rural poor. Emphasis should be on improving infrastructure of the village that would act as a catalyst for the development process (P. Cholan, O.T, 2008).

DISCUSSION AND CONCLUSION

Village Surveys are a great way to understand and experience the grassroots conditions of the villages. It also gives an opportunity to understand the psyche of a rural individual and his/her thinking about the prevailing socio-economic conditions. At the same time it is a great way to know the status of implementation of various developmental programmes operational on ground and make timely appraisals.

Nearly all villages represent a mixed picture of rural Karnataka in the sense that while infrastructure and basic amenities have been taken care of very well, the scourge of poverty is yet to be eliminated. Sectors like health and education are not in a pathetic condition as in some other parts of the country. People have been benefited by way of high level of awareness and motivation to explore the newer areas.

But, it seems that management and focus of these facilities is in not the desired condition. For example, primary education is in a pathetic condition as compared to upper and higher education. Again villages do not have a primary health centre even the larger villages. Although the closeness of the Community health centres has compensated it to a large extent. In the points that follow, all recommendations from the probationers have been compiled to get a clearer picture of the conditions of the villages.

- The villages need better coordination of the facilities available in the sectors like education and health, so that, these are optimally used.
- Government needs to encourage and provide self-employment opportunities Group activities like SHGs can prove to be very crucial in this regard.
- Although villages enjoy better connectivity, a systematic market linkage for various crops is not in place. Without marketing facilities no amount of entrepreneurship can achieve success.
- In view of the proximity of the villages to the town and city markets, farmers should be encouraged to move towards cash crops rather than production of foodgrains. Production of vegetables, floriculture etc. can be very rewarding in the village as quick transportation will not be a problem for the villagers.
- Capacity-building at the grassroots, level is a must. At the Gram Panchayat level, such capacity-building should take place for both, skills and attitude. Among the skills, accounting practices need to be paid attention on. Attitudinal training should aim at making the members more and more apolitical so that they function as a coherent unit dedicated to the well-being of the villagers.
- Participation of Panchayat should be more active in the higher level planning, i.e. at the Taluk and Zilla Panchayat levels by involving them through feedbacks.
- People need to be made aware of their rights and responsibilities as far as effective functioning of the Panchayats is concerned. Members from deprived sections

like the women and those from backward sections need to be given intensive training by the state.

- Large scale citizen awareness campaigns need to be built upon in order to generate demand for NREGA. Either a group of volunteers who take up such village level campaigns to educate the citizens or by informing panchayats on their responsibilities are the two ways awareness can be generated.
- Institutional capacities of the Gram Panchayats need to be improved. Panchayats are identified as the key implementation organization for NREGA. There is a need to effectively use this money to generate employment as well as create productive assets.
- Efforts should be made in all the states "to appoint technical staff to support the planning of large scale civil works as well as technical audit of works done for final payment. Similarly, accounts also need to be properly audited on a regular basis to maintain highest standards of financial accountability" (Planning Commission, p. 100).
- "Inclusion of some civil society representative—district collectors, district level panchayat presidents etc. in the planning process is essential so that diverse stakeholder concerns are expressed and incorporated. The meetings of the NREGS State Committee must happen on a fixed date and periodically, so that, such committees do not remain as a mere formality or a clearing house or the policy decisions proposed by the executives" (empowerpoor.org).
- The primary requirement of any place is connectivity. The village hamlets are situated at a lot of distance from each other in most of the cases. Good all-weather roads is a must under such conditions. SGRY needs to be implemented more efficiently. Arbitrary use should be curtailed and put only in beneficial projects. The programme needs to be promoted as a supplementary income generating prospect. People can be employed for shorter hours at the same wage rates.
- The Total Sanitation Campaign needs to be escalated and people need to be made aware of the same. The focus has to be on not merely the individual households, but institutional and community sanitation needs to be stressed.

To conclude, the state of Karnataka has succeeded in effecting significant improvements in the living conditions of its people during the last four decades; it is evident from the number of indicators related to literacy, health, education and other infrastructural facilities and quality of life. The state needs to build on its strengths, have a satisfactory economic growth in the tertiary sector and also take up new development initiatives. Such initiatives are important to ensure the social and economic development of the people of Karnataka. It is also imperative for the upliftment of the women and the backward classes of the society. The state government should work in coordinated manner with the SHGs and the NGOs since such institutions work at the grassroots level and are highly participatory in nature. Every state in the country has the potential to improve and adapt to the changing times. The Central Government has rolled out a number of schemes and programmes to alleviate the conditions of the poor and it is now the responsibility of the state governments and the local authorities to encash on these opportunities.

BIBLIOGRAPHY

Banerjee, A.V. (1999). "Prospects and Strategies for Land Reforms", In B. Pleskovic and J. Stiglitz (eds.), *Annual World Bank Conference on Development Economics 1999*. Washington, DC: World Bank, pp. 253-284.

Banerjee, A.V., P.J, Gertler, and M. Ghatak (2002). "Empowerment and Efficiency: Tenancy Reform in West Bengal", *Journal of Political Economy*, Vol. 110, No. 2, pp. 239-280.

Bardhan, P. and D. Mookherjee. (2005). "Political Economy of Land Reforms in West Bengal 1978-98", *Working Paper*, University of California, Berkeley and Boston University.

Besley, T. and R. Burgess (2000). "Land Reform, Poverty Reduction, and Growth: Evidence from India", *Quarterly Journal of Economics*, Vol. 115, No. 2, pp. 389-430.

Conning, J. and J.A. Robinson (2005). "Property Rights and the Political Organization of Agriculture", Forthcoming, *Journal of Development Economics*.

Economic Survey. Government of Karnataka, Finance Department, India. 2011-12. Government of Karnataka (1999): Human Development in Karnataka 1999, Planning Department, Government of Karnataka, Bangalore.

India, Registrar General (2011). *Census of India*, 2011. India, *Provisional Population Totals, Paper 1 of 2011, Series 1.*

India, Registrar General (2011). Census of India, 2011. Karnataka, *Provisional Population Totals.*

India, The *Gazette of India* (2009). Right to Education Act, 2009, Ministry of Human Resource Development. New Delhi.

Kapila, U. (2009). *Indian economy since Independence*. Academic Foundation.

Myles, F. Elledge (EHP). (2003). International Water and Sanitation. Reviewed by Roland Schertnlib (SANDEL), IRC International and Sanitation.

Ramasubban, Radhika (1982). *Public Health and Medical Research in India.* Saree Report R4: Swedish Agency for Research Cooperation with Developing Countries. Stockholm.

Rosenzweig, M. and H. Binswanger (1993) "Wealth, Weather Risk, and the Composition and Profitability of Agriculture", *Economic Journal*, Vol. 103, pp. 56-78.

Shaban, R.A. (1987). "Testing Between Alternative Models of Sharecropping", *Journal of Political & Economy*, Vol. 95, pp. 893-920.

State Domestic Product (2001-02). *Directorate of Economics and Statistics*, Karnataka, 2003, Bangalore, p. 62.

World Bank (1993). *Staff Appraisal Report, India: Karnataka Rural Water Supply and Environmental Sanitation Project.* (Report No. 11450-IN) Infrastructure Operations Division Country Department II – India. New Delhi: South Asia Regional Office.

World Health Organization and United Nations Children Fund (2000). *Global Water Supply and Sanitation Assessment 2000 Report.* Geneva, Switzerland: WHO.

4

Socio-Economic Status of Rural Development of Kerala

C.E. AJITH KUMAR

INTRODUCTION

Constitution of India—Setting the Mandate for Governance

The political wisdom that the economic slogans of mass appeal could ignite the fire of freedom struggle among the toiling rural masses of the countryside was dawned upon the Indian National Congress mainly with the conclusion of their Karachi (special) session (1931), by which time '*purna swaraj*' was declared the birth right of the natives. Ownership and management of land, full employment, removal of inequalities in resource distribution and equal opportunities to development to all are some of the slogans that whipped up passion for self-rule among the rural poor which eventually took them to freedom struggle. The huge public opinion thus generated in the country and outside and the widespread crave for Independence expressed through non-violent and occasionally violent mass upheavals also provided the much wanted bargaining power for the Indian National Congress in the bilateral talks for according the natives the dominion status and later the independence from the British rule. During the Constituent Assembly debate Resolution on Aims and Objective on (5th-13th December, 1946) moved by Pandit Nehru (United Province) proclaimed: "This Constituent Assembly declares its firm and solemn resolve to proclaim India an Independent Sovereign Republic and to draw up for her future governance a

Constitution.... (4) wherein all power and authority of the Sovereign and Independent India, its constituent parts and organs of government are derived from the people. The Government of India in its 'Resolution setting-up the Planning Commission of India' on 15th March, 1950 observed that the Constitution of India had guaranteed certain Fundamental Rights to the citizens of India and spelt out certain Directive Principles of State Policy. It directs the State to strive to promote the welfare of the people by securing and protecting as effectively as it may a social order in which justice, social, economic and political, shall inform all the institutions of the national life. The objectives of these policies will be towards securing, among other things: (a) that the citizens, men and women, equally, have the right to an adequate means of livelihood; (b) that the ownership and control of the material resources of the community are so distributed as best to subserve the common good; and (c) that the operation of the economic system does not result in the concentration of wealth and means of production to the common detriment.

It was, therefore, not considered a charity or largesse towards the Indian poor when the Parliament adopted a resolution in 1954 containing the clause that the objective of economic policy should be to build a socialistic pattern of society. While opposing an amendment of the draft of the Constitution to include the word "socialist" by Professor K.T. Shah in the Constituent Assembly, Dr. B.R. Ambedkar amazed that if the directive principles of state policy that were already enunciated in the draft "were not socialistic in their direction and in their content" what more socialism could be. Thus, even without the 42nd Amendment of Constitution (1976) that made the country a "Socialist Democratic Republic" (Preamble), the architecture of the Constitution of India envisaged a 'socialist pattern of development. Having regard to these rights and in furtherance of these principles as well as of the declared objective of the Government to promote a rapid rise in the standard of living of the people by efficient exploitation of the resources of the country, increasing production, and offering opportunities to all for employment in the service of the community, the government have set-up the Planning Commission with mainly seven specific objectives.

In December 1954, Parliament adopted a resolution which contained the following clauses:

1. The objective of economic policy should be a Socialistic Pattern of Society; and
2. Towards this end, the tempo of economic activity in general and industrial development in particular should be stepped up to the maximum possible extent." (ref: FYP-4 chap. 1; *Industrial Policy Resolution* 1956, p. 1).

The Constitution of a country enunciates the purpose and philosophy of governance of the country. It forms the basic rule book for planning and administration of the country. Thus, in a sovereign democratic socialist country whose power and authority are derived from its people, the philosophy and principle of governance is to usher in an era of secure and decent life of higher quality for the common man. The electoral system of the country based on universal adult franchise ensures that the will of the majority prevails over all other considerations. The groups of people like the skilled and unskilled wage earners, small peasants, petty craftsmen etc., who were marginalized hitherto, form the majority in number in the country. Their ambition and expression of their will should, therefore, find a prime place in the policy and agenda of governance of the country. In India, the above stated objectives remain to be the main theme and purpose of governance of the country in all policy documents. The economic policy is to build a socialist pattern of society, so that the trend of concentration of wealth is arrested and equality of opportunities for development for all the citizens is ensured. The governance process like, the assessment of resources available, planning as to how these resources should be utilized so as to "subserve" the common good and implementing the decided agenda for development could be best done by ensuring the participation of the people in such processes at grassroot level in the countryside. The 73rd and 74th Constitutional Amendments in India put forward the objective of democratic decentralization.

Inclusive Development and Poverty Alleviation Measures in India and Kerala

The ultimate objective of governance is human development or increased social welfare and well-being of the people. Improved education and health of the people will increase the quality of life of the people, which in turn, enhances productivity and output growth in a sustainable manner. However, the fruits of high growth need to be shared equitably among all particularly the weaker and hitherto marginalized classes of the society. Development should reach them and they should feel it tangibly. Poverty is a denial of choices and opportunities, a violation of human dignity. In India, a minimum level of consumption expenditure is determined on the basis of calorie requirements. The Planning Commission of India has defined poverty line on the basis of recommended nutritional requirements of 2400 cal/person/day in rural areas and 2100 cals/person/day in others. Viewing from the perspectives of the constitution of the country and the planning process that the country followed over the decades, poverty is immoral, and its persistence can not be tolerated any longer in a civilized society, not to speak of a socialist democratic country like India. Food and livelihood sufficiency should hence be the primary mandate of a responsible government. Table 4.1 provides the cost of eradication of poverty in India once and for all. Table 4.1 shows that it now costs the nation only 0.43 per cent of GDP, or Rs. 39,000 crores to remove the poverty from the land, for ever.

Table 4.1: Cost of poverty removal in India, 1983-2011/12

	1983-84	*1993-94*	*2004-05*	*2007-08*	*2009-10*	*2011-12*
Population (in million)	723	892	1089	1138	1176	1200
Percentage poor (Tendulkar line)	58.5	47.8	37.1	27.9	23.5	19
Poor Population (in million)	423	426	404	318	276	228
Poverty line (Rs. per month)	114	271	488	591	723	886
Per cent poor gap	29.8	24.1	21.5	18.5	18	16
Cost of removal of poverty with perfect targeting ('000 cr)	17	33	51	42	43	39
Nominal GDP ('000 cr)	221	866	3130	4700	6539	8974
Perfect targeting (% of GDP)	7.8	3.86	1.63	0.89	0.66	0.43

Source: Bhalla, Surjith S., 2011. *Inclusion and Growth in India: Some facts, some conclusions*. Asia Research Centre Working Paper 39. London.

India is a socialist country and a signatory to the UN Declarations. It is, therefore, bound by its Constitution, UN treaties and UN development goals to eradicate poverty in a specified time frame. In a state where government is made accoutable to its citizens—it being a democracy—it is barbaric and immoral to leave a considerable section of the citizens of the country who have voted them to power, hungry. Therefore, the amount that is to be spent to drive the huge mass of poor people out of poverty cannot be regarded as a liability. An investment into human capital will return duly as the most valuable performing asset. Hence, a developing and responsible government must fix priority to poverty eradication and social attainments while allocating the available resources. But the successive governments of India have failed to find funds to source fully the poverty eradicating operations of the country. On the other hand, the aggregate revenue foregone from central taxes (both direct and indirect) to Rs. 5,73,626.7 crore for 2012-13 while the total receipts in the form of tax revenues of the government in the year was around Rs. 11 lakh crore. Moreover, the total revenue foregone is showing an upward trend, both for direct and indirect taxes. About one-fifth of the total revenue thus forgone was by way of exempting the personal and corporate income tax (Union Budget 2013-14, Annexure 12). This kind of selective dissemination of state charity to corporate entities will impoverish the country to find resources for poverty reduction, create employment generation to the people and invest in human capital development programmes. This will also drain these beneficiary companies of their energy and wits to stand the competition they might face in the post-reform global corporate climate and upsets the prospects of their competing companies to thrive. In fact, this kind of arguments were raised by some economists against the cause of farmers who were succumbed to pressures of competition from abroad where the farmers were, both overtly and covertly, offered state support profusely to withstand the pressure in the face of neo-liberal interventions of removing trade barriers. In the long run, such state-favour to some corporate entities will end up in unhygienic polarization in the business climate and retard the process of economic growth. This limits further the sources of funds for poverty eradication efforts of the state.

A Profile of Rural Development Programmes over the Past 50 years of Planning

Table 4.1 looks at the progress under major rural development programmes. These programmes have been restructured on many occasions. Till the Fifth Plan Period, programmes like Small Farmers Development Agency (SFDA), Marginal Farmers and Agricultural Labourers (MFAL), Crash Scheme for Rural Employment, Food for Work Programme were in operation for specific periods, however, these generated employment on a very small scale. In the Sixth Plan, the major programmes for upliftment of rural poor were the Integrated Rural Development Programme (IRDP) and allied programmes, National Rural Employment Programme (NREP) and Rural Landless Employment Guarantee Programme (RLEGP). While these programmes continued in the Seventh Plan, the NREP and the RLEGP were merged into a single wage employment programmes called Jawahar Rozgar Yojana (JRY). The Indira Awas Programme (IAY) and Million Wells Scheme were also launched during the Seventh Five Year Plan. In the Eighth Plan the programme of Employment Assurance Scheme (EAS) was added. The year 1999-2000, in the Ninth Five Year Plan, witnessed the restructuring of the major rural development programmes, the IRDP along with the allied programmes of TRYSEM, DWCRA etc. and MWS have been merged into the Swaranajayanti Gram Swarozgar Yojana (SGSY) while the JRY has been redesigned as Jawahar Gram Samriddhi Yojana (JGSY).

Since 1970, Government of India has implemented a number of programmes designed to eradicate poverty. In many cases, these programmes have made an impact. Some of the poverty alleviation programmes in rural areas are free mid-day meals to primary school children, institution of supplementary nutrition programmes for pregnant mothers and pre-school children from poor households, granting of old-age pension to rural workers in a number of occupations and the implementation of MNREG A programme. The Government of India, Ministry of Rural Development has launched a new programme known as 'Swarnajayanti Gram Swarozgar Yojana' from 1st April, 1999 to bring assistance to poor families (swarozgaries) for them to earn appreciable level of income, by providing them income-generating assets through bank credit and government subsidy. SGSY was launched by restructuring the existing schemes, namely IRDP, Training of Rural Youth for Self-Employment (TRYSEM), Development of Women and Children in Rural Areas (DWRCA), Supply of Improved Toolkits to Rural Artisans (SITRA), Ganga Kalyan Yojana (GKY) and Million Wells Scheme (MWS). The objective of Indira Awas Yojana (IAY) is primarily to help construction of dwelling units by members of SC/ST, Free bonded labourers and also non-SC/ST rural people below poverty line by providing them with grant-in-aid. The IAY was launched in 1980 as a cash subsidy based programme, under which assistance is provided to BPL families for constructing dwelling units on their own using design and technology. MNREGA was launched in February 2006 in 200 most backward districts in the first phase and was expanded to 330 districts during 2007-08. The coverage was extended to all rural districts of the country in 2008-09. During the year 2008-09 more than 4.51 crore households in India were provided employment under the scheme. As against the budgeted outlay of Rs. 39,100 crore for the year 2009-10, an amount of Rs 24,758.5 crore has been released to the States/UTs in India till December 2009. During the year 2009-10, 4.34 crore households have been provided employment under the scheme. Out of the 182.88 crore person-days created under the scheme during this period, 29 per cent and 22 per cent were in favour of SC and ST population respectively and 50 per cent in favour of women (Economic Survey, 2009-10). However, even the financial efficiency of these projects has been very poor for many States. For instance, in Kerala, out of the total fund made available in 2009-10 of Rs. 37273.94 lakh more than two-third of which was from Central release, only 56 per cent could be spent by the State *(Economic Review,* 2010).

Table 4.2: Central Government Spending on Rural Development

(Rs. Crores)

	2000-01	*2013-14*
Ministry of Rural Development	11,791	95,516
Department of Rural Development	8888	74,478
Department of Land Resources	801	5773
Department of Drinking Water Supply and Sanitation	2101	15,266
Ministry of Water Resources (AIBP)	1856	1660
Department of Telecommunication	—	2697
Ministry of Power (Rural Electrification)	714	4041
Ministry of New and Renewable Energy	17	118
Ministry of Panchayati Raj	—	7001
Actual total rural development expenditure by GoI	14378	111033
GDP at market price—current price	22,168,652	10,028,118
Rural development expenditure as % of GDP	0.7	0.4

Source: IDFC., 2014: *India Rural Development Report* 2012-13.

India's spending on rural development comes to 0.4 per cent of GDP, as of 2013-14. Table 4.2 gives an account of the various amount spent by various ministries and departments for implementing rural development schemes. Though the pattern shows that there occurred a steep increase in the nominal expenditure for these schemes, the actual share of the total rural development expenditure by the Government of India comes to only 0.4 per cent in 2013-14, while it was 0.7 per cent during 2000-01. The social protection schemes of the nation constitutes approximately 1.6 per cent of GDP only. The schemes can be broadly categorized as promotional, protective or preventive, depending on the type of intervention (World Bank, 2011).

Table 4.3: Major Central Social Protection Schemes

Type	*Scheme*	*Entitlements*	*Expenditure (Rs. crores)*	*Targeting mechanism*
Promotional	National Rural Livelihood Mission—Aajeevika	Targeted livelihood promotion scheme for groups and some individuals. Targeted skill and promotional placement for rural poor and youth individuals	2392	One member of each household
	Mid-Day Meals Scheme	School feeding programme for children in grades 1 to 8	9891	Government and aided schools
	Conditional Cash Transfer—Janani Suraksha Yojana	Conditional cash transfer to pregnant women to promote institutional delivery	1606	BPL and women in low performing states
Preventive	Mahatma Gandhi National Rural Employment Guarantee Scheme (MGNREGS)	Self-targeted public works programme	29,213	Entire rural population willing to work
	Rashtriya Swasthya Bima Yojana (RSBY)	Subsidised health insurance	926	BPL population
	Public Distribution System (PDS)	Subsidised food distribution	72,822	BPL population. In some states, includes vulnerable such as SC/STs, widow, old age protective and disabled
Protective	Indira Awaas Yojana (Rural Housing)	Subsidised housing for rural poor	9,872	BPL population
	National Social Assistance Programme	Social pensions to widow, oldaged and disabled and BPL disabled	6608	BPL old aged and BPL disabled

Source: IDFC., 2014: *India Rural Devolopment Report* 2012-13.

As per the United Nations Development Programme (UNDP), Human Development Report (HDR 2009), the Human Development Index (HDI) for India in 2007 was 0.612 on the basis of which India was ranked 134 out of 182 countries listed, placing it at the same rank as in 2006 and in the category of Medium Human Development. Some countries in Asia with moderate growth rate like Sri Lanka and Indonesia performed much better in HDI than India. They registered an HDI of 0.759 and 0.739 respectively in 2007. The HDI of UNDP is based on three indicators, namely GDP per capita (PPP $), life expectancy at birth, and education as measured by adult literacy rate and gross enrollment ratio (combined for primary, secondary and tertiary education). Equity was not a deciding parameter of HDI.

However, it could be seen from Table 4.4 that despite its sub-optimal income growth pattern (as demonstrated early), the State of Kerala has managed to reduce poverty over the decades, and, as of now (2007-08) it is only 10.2 per cent, which is about one-third of the national level. The per cent of severely poor is not only substantively lower but is steeply sliding with the current level at 3.5 per cent only. Poverty in India is on a course of fast decline. But even this reduced level of poverty is unjustified in India, a nation whose income growth has been spectacularly large during the last decade.

Table 4.4: Per cent of poor population (Tendulkar line) in Kerala and India

	Poverty ratio				*Per cent of severely poor*		
	1983-84	*1993-94*	*2004-05*	*2007-08*	*1993-94*	*2004-05*	*2009-10*
Kerala	53.2	35 (–410)	19.7 (–5.09)	10.2 (–19.7)	13.3	7.5	3.5
India	58.5	47.8 (–2.0)	37.1 (–2.28)	27.9 (–9.06)	22.8	16.3	11.3

Note: Values in parentheses are the respective compound annual growth rate.

Kerala is ranked first with regard to the human development index (HDI) of the States in India. The major parametres leading to this achievement of Kerala are presented in Table 4.5. It could be seen from the Table that Kerala's achievement out-performed the average performance in India in an amazing manner. Only 1 per cent of the

Kerala population was entangled in the lowest wealth quintile in India. The per capita GDP of the State during 2006-07 was 1.66 times that of the nation. The per capita median income in 2004-05 also was 1.66 times larger. The social development indicators related to human capital and health also were remarkably better in Kerala.

Table 4.5: Selected Development Indicators for Kerala and India (2005)

	Kerala	*India*
Female literacy% age 15-49	93	55.1
Children age 6-14 in school 2005-06	97.7	79.6
Children age 8-11-simple test 2005-05%	82	54
Under 5 mortality% 2005-6	16.3	74.3
Young children fully immunised	75.3	43.5
Adult women with low BMI	18	35.6
Population below poverty line% 2004-05	19.6	37.2
Population (%) in lowest wealth quintile 2005-6 in India	1	20
Median per-capita income 2004-05 (Rs/year)	9987	5999
HDI 2004-05	0.98	0.41
HDI rank among Indian States	1	

Table 4.6: Inequality and Growth in MPCE in Kerala and India

Gini coefficient of Inequality		*Rural*			*Urban*		
		1993-94	*2004-05*	*2009-10*	*1993-94*	*2004-05*	*2009-10*
	Kerala	26.53	33.74	34.99	31.38	38.48	39.9
	India	26.53	27.36	27.58	32.05	35.57	37.06

Growth rate in MPCE		1993-94 to 2004-05	2004-05 to 2009-10	1993-94 to 2004-05	04-05 to 09-10
	Kerala	3.08	3.46	3	3.34
	India	1.31	1.78	2.05	2.5

Table 4.6 shows how the state of Kerala performed over the years in terms of two major parametres of social development. It could be read from Table that the Gini coefficient of inequality in Kerala, although, comparable with the national level, had increased sharply, particularly in the rural area. The rise in inequality was more visible in urban area, especially in the early post-reform period. The rural

monthly per capita expenditure (MPCE) had been the highest in Kerala among all major States in India. The growth in MPCE had been much faster in Kerala than that of the all-India level.

AN OVERVIEW OF KERALA: THE GEO-POLITICS AND SOCIAL ATTAINMENTS

Kerala is a state in the Indian Union that came into existence on November 1, 1956, consequent on the implementation of the State Reorganization Act of 1956. The re-organization was done on linguistic basis, by merging the Malayalam speaking regions, namely, the Thiru-Kochi State of the Indian Union, the Malabar district of the erstwhile Madras province and the south Kanara taluk of Kasaragod. Kerala is the twelfth largest state by population in India and is divided into 14 districts, 21 revenue divisions, 14 District Panchayats, 75 taluks, 152 CD blocks, 1453 revenue villages. There are 978 gram panchayats, five corporations, sixty municipalities and one Township in Kerala. Malayalam is the most widely spoken and the official language of the state. It is the official language except where English and the minority languages of the state, namely Tamil and Kannada, were used as provided by law (Official Languages Act, 1969). The state capital is Thiruvananthapuram. Other major cities include Kochi, Kozhikode, Thrissur, and Kollam.

Kerala is a land highly diversified in its physical features and agro-ecological capabilities. The undulating topography ranges in altitude from below the sea level (MSL) to 2694 above MSL. This much altitude difference across a geographical width of 32-130 km of the state make its west-ward rivers that originated in the Sahya mountain peaks on the east flow across the width (West-East orientation) of the state and attain great speed during its course to Arabian sea on the west. These rivers, therefore, carry with it the top soil consisting of sand and silt on the mountains and their valleys that are rich in minerals and deposit them on the coast. The east-ward rivers of Sahya-origin take a longer course, flow through the neighbouring States also before they join the Cauvery to drain finally into the Bay of Bengal.

Based on the topography, the land resources of the state fall generally into four well-defined natural divisions: (i) the lowlands (< 7.5 m from MSL) bordering the Arabian sea, (ii) the midlands

(7.5 to 75.0 m above MSL), (iii) the high land (75 to 750 m above MSL), and (iv) the high ranges (> 750m above MSL). These zones run parallel across the length of the State (North-South orientation). The low land region comprising about 10 per cent of the total area of the state supports about one-fourth of the state population. The midland plains covering about 42 per cent of the land mass have an undulating terrain intersected by many rivers, small hills and valleys. About 60 per cent of the state population inhabits this region. The high lands comprise mainly the hilly tract on the western side of the Western Ghats. It consists of about 43 per cent of the land of the state and supports about 15 per cent of the population which includes many hill tribes. The mountainous high ranges mainly composed of the two hilly districts, viz. Wayanad and Idukki and the eastern parts of the other eastern districts.

Traditionally, when only gravity-driven water flow was the only source for irrigation of crops in Kerala region, the type of soil, the elevation of the region and the presence of the river-backwater systems determined the cropping pattern that was followed in a particular land in these regions. However, the major and minor irrigation dams of Kerala that were constructed with a view to bring large areas under irrigation have in fact failed to add to the acreage of the crops, especially the water-intensive ones like paddy. While in the lowland regions where the type of soil is sandy to sandy-loam and riverine alluvium (soil order: *Entisol*) the crops like paddy, sugarcane and coconut are preferred, the midland zone supports many seasonal crops like rice, vegtables, sesamum etc., annual crops like tapioca, banana, ginger and perennial crops like arecanut, coconut, pepper, cashew and rubber. The lowland is often subjected to salinity intrusion. Rice and coconut are the important crops grown in the lowlands. Kolelands of Thrissur and 'padasekharams' (large extent of paddy fields below MSL) of Kuttanad are situated in the lowlands. Still higher, on the hilly tract, the soil is mainly of forest loam which is generally rich in organic matter, the plantations of tea, coffee (*robusta* variety), cardamom and rubber are prevalent. The cooler, humid climate in high ranges are generally tolerable only for certain special crops like tea, coffee (*Arabia*), some fruit crops and cardamom and even rubber is a hardly preferred crop there.

The lowlands are characterized by numerous lagoons and backwaters, such as the Vembanad, Ashtamudi lake etc., which receive drainage from many of the west-flowing rivers—all fed by the two monsoons available to the state, the south-west (normal date of onset is 1st June) and north-east. The backwaters are connected by a network of artificial canals which help inland navigation for a length of about 558 km. The inland canal system, navigable round the year, extends from the capital (Thiruvananthapuram) city in the south to Kochi and further to Badagara in the north by the Kochi-Ponnani-Badagara canal system. The important peaks in the Western Ghats are the Anamudi (2694 m), Mukunni (2550 m) and Nilgiris (2470 m). The Palaghat Gap with the width of about 32 km is the largest gap in the Western Ghats. In addition, there are a few other passes in the Ghats such as Aramboli, Kumili, Kambam, Thevaram, Bodinaikannur, Karkkur, Periya, Perambadi etc.

Beginning at least from the late medieval period, the political conditions prevailed in the three geographic regions of the present Kerala state came to be vastly different. Though Travancore region had experimented with popular assemblies from as early a period as 1888, the idea of democratic control of the administrative machinery got transformed into organized political activity only by the 1930s. The community-based mobilization and struggles for communal control of the executive during the period by the major communities like, Ezhavas, Christians, Nairs and Muslims, led to an arrangement of proportional representation or quota in the legislative assembly. After the Vikom Satyagraha (1924), a political congress was launched and this formed the consolidating force behind the mass uprisings against many social and economic evils afflicted the region during the time. The temple entry proclamation (1937) and communal representation in the legislature followed. Toeing the spirit of national movement spread in northern regions of the country the Travancore State Congress was formed which demanded the resignation of the *Dewan* of Travancore. Mobilisation of the labourers in agricultural and traditional industry sector ignited many labour agitations and the radical elements in the State Congress outfit found the situation conducive to show solidarity to the Indian Communist movement. The growing disenchantment among the tenants with the implementation of the Malabar Tenancy Act (1929) and the political climate that emerged out of the Guruvayoor Satyagraha (1931) infused new energy and confidence among the Socialists in the Congress in the Malabar region. The State unit of the CPI spearheaded the activities to break the barriers of casteism and communalism and forge mass organization of the working class.

The whole Kerala region was on the throes of a struggle for change, the most important areas of change being land distribution and improvement of the socio-economic conditions of the working class. Reformation in the areas of education and health was also among the major socio-political exigencies. Since Independence, the three administrative units of Travancore, Cochin and Malabar were brought into the single state of Kerala in 1956, consequent on the 're-organisation of states in India on linguistic basis'. But the interim period during 1949-1956 when the two princely states of Travancore and Cochin were integrated into a single political State called 'Thiru-Kochi' State, the region was writ with intense political rivalry on caste lines. Seven governments were brought down during this period (Kerala Development Report 2008). Emergence of the newer political parties on communal basis eroded the mass base of the mainstream political parties and it became impossible for the established mainstream parties to form the government after elections, but for the alliance with these newly evolved parties, based on expediency and setting aside the yawning ideological differences. Coalition politics have come to stay in Kerala immediately after the formation of the State. Kerala could thus be regarded as the cradle for 'coalition polity' in the country.

The course of economic growth of Kerala in relation to that of the nation is depicted in Table 4.7. It could be seen from the Table that the early Five Year Plan (FYP) periods in Kerala witnessed slow growth in Gross State Domestic Product (GSDP) and per capita income (PCI). The growth momentum took a sharp increase after the Sixth Five Year Plan period. Kerala's performance in the last decade was spectacular, and it was higher than the overall national GDP growth. The growth of Kerala was different from that of the nation. Contrary to the pattern of growth and the sources of income in the overall economy of the nation, the main sources of GSDP of the State were income from plantation sector and the service sector which boomed in the post-reform period due to the boost in the foreign remittance-driven consumption expenditure. Despite the cynical approach to the Kerala model of development by the mainstream economists, Kerala economy flourished in terms of the GSDP and its growth. Unlike the case with the Indian economy, Kerala, traditionally a more globalised economy, remained unfazed even with the rough weather experienced in the economy of the global leaders in late 2000s.

Table 4.7: Growth Targets and Achievements (% per year) of National Income of India and CAGR of GSDP (at 1990-2000 prices) of Kerala and the CAGR in per capita income (PCI) of India and Kerala during the Five-Year-Plan periods

Plan	*India*			*Kerala*	
	Target	*Actual*	*Per capita income*	*GSDP*	*PCI*
First Plan (1951-56)	2.1	3.6	1.8	3.4	1.2
Second Plan (1956-61)	4.5	4.2	2.1	1.8	–0.4
Third Plan (1961-66)	5.6	2.8	0.2	2.5	0.2
3 Annual Plans (1966-69)	—	3.8	1.5	5.6	3.2
Fourth Plan (1969-74)	5.7	3.3	1	2.373	3.3
Fifth Plan (1974-79)	4.4	4.7	2.7	0.614	–0.4
Annual Plan (1979-80)	—	0.0	–8.2	1.011	1.01
Sixth Plan (1980-85)	5.2	5.7	3.2	1.136	1.2
Seventh Plan (1985-90)	5	5.8	3.6	3.593	3.0
2 Annual Plans (1990-92)	—	3.4	0.6	4.784	1.04
Eighth Plan (1992-97)	5.6	6.5	4.1	5.934	5.3
Ninth Plan (1997-02) $	6.5	5.7	3.5	5.066	4.3
Tenth Plan (2002-07)*	8	7.6	—	8.855	1.2
Eleventh Plan (2007-12)	9	8.0	—	—	—

$ The growth targets were set with respect to national income.

* For Tenth Plan, growth rate is average of first four years.

Source: 1. Statistical data from Economic Review 1968, 1982, 1987, 1994, 1997, 2000, State Planning Board, Statistics for Planning 1977, Department of Economics and Statistics, Kerala.

2. Source for Kerala data on GSDP from Fourth Plan: DES., 2010. Gross State Domestic Product of Kerala from 1970-71 to 2008-09.

3. GoI., 2001. Indian Planning Experience: A Statistical Profile. Planning Commission, New Delhi (for growth of National Income, Per capita income and agricultural and foodgrain production up to 2001) Tata Services, 2001. Statistical Outline of India 2001-2002. Department of Economics and Statistics, Mumbai.

4. Source for foodgrain production of Kerala: Shyjan, D. (2007). Public Investment and Agricultural Productivity: A state-wise analysis of foodgrains in India. Working paper No. 387. Centre for Development Studies, Thiruvananthapuram.

Demography

Kerala is one of the most populous states in India. Population density in Kerala has been almost three times than that of the whole country all through these decades, and currently (2011) it is 859 (against 382 of the country). Yet, a comparison of demographic parametres of India with Kerala places the state in an envious position. Sex ratio has always been favourable to women. In that respect also it stands distinct from that of other states in India. While the decadal population growth rate of Kerala was considerably higher than that of the average Indian level till the 1971 census, it entered a decelerating phase thence. Although Kerala has continued with its impressive show to register a growth rate of just above 4.9 per cent during 2010-11, the decadal growth rate of Bihar, Chhattisgarh, Jharkhand, Rajasthan, Uttar Pradesh and Madhya Pradesh are above 20 per cent, a level which Kerala and Tamil Nadu were 40 years ago. This spectacular performance in population front could not be achieved in state GDP growth.

Table 4.8: Trend in Population Parametres of India and Kerala over the Decades

Year	*1950-51*	*1961*	*1971*	*1981*	*1991*	*2001*	*2011*
India							
Population Mn	361.1	439.2	548.2	683.3	846.4	1028.7	1210.2
Annual growth (exp)%	1.25	1.96	2.20	2.22	2.16	1.97	1.64
Sex ratio (F per 000M)	946	941	930	934	927	933	940
Population density	117	142	177	216	267	325	382
GDP at factor cost-Constant prices Rs. Bn.	2247.86	3298.25	4741.31	6419.21	10835.72	18643	44937.43
Kerala							
Population Mn	13.549	16.904	21.347	25.451	29.074	31.841	33.388
Annual growth (exp)%		2.24	2.36	1.77	1.34	0.91	0.476
% of Population of India	3.75	3.85	3.89	3.72	3.44	3.1	2.76
Sex ratio (F per 000M)	1028	1028	1016	1032	1036	1058	1084
Population density	349	435	549	655	748	819	859
GSDP at factor cost-Constant prices Rs. Bn.				341.1	469.55	798.08	1702.37
% GDP of India				0.4	0.27	0.17	0.07

Source: Census of India Reports.

Agriculture and Food Security

Food security of its citizens is considered as the most important parameter for responsible governance of a civilized society. FAO conceives food security as a guarantee of food to all citizens at all times. Food availability is not the only aspect that is to be ensured for food security, but the capability of the people to access food and ensuring stability of such capability also. Table 4.9 presents the trend of the food security of India and Kerala over the decades, with reference to the seven parametres relating to food security. Two important observations could be made from the Table. The per capita food availability in India is not always on an increasing trend, though food was already taken by many planners and development strategists for granted. As early from 1980s there is a sense of complacency towards growth in foodgrain production ostensibly on the ground that the nation had already attained a stage of foodgrain sufficiency. The per capita net sown area (NSA) also showed an alarmingly declining trend.

Table 4.9: Population and food security parametres of Kerala (region) and its growth over the decades

Year	*1950-51*	*1961*	*1971*	*1981*	*1991*	*2001*	*2011*
India							
Foodgrain Mn T	50.82	82.02	108.42	129.59	176.39	196.81	244.49
FG area Mn ha	97.32	115.58	124.32	126.67	127.84	121.05	125.73
FG yield t/ha	522	710	872	1023	1380	1626	1945
Per capita FG in Kg		186.73	197.79	189.65	208.4	191.31	202.03
Per cap FG area ha		0.263	0.227	0.185	0.151	0.118	0.104
Net sown area Mn ha	118.75	133.2	140.86	140.29	143	141.37	140.3
Per capita NSA ha		0.303	0.257	0.205	0.169	0.137	0.116
Kerala							
Foodgrain (FG) Mn T	0.736	1.091	1.323	1.318	1.111	0.765	0.548
FG area Mn ha	0.758	0.835	0.927	0.825	0.592	0.365	0.222
FG yield t/ha	971	1307	1427	1598	1877	2097	2472
Per capita FG	54.32	64.54	61.98	51.79	38.21	24.03	16.43
Per cap FG area ha	0.056	0.049	0.043	0.032	0.02	0.011	0.007
Net sown area Mn ha	1.117	1.924	2.172	2.180	2.247	2.206	2.101
Per capita NSA ha	0.082	0.114	0.102	0.086	0.077	0.069	0.063

Source: Compiled from various Government of Kerala Publications.

Kerala had always been a food-deficit state, right from its formation, though foodgrain yield in the State has been substantially better than that of the nation. Per-capita foodgrain production is too low when compared with the level of requirement. The trend is declining at an alarming rate.

Table 4.10 provides the annual compound growth rates of population and food security parametres of Kerala. The GSDP growth from 1980 has been appreciable though below the national growth. But it far outpaces the growth in population. The population density is declining at a gratifying rate. But the foodgrain situation, as mentioned above, is quite alarming since 1970s up to which it could, by and large, keep pace with the growth in population. Though yield growth has been satisfactory all through the decades, especially in comparison with the population growth, per capita foodgrain production is on a free fall. This is mostly because of the per capita steady decline in the area under foodgrain cultivation. The negative growth and the low levels of current per capita NSA and foodgrain production suggest that Kerala survives only because of the supplies from outside. If purchase parity of foodgrains through current channels of supplies is lost against the income sources the state now enjoys, like foreign remittance and rubber incomes, the food security of the State would be in utter peril. Development means nothing if the state remains complacent on the food front.

Table 4.10: Annual compound growth rates (%) of Population and food security parametres of Kerala over the decades

Year	*1950-60*	*1960-70*	*1970-80*	*1980-90*	*1990-2000*	*2000-10*
Population Mn	2.24	2.36	1.77	1.34	0.91	0.48
Sex ratio (F per 000M)	0	–0.12	0.16	0.04	0.21	0.24
Population density	2.23	2.35	1.78	1.34	0.91	0.48
GDP at factor cost-Constant prices Rs. Bn.				3.25	5.45	7.87
Food grain (FG) Mn T	4.01	1.95	–0.04	–1.69	–3.66	–3.27
FG area Mn ha	0.97	1.05	–1.16	–3.26	–4.72	–4.85
FG yield t/ha	3.02	0.88	1.14	1.62	1.11	1.66
Per capita FG	1.74	–0.4	–1.78	–2.99	–4.53	–3.73
Per cap FG area ha	–1.33	–1.3	–2.91	–4.59	–5.8	–4.42
Net sown area Mn ha	5.59	1.22	0.04	0.3	–0.18	–0.49
Per capita NSA ha	3.35	–1.11	–1.69	–1.1	–1.09	–0.91

Source: Computed by the Author.

Table 4.11 gives the district-wise demographic details. The districts are arranged in their order of locations in the state from south to north. As noted above, Kerala's population growth is very slow since 1970, in comparison with that of the nation. But it is not even across all the districts in Kerala. Malappuram, Wayanad and Kasaragod districts registered higher growth than that of the nation (12.15%) during the period. Generally, the northern districts have higher growth in population. Though Alappuzha has the second lowest population growth during the period, the population density is the largest in the district in 1991. The trend is not seen to have reversed after a decade also.

Table 4.11: Population (in lakhs) and its Growth, of Kerala and its districts

Districts	*Area (sq. km.)*	*Population*		*% Population*	*Population growth%*	*Poplation density (per sq km)*	
		1991	2001	2001	1991-2000	1991	2001
Thiruvananthapuram	2,192	29.47	32.35	10.2	9.8	1,344	1,476
Kollam	2,491	24.08	25.84	8.1	7.3	967	1,038
Pathanamthitta	2,642	11.88	12.32	3.9	3.7	450	574
Alappuzha	1,414	20.01	21.05	6.6	5.2	1,415	1,496
Kottayam	2,203	18.28	19.53	6.1	6.8	830	722
Idukki	5,019	10.78	11.29	3.6	7	215	252
Ernakulam	2,407	28.17	30.98	9.7	9.1	1,170	1,050
Thrissur	3,032	27.37	29.75	9.3	8.7	903	981
Palakkad	4,480	23.82	26.17	8.2	9.9	532	584
Malappuram	3,550	30.96	36.3	11.4	17.2	872	1,022
Kozhikode	2,344	26.2	28.78	9	9.9	1,118	1,228
Wayanad	2,131	6.72	7.87	2.5	17	315	369
Kannur	2,966	22.52	24.12	7.6	7.1	759	813
Kasaragod	1,992	10.72	12.03	3.8	12.3	538	604
Kerala	38,863	290.99	318.39	100	9.4	749	819
CV (%)	34.2	36.7	37.9	37.9	40.5	43.87	42.04

Source: Census Reports

The income and poverty status of the districts of Kerala are presented in Table 4.12. Generally, southern districts of Kerala are richer ones during both the years. By and large, the growth levels also follow the same pattern. Barring one or two districts, poverty in southern districts is comparatively lesser than that of northern ones.

Table 4.12: District-wise Per Capita Income in Real Term (in Rs.) and Poverty

Rank (2006-07)	Districts	2005-06	2006-07	Growth Rate	Poverty %	Rank of Poverty-lessness
15	Malappuram	18,024	19,124	6.1	19.7	9
14	Kasaragod	22,549	23,928	6.12	26.5	14
13	Kollam	23,154	24,580	6.16	3.5	1
12	Palakkad	23,518	24,903	5.89	13.4	7
11	Alappuzha	24,198	25,686	6.15	20.3	11
10	Kozhikode	24,691	26,238	6.27	19.9	10
9	Kannur	24,874	26,412	6.18	24.7	12.5
8	Wayanad	25,213	26,694	5.87	24.7	12.5
7	**State**	25,657	27,284	6.34		
6	Thrissur	26,599	28,301	6.4	11.1	6
5	Thiruvananthapuram	26,726	28,526	6.74	6.3	4
4	Pathanamthitta	27,131	28,979	6.81	10.5	5
3	Idukki	28,983	30,605	5.6	5	2.5
2	Kottayam	28,840	30,626	6.19	5	2.5
1	Ernakulam	36,520	39,034	6.88	13.8	8
	India				**26.1**	

Source: Kerala Economic Review (2007).

DEVELOPMENT AND PARTICIPATORY GOVERNANCE IN KERALA: A STUDY OF SELECT VILLAGES

Revenue and Land Administration

Even with the sub-national growth in GSDP the state of Kerala could maintain high levels of human development indicators, placing the State on a par with developed countries having high GDP growth. This model of development named in late 1970s 'the Kerala Model of Development' was later celebrated during many academic and development discourses in the country, and the success of the model was greatly attributed to the legacy of 'public action' (Dreze and Sen 1989). Per capita availability of land being the lowest among that of Indian states, land question is crucial to Kerala's development, particularly if it is to be inclusive. Kerala Land Reforms (Amendment) Act, 1969 was land mark legislation in Kerala that abolished the centuries-long landlordism in the region. It provided for vesting of private lands in excess of a prescribed limit to the government and distributing it to the landless. It also prohibited tenancy. However, there is a growing body of opinion among planners of inclusive development that if tenancy is allowed and land is given to small entrepreneur's groups of the landless poor like *Kudumbasree* units the sluggish growth in agricultural sector due to resentment among some large farmers towards cultivation could be partially overcome. Land in Kerala has been fragmented and continuously changed hands.

The issue of land relations and land management in Kerala has been key to revenue administration even from the post-medieval period of Kerala history. The following chart shows the major initiatives taken towards revenue settlement in Kerala region during the eighteenth century AD and afterwards.

Period	*Details of settlement work done*
1738 to 1748	Settlement of lands belonging to the Sree Padmanabha Swamy Temple was done. No measurement of land was conducted.
1712	A complete survey and settlement was conducted. The survey was a (Record of what is heard) (Kettezhuthu) and was based on discussions with the landholders. The Landholders were issued *Pattas* after settlement.
1775	Ramayyan Dalava conducted a complete survey and settlement holders were issued *Pattas*. The nature of the survey is unknown.
1801	A complete survey was conducted. This was a "Kandezhuthu" (record of what is seen). The tenures were similar to the previous settlement. *Pattas* were issued after this settlement.
1817	This was only a settlement of garden lands. *Pattas* were issued subsequent to the settlement.
1836	Complete resurvey of garden lands was conducted. Side measurements were made with a '10' feet rod. *Pattas* were issued subsequent to the settlement.
1882/1909	A scientific survey was conducted and *Pattas* were issued to the landowners.

(Contd.)

Period	*Details of settlement work done*
1905-1909	(1) Survey was conducted in Cochin following the Settlement Proclamation of 1905. (2) Malabar during 1926-1934 according to Resettlement Manual 1936. In all the regions settlement was conducted after land survey. The survey records in all the regions were maintained according to Land Record Maintenance Rules in the respective regions.
1966	After formation of Kerala, elaborate survey of Government lands and occupation in Government Lands was conducted under Plan Schemes but most of these records were not finalized and given effect in the Revenue Administration. In 1966, a general resurvey of the State was commenced and the resurvey of 652 villages has been completed and given effect in the Revenue Administration.
1966	In resurvey, each Taluk was divided into main circuits with an approximate area of 150 sq. km. and each main circuit is connected with the GT station established by the Survey of India so as to provide geographical co-ordinates to all survey points. According to the present system of survey, each taluk is divided into blocks of approximately 1000 hectares. Then each block is divided into Khadom with an area of 25 to 40 hectares. Each Khadom is sub-divided into survey numbers of approximately 4 hectares in dry land and 2 hectares in wet land.

Source: Randhir Kumar Singh, 2008. Village Report: Edakkad, Kannur, pp. 25-30.

It could be seen from the history of revenue settlement procedure as shown in the above chart that the settlement and the regime of ownership rights that was instituted during a period dated back the time of formation/consolidation of territories that later formed the principalities in Malabar, Cochin and Travancore which later amalgamated into the state of Kerala in Indian Union had been the basis of land ownership claims in Kerala even now. The tiller and the labourers who created all the use values out of land remained out of bounds of the land reform measures carried out even in post-formation of Kerala. Initiatives towards settlement and updating land records could not be taken to its logical conclusion as yet. In fact, the celebrated land reforms legislations in Kerala were all founded on the land survey conducted many decades prior to its formation when the social sensibility towards equality of opportunities for development and equity in land access were not dawned upon as an issue of social rights.

Village office is the basic unit of revenue administration in Kerala. Moreover, the district administration implements many welfare schemes for the people in the village through the village office. It is the custodian of all records related to the land of the village and maintains them. It also collects revenues like basic tax, water cess etc. It recovers revenue if a resident of the village is adjudged to have defaulted in paying the tax due to the government, or commits any kind of civil offences that led to a revenue loss to the government, or any other citizen. It even conducts on-site inquiries on matters referred to it from higher authorities on criminal or civil justice petitions. As part of the maintenance and administration of the *puramboke* land (barren, unused land in the village owned by the government) the village officer keeps vigil against the encroachment on *purmboke* land and is the authority to collect fines imposed on such encroachment. The state of Kerala had enacted much legislation with the intention of upholding justice in the distribution of land and its sustainable common use. Some legislation even sought to protect the ecology and food security system of the State. Some other legislations are more or less outdated and have a disconnect with ground reality. For instance, *Kerala Land Utilisation Order, 1957* (the paddy lands cannot be used for other crops in the paddy season, therefore, the farmers are leaving the land fallow). The village officer is the revenue authority to see and ascertain itself that no provision in such Acts of the State is not violated. In other words, the village office is the nearest seat of power and protects citizen's interests on land. Though the powers are vested either with Tahsildar/RDO/Collector, Village officer is the one implementing these land laws or in most cases action is taken by the concerned authority on the basis of the Village officer's report. The scientific survey of land masses equipped the State to realize the objectives envisaged in the Land Reforms Act (The Kerala Land Reforms Act, 1963) in a meaningful way. The legislations like

The Kerala Land Conservancy Act, 1957; *The Kerala Escheats and Forfeitures Act*, 1964; *The Kerala Revenue Recovery Act, 1968*; *The Kerala Land Assignment Rules, 1968* etc. gave the government ample space to conserve, improve and manage the lands vested with her. The very recent *The Kerala Conservation of Paddy Land and Wetland Act, 2008* is a landmark Act to conserve the paddy land and wetland and to restrict the conversion or reclamation thereof, in order to promote the growth in the agricultural sector and to sustain the ecological system in the State.

Almost all village offices in Kerala are housed in well-constructed buildings. However, considering the kind and enormity of office records they have to manage, the office space available in these buildings is undoubtedly a serious constraint. Other problems like the lack of sufficient number of office furniture to accommodate the staff and the large number of visitors, proper storage space and shelves to keep the records safe and easily retrievable etc. are also serious limitations of the working condition of the village office. As part of the ADB-funded Modernisation of Government Programme (MGP) the Taluk offices have been fully computerized and the file movement takes place through the Taluk Suite System software. The vision of the district administration is to complete the implementation of the Village Suite Software which will automate the entire work flow in the Village office. Computerization of land records is going on at a fast pace. However, the connectivity to all the villages still poses a challenge to set-up the K-Swan network (Report of Avinissery village).

Participatory Governance of Kerala Villages

The recent experiments of democratic decentralization in Kerala could be qualified as a direct attempt at deepening democracy in the State by augmenting the space for public action and people's participation in governance in general and planning in particular (Kerala Development Report 2008). Based on these Amendments, the Kerala Panchayati Raj Act, 1994 and Kerala Municipalities Act, 1994 were passed. An important change brought in by the 1994 Acts has been the detailed listing of functions, responsibilities and powers to be transferred to the local self-governments (LSGs). Based on the recommendations of the State Government appointed S.B. Sen Committee (1996) an Amendment Act (1999) was legislated to give more autonomy to the LSGs by curtailing the regulating power of the

State. On the eve of the Ninth Five Year Plan (1996) a major step, by name 'People's Plan Campaign', was initiated by the State to usher in a phase of decentralization in the process of State governance. It is basically a process by which the functions and resources of the State is devolved to the elected governments at the lower levels so as to facilitate greater direct participation by the citizens in governance including fixing of local priorities, identification of feasible schemes, selection of beneficiaries of government funded schemes, monitoring of implementation, etc. The plan was to devolve 35 to 40 per cent of the State's plan funds in the form of grants-in-aid to the LSGs. Evolving a working methodology for participatory planning was one of the major priorities in Ninth Plan. During the Tenth Plan, institutionalization of the methodology of decentralized planning already evolved was given greater stress. In the Eleventh Plan, the entire process was revamped laying increased stress to the concept of 'people's planning' and the institutionalization of decentralization of state power is completed.

Table 4.13 provides the list of various sources of funds for the panchayats. Apart from this fund from the public, village panchayats get fund from the State Government by way of Establishment Grant, Road Maintenance Grant, Vehicle Tax Compensation, Minor Irrigation Grant and Basic Tax Grant. However, the collection rate of tax in villages is not full. For instance, in Eruthempathy village the collection rate is only about two-thirds of the total demand of Rs. 2,65,345 (village report, 2005-06). They also receive special grants like building grants, lighting grants, construction of bridges and culverts grant and grant for maintenance of burial and cremation grounds.

The figure of Local Governance Structure (LGS) in Kerala given below depicts the hierarchical structure of various LSG Institutions. The 1994 Act (as amended in 1999) do not prescribe any hierarchical control of iSGs belonging to higher tiers over the lower tiers. In other words, the village panchayats (Grama Panchayats) and block panchayats are free from the control of District Panchayat, but bound to accept the district perspective plan that is chalked out by the District Planning Committee. An analysis of the total plan grants to LSGs during the late 1990s period, as provided in the Kerala Development Report 2008, who sourced their data on the Second State Finance Commission Report, Kerala 2001) showed that while about one-fifth of the total State Plan size is allotted to village panchayats, the total grant to block and district panchayats were only about half of what

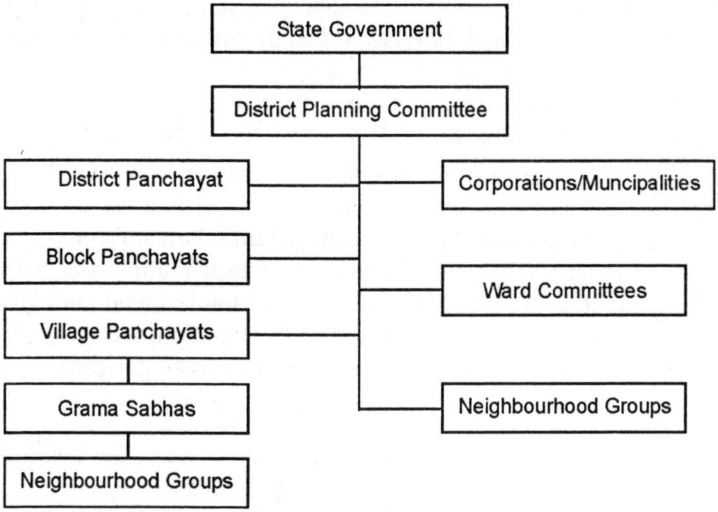

Fig. 4.1: Local Governance Structure in Kerala

Table 4.13: Sources of funds collected from the public and the rate of levy

Name of tax	*Target population*	*Rate per annum*
Profession tax	Employees, merchants, agriculturists and professionals having a half-yearly income of more than Rs. 2400	Max. Rs. 1250
Entertainment tax	Theatre owners	20.88 per cent of gate collection
Vehicle tax	Owners of bicycles, horse carts, bullock carts	
Licence fee	On hotels, teashops, grocery shops, rice mills, saw mill etc. for issue of licence	
Market fee	On vegetable market etc.	Depends on the area
Rent on Land and Buildings	For the use of *puramboke* (government) land to set-up market stalls, soft drink stalls etc.	
Sale proceeds	On sale of coconut, tamarind, mango trees etc.	Through public action
Stamp duty	On transactions taking place in the panchayat	Registrar allocates 90 per cent of stamp duty

Source: Singh, Balkar, 2006 Village Report – Kizhakkambalam village.

the village panchayats enjoyed. Though the LSGI share in State plan was about 39 per cent in 1997-98, it had declined to 32.32 per cent during 2000-01. Other than the State allocation of grant-in-aid, the village panchayats receive revenue from the public by way of panchayat tax, building tax, entertainment tax, profession tax etc.

The expenditure pattern of grama panchayats from 1993-94 to 1998-99 showed that about one-half of total expenditure of grama panchayats was spent on establishment and for salaries. Trend is seen to be increasing in favour of this head of expenditure. The roads consume another big share (19 to 28% of the total expenditure). The other essential services like public health/sanitation, water supply/ drainage and street lighting incur a share of 13 to 16 per cent.

However, the ideal conceptualization of democracy as the

Table 4.14: Trend in the Devolution of Resources to Local Governments (by the Kerala State Government 1997-98 to 2011-12)

Year	*Ratio of LG Plan Grant State Plan Outlay*	*Total Transfers to LGs Plan + Non-Plan as Percentage of SOTR*	*Per Capita Transfers (Rs.)*	*Per Capita Transfers in Real Terms on 1993-94 Prices (Rs.)*
1997-98	26.23	23.24	337.07	337.07
1998-99	30.65	28.7	429.89	339.81
1999-2000	31.38	27.45	459.24	342.41
2000-01	29.56	24.95	471.97	344.88
2001-02	28.19	21.79	415.91	347.21
2002-03	33.33	24.84	584.51	350.81
2003-04	29.73	22.53	587.22	353.94
2004-05	28.13	20.99	606.06	357.02
2005-06	25.61	20.78	654.75	360.05
2006-07	22.54	17.17	660.48	363
2007-08	22.14	16.63	732.47	365.91
2008-09	21.69	15.36	791.5	368.78
2009-10	20.65	15.56	872.3	371.58
2010-11	22.72	14.87	1040.46	374.31
2011-12	23.24	15.45	1280.27	376.93
15-Year Ratio	**24.98**	**18.48**	**624.82**	**356.91**

Note: SOTR-State's Own Tax Revenue.

Source: 1. Worked out from CAG Reports for various years and Government of Kerala (2011) and SOTR from Budget in Brief (various years), Government of Kerala.

2. Oommen, M.A. 2014. Deepening Democracy of Local Governance: Challenges before Kerala. *Economic & Political Weekly*. June 21, 2014, Vol. XLIX, No. 25: 42-46.

government of the people, by the people, for the people assumes meaning and content only when its practice enhances the quality of life that the people live. While participatory democracy has powerful theoretical arguments, its empirical basis continues to be weak (Oommen, 2014). Table 4.14 gives an account of how much share of the state resources the people in the country side get who are supposed to decide their own destiny by participating directly in LSGs. The major finding of this study was that despite the growth that was nearing a rate of 9 per cent and the rhetoric of inclusiveness of growth, there was virtually no improvement in per capita transfers to LSGs when they were measured in 1993-94 prices.

Thus, it is clear that though the Panchayati Raj Act, 1994 and its Amendment Act, 1999 have envisaged to siphon off a large share (30-40%) of the state plan fund to LSGI where the grassroots level people in the countryside participate directly in the process of governance, the actual allotment is on a steady decline. Moreover, the major share of amount granted is spent towards establishment and salary in the LSG institution, and the people at the grassroots level is left with a paltry 13 to 20 per cent of the total expenditure. There are 5,010,259 households in rural Kerala and 1,716,097 households in urban area (Census 2001; Panchayat Level Statistics 2006). While the population of rural area in Kerala was 23,5,74,449 in the urban area it was 82,66,925. The average geographical area of a grama panchayat is 32,889.39 ha, a block panchayat has 25,562.48 ha and a district panchayat has 2,77,535.5 ha area. There are, in average, 5,015 households in a grama panchayat, 32,962 households in a block panchayat and 3,57,876 households in a district panchayat. The average total grants-in-aid allocation for a grama panchayat in 2006-07 was about Rs.1,573 per household, Rs. 399 per household in a block panchayat and Rs. 411 per household in a district panchayat. While an amount of Rs. 2,382 was allocated as total grants-in-aid for the year 2006-07 for a rural household for local-self-governance, an amount of Rs. 1,203 was allocated for an urban household (computed by the author from the data sourced from Statistics for Planning 2009 and Panchayat Level Statistics 2006). 'Self-governance' is thus, by no means, a cost-free affair. Of the total grants-in-aid allocated, about 29 per cent comes from the SCP fund and about 5 per cent comes from TSP fund.

It may be noted from the above section that the grama panchayat is the basic unit of administration in the state. It has the autonomous power to collect revenue from its citizens, receive grant-in-aid from the state plan fund and also to decide and spend the financial resources on various items of development in the panchayat. On the other hand, villages are units of revenue settlement, mainly land tax and other related items. While in Kerala there are 999 grama panchayats, it has 1452 revenue villages. Thus the geographical boundaries of these government institutions are not co-terminus.

Method of the Village Study

The salient findings of the study on the villages of Kerala are presented in this section of the paper. These studies were undertaken by the IAS probationers who belonged to Kerala cadre, and who joined the service during the period from 2007 to 2011. The studies were part of the induction training they had undergone at LBSNAA, Mussoorie, during the period. This paper covered 14 studies, each done by a probationer. Each officer had studied one Kerala village of his choice. Thirteen villages were covered. In fact, the study area is not confined to the boundary of a particular village, but the grama panchayat area which houses that village. As there were no specific guideline to the investigating probationary officer from any quarter for selection or exclusion of any particular village from the set of all 1452 villages of Kerala, and the officers, for themselves, did not seem to have any specific affinity of sorts towards any village, it could be assumed that the villages were chosen randomly. Therefore, the findings that emerge from these studies could portray, with sufficient degree of confidence and generality, as to how an ordinary Kerala village lives.

This section describes the current socio-economic status of the State from the development perspective, as it envisaged in the Constitution and other plan documents, and which were spelt out in the beginning. Though the report of all the village studies contained an overview Kerala, all the details as given in them could not be compiled in a common template of subject organization so as to enable the reader to have a comparative assessment across the villages. At least in some cases, the information provided appeared non-comparable. Many of the Tables in this and previous sections were adopted from the forthcoming too primary or redundant book by M.

Lathika and C.E. Ajith Kumar on Kerala Agriculture. The authors of the village study reports are listed below:

Sl. No.	*Name of the Probationer*	*Year*	*Name of the village/Grama Panchayat*	*Name of the district*
1.	Dr. Rathan U. Kelkar	2005	Edakkad	Kannur
2.	Dr. Balkar Singh	2006	Kizhakkambalam	Ernakulam
3.	Mr. P. Nath	2007	Narikkuni	Kozhikode
4.	Mr. Ajith Kumar	2008	Kumbalangi	Ernakulam
5.	Mr. K. Biju	2008	Eruthempathi	Palakkad
6.	Mr. Randhir Kumar	2008	Edakkad	Kannur
7.	Mr. Patil Ajit Bhagawantrao	2009	Elankunnapuzha	Ernakulam
8.	Mr. N. Parasanth	2009	Ramanattukara	Kozhikode
9.	Mr. Kesavendra Kumar	2010	Chellanam	Ernakulam
10.	Mr. Harikishore	2010	Kizhakke Kallada	Kollam
11.	Mr. Balukiran	2010	Farooq	Kozhikode
12.	Mr. M.G. Rajamanikkam	2010	Avinisserri	Thrissur
13.	Dr. A. Kowsigan	2011	Elankunnapuzha	Ernakulam
14.	Mr. T. Mitra	2011	Mayyanad	Kollam
15.	Mr. Venkitesapathi	2011	Kodancherry	Kozhikode

From the list given, it could be discerned that the village study could not be conducted so as to cover the State evenly. None of the villages in some districts of the state were studied. The study on the villages Edakkad and Elankunnapuzha were done by two probationers each. While the third chapter presents some basic information of the villages covered in the village study reports. Four panchayats in Ernakulam district, four in Kozhikode, two in Kollam and one each in Kannur, Palakkad and Thrissur have been covered here. The same parametres for socio-economic status and development of the village are presented for all the villages. Moreover, the same information relating to the Block Panchayat in which the grama panchayat is structurally included is also given along with the details of the grama panchayats. The data on the block and district panchayats are adopted from the respective 'Panchayat Level Statistics' of the department of Economics and Statistics, Government of Kerala. The information of the district under which these panchayats come has also been given. This will provide the scope to have an assessment of the panchayats in comparison with the block panchayat and district panchayat under which the grama panchayat is included. This section provides information about the village, which are given district-wise.

The main feature of the study of all the probationers is that each of them made detailed study of certain cases in the village which they found either that it would demonstrate the living conditions of some specific section of the village population in its true colour and detail, or that the cases are models to replicate in a developing society. The probationers have made many visits to the village to study these cases in detail and they have also used case study tools like focus group discussion, interview etc.

As noted elsewhere, the village studies that are covered in this volume did not encompass all the districts. Villages in some districts were more represented. The main districts that are covered by the village studies are Kozhikode, Ernakulam, Kollam and Kannur. The number of local self-government institutions in the State and these main districts are presented in Table 4.15.

Table 4.15: No. of Local Self-government Institutions in Kerala and Selected Districts

Administrative	*State*	*Eranakulam*	*Kozhikode*	*Kollam*	*Kannur*
1. Number of Revenue Divisions	21	2	1	1	1
2. Number of Taluks	63	7	3	5	3
3. Number of Revenue Villages	1452	117	117	104	129
4. Number of Corporations	5	1	1	1	—
5. Number of Corporation Wards	316	71	55	52	—
6. Number of Municipalities	53	8	2	2	6
7. Number of Municipality Wards	1756	229	85	61	232
8. Number of Block Panchayat	152	15	12	13	9
8. Number of Block Panchayat Wards	2004	185	165	163	133
9. Number of Grama Panchayat	999	88	78	71	81
10. Number of Grama Panchayat Wards	16139	1363	1452	1226	1264
11. Number of Assembly Constituencies	140	14	12	12	10
12. Number of Parliament constituencies	20	2	2	2	1
13. Number of District Panchayat Wards	339	28	—	27	—

State-led Agrarian Reforms in Kerala Region

In Kerala, the origin of ownership in land was entangled in myth and mystery (Sankaranarayan and Karunakaran, 1985). One version how the high caste *Namboothiris* (Kerala Brahmins) who migrated to Kerala only during the ninth century (Logan, Malabar, Manual) acquired the *jenmam* right (absolute right) of all the cultivable private property in Kerala, owed its origin to the myth that Kerala was reclaimed from the Arabian sea by Parashurama, one of the mythological incarnations of Lord Vishnu, and gifted to Brahmins for cultivation. This mythical version of Kerala's origin seemed to have formed the basis and moral justification for centuries of blatant expropriation of surplus value of labour and the attendant suppression and denigration of lower caste natives by the Brahmin *janmis* (landlords). The colonial hegemony in Kerala not only patronized the highly hierarchical social structure built on castes which formed the basis of the cultivation and produce-sharing system, but also helped the *de-jure* native rulers assert their power of the state. Early in nineteenth century as the population grew and the pressure on land was intense unrest rose amongst the ryots. With the outbreak of Moppila disturbances beginning in 1836, the question of land reforms engaged the serious attention of the government and the public, leading to many ryot-friendly legislative and administrative measures in the Malabar region. Notwithstanding the early strides towards land reforms, the State, at the time of its formation, was a highly heterogeneous state with high inequality in the extent of land ownership and degree of tenancy liabilities both within and between its erstwhile regions. Kerala is acclaimed to be one of the few States in India where state-led land reforms measures were implemented rather effectively. The objectives of land reform legislations in India, or for that matter, any part of the world are mainly two: one, to redistribute land in a more equitable and operationally efficient way; two, to enhance agricultural productivity of land. The salient components of the land reform legislations, therefore, comprise the provision for fixity of tenure and land rent, fixing land ceilings, vesting the land in surplus of land ceiling limit to the government so as to enable them to distribute them among the landless poor other more needy people of the state. Viewing from this angle, the land reform measures as it was implemented in the State, cannot be regarded as a landslide success. Neither the equity in land access and entitlement is achieved nor the agricultural productivity is significantly raised, with the administering of major land reform measures in Kerala. In 1959-60, Lorenz ratio of land concentration was 0.7897 in Kerala and it was the highest among 14 major Indian states. Prior to the most seriously implemented land reform legislation was given effect to in Kerala (1970-71) the Gini coefficient of operational holdings was 0.647 in Kerala, while it was conspicuously lower (0.586) in India. The degree of land concentration had not changed much in Kerala (Gini coefficient was 0.636 against 0.641 in India, NSSO) even by 1991-92. The yield of all the crops that were seriously affected by the implementation of land reforms had not improved after 1975.

As already noted, the land reform measures of 1960s and 1970s exempted very large holdings of plantation crops from the ambit of land ceiling provisions. This seriously limited the scope of re-distribution of land to the real tillers. Moreover, neither of these Acts addressed the issue of giving ownership rights to the tribal people who live in forests and hill tracts of Kerala. About 25 per cent of the tribal people in Kerala live in the reserve forests. Non-tribal people from the plains migrated to these tracts and settled there, challenging the forest-based livelihood of the native tribal population who, for generations, made a subsistence living in the woods. It never dawned to them to procure ownership rights of the lands to which they had free and unconditional access either for cultivation or for other land-based economic activities like grazing, collection of forest produces. Moreover, their activities never tampered with the pristine ecology of forest lands, and remained rather the God-sent custodians of forest lands. However, the Kerala legislature passed the "Kerala Scheduled Tribes restriction on transfer and restoration of alienated land Act 1975" unanimously, and had included it in the Ninth Schedule to the Constitution. In practice, nothing occurred thereupon. But, on a clear direction by the High Court to implement the Bill before October 1996, the government hurried and amendment bill diluting many provisions giving land access rights to the tribal people who were alienated from the livelihood they enjoyed for generations were rendered totally helpless and landless (Task Force Report on Land Reforms and Agrarian Institutions 1997 of the State Planning Board).

The time-line of salient state-led measures for Land Reforms in Kerala

Year	*Name of Committee and its report in brief*
1	**2**
1852	Mr. Strange was appointed to suggest measures for defining the land tenures and to place them on a more rational basis.
1852	Sadar Adalat Court issued instructions on the basis of the report of Mr. Strange to the Civil Courts defining the main tenure established by usage and precedents. In the period that followed, the eviction of tenants steadily increased but they were restored by the *Janmis* (landlords) mostly after enhancing the rent rather than for cultivating the land directly. There were complaints of excessive rents and renewal fees levied by the *Janmis*. Moreover, with regard to the compensation for improvements, the tenants did not get adequate amounts. The cumulative effect of all these factors made the relations between the landlords and their tenants further strained.
1880	Mr. Logan was appointed Special Commissioner to investigate the land tenures and report on the adequacy of compensation allowed for the tenants' improvements. The recommendations of his report are as follows: (i) Fixity of tenures by legislation for actual cultivation of holding not more than 25 acres of wet land or 5 acres of dry land; and (ii) Rent to be equal to two-thirds of net produce.
1887	On the basis of the above recommendations, the Malabar Compensation for Tenants Improvement Act was passed. This Act no. 1 of 1887 was passed to prevent the growing practice of eviction, but experience of its working showed that it did not have the desired effect. The government then undertook an investigation into the causes of the failure of this Act. It was found that major cause of failure was inadequacy of compensation given by the Courts and further legislation was needed to rectify the defects.

(Contd.)

1	2
1900	Act no. 1 of 1900 was passed superseding the Act no. 1 of 1887. This Act was not effective in checking the arbitrary evictions. Melcharth was a usual phenomenon which helped the proprietors to bypass the provisions of the Act against evictions. Then several times it was tried to be rectified by legislations, but every time it could not fructify because of one or the other reasons.
1915	Collector Innes in his report to Madras Government on the working of the Compensation for Tenants Improvement Act, 1900, attributed the evils of Malabar tenancy system to insecurity of tenure, rack-renting, exorbitant renewal fees, social tyranny and miscellaneous exactions.
1924	Madras Tenancy Bill was introduced in Madras Legislative Council by Mr. M. Krishnan Nair. It had the intention to confer fixity of tenure and for fixing fair rent and withdrawal fees.
1926	Madras Tenancy Bill was passed by the Legislature, but Governor withheld his assent citing various inconsistencies in the Bill.
1927	The Raghaviah Committee was appointed to enquire into and report on the disabilities of the tenants of Malabar, the extent of unjustifiable evictions by the *Janmis* and necessity for protection of "Kanamdars" and on the best means of remedying their disabilities.
1930	Malabar Tenancy Act no. XVI was passed on the recommendations of the Raghaviah Committee. It conferred fixity of tenures on cultivating verumpattamdars, subject to their payment of fair rent and also one year rent in advance or otherwise furnishing security for the same, if demanded by the landlord. Within a few years of working of Malabar Tenancy Act, certain defects in the enactment became apparent.
1940	Malabar Tenancy Committee headed by Mr. Kutti Krishna Menon reported on the general question of tenancy in Malabar. It recommended many provisions for fixity of tenures, restricting the grounds for eviction of tenants, fixing

(*Contd.*)

1	2
	the fair rent, reducing the renewal fees for long-term tenancy etc. But the implementation of these recommendations was postponed due to War and after that it never came into being. However, certain amendments were done in the Act in 1945, 1951 and 1954 with a view to prevent eviction and for safeguarding the interest of tenants.
1956	Kerala State was formed and in 1957. The Kerala Stay of Eviction Proceedings Act, 1957 sought to provide for temporary protection of tenants, Kudikiddappukar and persons cultivating the land on minor sub-tenures at the will of the proprietors.
1958	The Compensation for Tenants Improvement Act superseded the Malabar Compensation for Tenants Improvement Act, 1900 and provided for compensation at the rate of fifteen times the net annual yield for trees planted by tenants and actual value of permanent structures put up by them. It also gave tenants the right to compensation for improvements effected by them, even if there was a contract to the contrary in the otli.
1960	The Kerala Agrarian Relations Act was passed. This was the first unified legislation which embodied in it the broad principles of land reforms as enunciated in Five Year Plans. However, this act was struck down by the Hon'ble High Court. In the light of the experience with the working of the Kerala Agrarian Relations Act, the State Government obtained the assurance to have a new Land Reforms Act included in the 9th Schedule of the Constitution.
1963	The Kerala Land Reforms Act, 1963 is a watershed in the history of land reforms in Kerala. After this several other acts came for specific purposes, but all were made taking into account the principles and objectives of the Kerala Land Reforms Act.
1969	Kerala Land Reforms (Amendment) Act. Provided for vesting in government all rights, title and interest the land owners and intermediaries over the holdings held. Tenants got full ownership of their tenanted lands; ceiling of land

(*Contd.*)

1	2
	holdings and taking over the distribution of surplus lands; fixity of occupation to the *kudikidappukars* (residents in the land of the landlord) and conferment of the right to purchase at one-fourth of the market rate the small extent of land ranging from 3 cents to 10 cents, in and around their hutment. More than 42 lakh tenants and about 5.3 lakh *kudikidappukar* were conferred ownership rights (Task Force Report). However, the exemption of plantations like rubber, tea, coffee etc. from land ceiling regulation, and the provision to consider supervision by landlords as a job equivalent to family labour have drained the steam out of the vigours of land reform measures.
1975	Kerala Scheduled Tribes Restriction on Transfer and Restoration of Alientated Act. To protect the right of the tribal people from alienation.
1996	Amendment to the Kerala Scheduled Tribes Restriction on Transfer and Restoration of Alientated Act, repealing many provisions that favoured the livelihood of tribal people.
2002	Kerala Land Reforms (Amendment) Bill granted exemption from ceiling provisions of the parent Act to lands planted with cashew, vanilla and medicinal plants.

Land Use and Management in Kerala

Table 4.16 shows the area under each class of land use in Kerala and the select districts. Only 54 per cent of the total geographical area in the state could be brought under cultivation.

However, owing to intensity of use which spread to 15.2 per cent of the total area, the gross cropped area is estimated at 69 per cent. Though Kerala is known for its dense ever green forests, now the area under forest covers extends only to about 28 per cent of the total area. By size, Palakkad is the largest district in Kerala and Alappuzha the smallest. All the four select districts are medium sized districts.

Table 4.16: Total geographic area of Kerala and selected districts classified by geographic classes

Administrative	*State*	*% share*	*Erana-kulam*	*Kozhikode*	*Kollam*	*Kannur*
Total Geographical Area (ha)	3885497	100	235319	233330	251838	296797
Dry area (ha) per ha of wet area	4.91		2.56	6.35	6.59	7.56
Forest Area	1081509	27.8	8123	41386	81438	48734
Land put to non-agricultural use	430084	10	51133	28813	27017	33700
Barren and uncultivable land	28891	0.6	1310	1342	275	3076
Permanent pastures and other grazing land	292	0	12	30	13	10
Land under misc. tree crops	10193	0.1	133	189	157	1121
Cultivable waste	70092	2.5	7142	1141	427	4524
Fallow other than current fallow	40917	1	2984	852	587	2680
Current fallow	68634	2	6279	1297	3874	3538
Net area sown	2154885	54	158203	158280	138050	199414
Area sown more than once	841408	15.2	55069	71548	51535	58129
Total cropped area	2996293	69	213272	229828	189585	257543
Coast length (km)	590		46	71		

Table 4.17: No. and average size (ha) of operational holdings in 3 block panchayats in Ernakulam district by size of holding, 2004-05

Size of class of holdings (ha.)	*No. of operational holdings*				*Average size (ha) of holding*			
	Pallur-uthy	*Vazhak-kulam*	*Vypin*	*District*	*Pallur-uthy*	*Vazhak-kulam*	*Vypin*	*District*
Below 0.5	11705	40129	40895	590609	0.035	0.094	0.05	0.079
0.5 to 1.0	130	2338	410	30806	0.746	0.684	0.666	0.692
1.0 to 2.0	65	827	180	16975	1.308	1.29	1.367	1.329
2.0 to 3.0	15	206	60	4814	2.6	2.369	2.45	2.3
3.0 to 4.0	15	55	5	1023	3.467	3.4	3.8	3.349
4.0 to 5.0	0	35	0	511		4.6		4,425
5.0 to 7.5	5	25	10	416	5.8	5.76	5.7	6.118
7.5 to 10.0	0	5	0	80		8.2		8.338
10.0 to 20.0	0	15	0	135		12.333		13.556
20.0 and above	0	0	5	60			50.2	78.567

Operational holdings in Kerala are relatively small. It is not different in the case of Ernakulam and its various villages we considered. About 98 per cent of holdings are of size less than 0.5 ha.

Demographic Profile of the Villages Studied

Four villages were selected from Ernakulam district for the village study programme of the IAS probationers. These four villages come under three block panchayats. The villages selected were Kizhakkambalam (Vazhakkulam block), Elamkunnapuzha (Vypeen block), Kumbalangy and Chellanam (both from Palluruthy block). The population in these villages range from 26,661 to 50,563 people. In all the villages, women outnumbered the males. Scheduled caste population is comparatively lesser in these villages, and scheduled tribe people are very few.

Table 4.18: Demographic status (2001 Census) of select Gram Panchayats of Ernakulam District along with the details of the respective Block Panchayats

Block/Panchayat/ Municipality		*Vazhakkulam Block*	*Kizhakkambalam*	*Vypeen Block*	*Elamkunnapuzha*	*Palluruthy Block*	*Kumbalangy*	*Chellanam*
Total Population	Total	205403	31631	197624	50563	62870	26661	36209
	Male	102187	15109	95973	24575	30712	12984	17728
	Female	103216	16522	101651	25988	32158	13677	18481
Scheduled Castes	Total	18774	2902	24063	4801	3773	2048	1725
	Male	9357	1471	11686	2364	1821	1001	820
	Female	9417	1431	12377	2437	1952	1047	905
Scheduled Tribes	Total	549	75	276	134	9	1	8
	Male	264	33	132	61	5	1	4
	Female	285	42	144	73	4	0	4

Source: GoK. 2006. Panchayat level Statistics. Ernakulam District 2006. Department of Economics and Statistics.

The team who headed to Kozhikode district studied four villages from three block panchayats of the district. Narikkuni (Chelannur block), Kodencheri (Kunnamangalam block), Feroke and Ramanattukara (Kozhikode block) were the villages selected. Kodencheri is a relatively large village, but with very low density of

Table 4.19: Structural profile of select Gram Panchayats of Kozhikode district along with the details of the respective Block Panchayats

Block/Panchayat	Chelannur Block	Narikkuni	Kunnama-ngalam block	Koden-cheri	Kozhik-ode Block	Feroke	Ramana ttukara
Area (Sq/km)	138.66	17.75	337.94	102.58	79.22	13.53	11.71
No. of wards	122	14	188	20	127	22	18
No. of women wards	44	5	66	7	45	8	6
No. of SC wards	14	2	19	1	8	2	2
Density	1503	1250	981	358	3777	3716	2599
No. of households	42961	4732	67379	7803	53199	8907	5724

Source: Ibid.

population (the next denser village has 1250 people/sq. km) residing in it. Number of households is also more in Kodencheri. Ramanattukara is the smallest village in the lot.

Narikkuni is the least populous village among the selected villages in Kozhikode. Feroke is the most populous village. Except for Feroke panchayat all panchayats have sex-ratio favourable to women. ST population is very few in number in all the villages except Kodencheri. The most striking feature of this Table 4.19 is that the child sex-ratio is favourable to men in all the villages.

Two villages were studied from Kollam district, which is a southern district. Mayyanad is coastal village while Kizhakke Kallada is a mid-land region. Mayyanad is relatively a village denser in population. Sex ratio in both the villages, as is the case with other districts studied, is favourable to women.

Only few people of Scheduled Tribes reside in the selected villages of Kollam. Though sex-ratio in these villages and the respective block panchayats is favourable to women, child sex-ratio speaks a different story. In this district also, as a whole, boys outnumbered girls.

In Kerala, grama panchayats are graded according to the revenue and administrative volume of the panchayat. Edakkad is a first grade panchayat, with an area of 18.27 sq. km, 5313 occupied residential houses and 6779 households. It is a moderately dense panchayat with sex-ratio hugely favouring females. The child sex-ratio favours boys in this district also. This indicates that the sex-ratio that has been always favourable to women all through the censuses conducted in Kerala since Independence, is set for tilt towards men, in the near future, particularly in the study districts.

Table 4.20: Demographic Status (2001 Census) of select Gram Panchayats of Kozhikode district along with the details of the respective Block Panchayats

Block/Panchayat		*Chelannur Block*	*Narikkuni*	*Kunnamangalam block*	*Kodencheri*	*Kozhikode Block*	*Feroke*	*Ramanattukara*
Total Population	Total	208450	22196	331381	35179	299238	50277	30440
	Male	100856	10890	164426	17513	146400	24672	15032
	Female	107594	11306	166955	17666	152838	25605	15408
SC Population	Total	22613	2972	33172	1776	16660	4659	3337
	Male	11018	1489	16052	889	8165	2302	1658
	Female	11595	1483	17120	887	8495	2357	1679
ST Population	Total	8	4	1549	835	86	1	16
	Male	4	3	764	414	37	1	9
	Female	4	1	785	421	49	0	7
Child Population (0-6)	Total	23989	2766	42505	4263	39408	6743	3826
	Male	12175	1391	21747	2250	20235	3461	1946
	Female	11814	1375	20758	2013	19173	3282	1880

Table 4.21: Structural profile of select Gram Panchayats of Kollam district along with the details of the respective Block Panchayats

Name of Panchayat/Block	*Kizhakke Kallada*	*Chittumala Block*	*Mayyanad*	*Mukhathala Block*	*District Total*
Area in Sq. Kms.	12.2	77.01	17.57	61.66	2491.08
No. of households	4970	28963	10092	37484	593314
Density of population/Sq. Km	1773	1632	2683	2799	1038
Sex ratio Females/1000 Males	1079	1068	1064	1050	1069

Table 4.22: Demographic status (2001 Census) of select Gram Panchayats of Kollam district along with the details of the respective Block Panchayats

Block/Panchayat/ Municipality		*Chittumala Block*	*Kizhakke kallada*	*Mukhathala Block*	*Mayyanad*	*District Total*
Total Population	Total	125680	21632	172605	47148	2459528
	Male	60772	10406	84199	22843	1188849
	Female	64908	11226	88406	24305	1270679
Scheduled Castes	Total	19325	4221	22234	5210	303562
	Male	9362	2054	10877	2592	147518
	Female	9963	2167	11357	2618	156044
Scheduled Tribes	Total	83	9	61	19	5107
	Male	39	6	21	10	2408
	Female	44	3	40	9	2699
Children age group 0-6	Total	13992	2335	20541	5483	278607
	Male	7146	1182	10458	2741	142109
	Female	6846	1153	10083	2742	136498

Table 4.23: Structural and demographic profile of the select Gram Panchayat of Kannur district along with the details of the respective Block and district Panchayat

Name of Panchayat/Block/ Municipality		*Edakkad Block*	*Edakkad*	*District Total*
Grade			Ist	
Area (in sq. km.)		142.4	18.26	2969.76
No. of wards		151	20	1504
No. of occupied residential houses		35889	5313	367668
No. of households		45785	6779	457368
Population density		1796	1991	812
Sex ratio		1124	1153	1090
Total Population in the age 0-6	Total	26685	4112	279495
	Male	13563	2101	142475
	Female	13122	2011	137020

Employment Status of the People in Villages

Table 4.24 shows that non-workers constitute about two-third of the that of the villages in Ernakulam district. These villages are having very low work participation rate, with women participation much less than their male counterparts,. Very few persons rely on traditional sectors like, agriculture, household industry like coir, candle making etc. for employment.

Table 4.24: No. of total workers and per cent of workers in different occupational categories, and the per cent of unemployed, Ernakulam

Block/Panchayat/ Municipality		Vazhakk-ulam Block	Kizhakka-mbalam	Vypeen Block	Elamku-Nna puzha	Pallur-uthy Block	Kumba-langy	Chell-anam
Total Workers	Total	72176	13001	66808	17233	22916	10080	12836
	Male	55752	8739	52913	13822	17802	7454	10348
	Female	16424	4262	13895	3411	5114	2626	2488
Main Workers (% of total workers)	Total	84.95	86.84	82.05	87.04	81.27	74.6	86.5
	Male	87.8	90.19	86.37	90.6	85.28	80.17	88.96
	Female	75.27	79.96	65.6	72.62	67.29	58.8	76.25
Main Cultivators (% of workers)	Total	6.09	10.54	0.8	0.59	1.25	1.06	1.38
	Male	5.92	13.38	0.71	0.49	1.28	1.04	1.44
	Female	6.73	3.96	1.24	1.09	1.1	1.17	1.05
Main Agricultural Labourers (% of workers)	Total	6.66	10.58	1.29	1	1.11	0.69	1.39
	Male	5.6	10.31	1.3	0.87	0.96	0.59	1.19
	Female	10.87	11.21	1.23	1.66	1.77	1.1	2.32
Main Household Industry (% of workers)	Total	2.53	1.76	2.36	1.99	2.31	3.8	1.31
	Male	2.23	1.52	2.19	1.59	1.88	3.53	0.81
	Female	3.7	2.32	3.21	4	4.21	4.86	3.69
Non-Workers (% of total population)	Total	64.86	58.9	66.19	65.92	63.55	62.19	64.55
	Male	45.44	42.16	44.87	43.76	42.04	42.59	41.63
	Female	84.09	74.2	86.33	86.87	84.1	80.8	86.54

Source: Ibid.

The employment pattern in Kozhikode (Table 4.25) villages follows, by and large, the same as that of the villages in Ernakulam district, with very low work participation rate, women participation much less than their male counterparts, and too meagre participation in traditional sector. In fact, work participation rate is slightly lesser in Kozhikode villages than that of the Ernakulam villages.

Villages in Kollam district also do not present a different picture than that of the villages in either Ernakulam or Kozhikode villages.

Table 4.25: No. of total workers, per cent of workers in different occupational categories, and the per cent of unemployed in Kozhikode

Block/Panchayat/ Municipality		*Chela-nnur Block*	*Nari-kkuni*	*Kunnam-angalam Block*	*Koden-cheri*	*Kozhi-kode Block*	*Feroke*	*Raman-attukara*
Total Population	Total	208450	22196	331381	35179	299238	50277	30440
	Male	100856	10890	164426	17513	146400	24672	15032
	Female	107594	11306	166955	17666	152838	25605	15408
Total Workers	Total	59936	6053	93421	11787	82953	13246	8410
	Male	51547	5224	80353	9452	73774	11825	7309
	Female	8389	829	13068	2335	9179	1421	1101
Main Workers (% of total workers)	Total	76.99	71.42	77.3	78.66	85.15	80.01	86.74
	Male	78.49	73.18	78.98	82.38	86.38	80.94	88.12
	Female	67.81	60.31	66.94	63.6	75.22	72.27	77.57
Main Cultivators (% of workers)	Total	3.21	7.24	3.87	4.56	0.34	0.53	0.57
	Male	3.45	7.6	4.16	5.24	0.36	0.58	0.62
	Female	1.74	4.95	2.09	1.84	0.17	0.14	0.27
Agricultural Labourers (% of workers)	Total	5.16	11.15	7.14	7.83	1.27	2.79	2.96
	Male	5.32	11.31	7.37	8.1	1.33	2.98	3.15
	Female	4.18	10.13	5.78	6.72	0.8	1.27	1.73s
Main Household Industry (% of workers)	Total	1.26	2.28	1.37	0.94	1.83	1.67	2.9
	Male	1.13	2.24	1.21	0.56	1.66	1.42	2.63
	Female	2.06	2.53	2.36	2.48	3.15	3.73	4.72
Non-Workers (% of total population)	Total	71.25	72.73	71.81	66.49	72.28	73.65	72.37
	Male	48.89	52.03	51.13	46.03	49.61	52.07	51.38
	Female	92.2	92.67	92.17	86.78	93.99	94.45	92.85

Source: Ibid.

Agriculture offered them very few work days. The employment situation in Mayyanad is still worse, with only 0.8 of the workers resort to cultivation, and only about 3 per cent of them having opportunities in agricultural sector as labourers. Three-fourths of the workers do find jobs in sectors other than agriculture and household industry.

Employment scene in Kannur also closely resembles the ones in villages in other districts. Very few people take up cultivation as an avocation. Joblessness can almost be said to be a rule in Edakkad village. It could be seen from Table 4.24 to 4.27 that non-workers constitute a huge majority of the population in the villages of the four districts studied. But for a village in Ernakulam district, all villages are having more than *two-third* of the population are non-workers. Also, the main workers constitute *four-fifths* of the workers

Table 4.26: No. of total workers, per cent of workers in different occupational categories, and the per cent of unemployed in Kollam villages, and the respective blocks

Category		Chittumala Block	Kizhakke Kallada	Mukhathala Block	Mayyanad
Total Population	Total	125680	21632	172605	47148
	Male	60772	10406	84199	22843
	Female	64908	11226	88406	24305
Total workers	Total	34.48	32.43	32.23	28.22
	Male	47.34	44.62	46.18	44.45
	Female	22.45	21.13	18.94	12.97
Main workers	Total	78.19	80.04	77.39	83.33
	Male	78.67	78.46	76.61	83.32
	Female	77.24	83.14	79.18	83.38
Main Cultivators	Total	2.04	3.31	1.19	0.68
	Male	2.82	4.61	1.53	0.8
	Female	0.51	0.76	0.4	0.32
Main Agricultural Labourers	Total	4.7	6.83	5.35	2.98
	Male	6.68	9.78	7.39	3.8
	Female	0.78	1.05	0.6	0.32
Main Household Industry	Total	2.51	1	2.05	4.37
	Male	2.19	1.1	2.32	4.17
	Female	3.14	0.8	1.41	5.01
Main Other Workers	Total	68.93	68.91	68.8	75.3
	Male	66.97	62.98	65.37	74.55
	Female	72.8	80.52	76.77	77.74
Non-Workers	Total	65.52	67.57	67.77	71.78
	Male	52.66	55.38	53.82	55.55
	Female	77.55	78.87	81.06	87.03

in almost all the villages, indicating that a majority of the workers do jobs of permanent nature. The female participation is considerably in lesser degree than that of males, for all categories of occupation. The share of women non-workers is almost the double as that of their men counterparts. Cultivators and agricultural labourers have only a miniscule representation in the worker population. Agriculture is no longer an asylum for employment for the job-seekers in these villages. Even the youngsters whose parents had been making a living out of these sectors have detested from taking up jobs in these sectors. There are reports that youngsters in Kerala show little inclination to traditional jobs in sectors like agriculture, coir and cashew. A study by Lathika (2013) has dwelled deep into the problem and identified

Table 4.27: No. of total workers and per cent of workers in different occupational categories, and the per cent of unemployed, Kannur

Block Panchayat/Municipality	*Category*	*Edakkad Block*	*Edakkad*
Population	Total	233921	36358
	Male	110057	16888
	Female	123864	19470
Total Workers	Total	69248	10031
	Male	52320	7930
	Female	16928	2101
Main Workers (% of workers)	Total	88.3	89.72
	Male	90.46	91.19
	Female	81.59	84.2
Main Cultivators (% of workers)	Total	0.76	0.12
	Male	0.71	0.15
	Female	0.93	0.01
Main Agricultural Labourers (% of workers)	Total	4.11	1.34
	Male	3.69	1.39
	Female	5.42	1.14
Main Household Industry (% of workers)	Total	3.6	3.2
	Male	2.69	2.99
	Female	6.42	4
Non-Workers (% of Population)	Total	70.4	72.41
	Male	52.46	53.04
	Female	86.33	89.21

the push and pull factors towards jobs in traditional sectors. Seasonality of these jobs, lesser income, high degree of physical exertion, little social values and dignity attached to these jobs were found to be the major causes for hesitation for entry into these kinds of jobs.

Literacy and Education in Villages

Kerala is the only State in India that is declared as a 'totally literate state' as early in 1990s. Table 4.28 shows that many villages in Kerala has literacy rate more than 90 per cent. The salient thing about this is

Table 4.28: Literacy and Education in Kerala villages

Panchayat	*Year*	*Literacy rate*	
		Literacy %	*Gender disparity (%)*$^{\$}$
Edakkad	2005	90	2.2
Kizhakkambalam	2006	93	—
Narikkuni	2007	92	
Kumbalangy	2008	83	2.4
Eruthempathy	2008	93.5	—
Ramanattukara	2009	83	3
Kizhzakke Kallada	2010	83.4	2
Feroke	2010	98.5	—
Avinisserry	2010	83.4	2.8
Kodancherry	2011	83.4	2

Note: \$: Gender disparity = $(l_m - l_f)/l/2*100$, where l_m, l_f and l are literacy rates of male, female and persons respectively.

Source: Village reports.

that the achievement is almost gender-neutral. The gender disparity index worked for the villages (from where literacy rate of that of both men and women were known) was very low, ranging 2-3 per cent only. It could be seen from Table 4.5 that literacy of women of 15-49 age is as high as 93 per cent in Kerala (2005), while it is 55.1 per cent in India, as a whole. But this advantage of higher level of literacy and primary education could not be made use of by the women in Kerala in the employment aspect. In that sense, education goes waste without finally being employed in any kind of gainful employment.

Table 4.29 is compiled from the village reports, and the basic information regarding school education and management was collected by the probationers by making many visits to the respective schools (mainly government and aided) in person. Some general yet very significant observations could be made out of this Table. The facility of government/aided school system in the village is poorly utilized by the children around, despite many incentives and concessions being offered to them. The participation of girls is comparable to that of boys in these schools. The negligible rate of drop-out in the schools points to the fact that it was only the initial perceptions of these schools that put barriers for the parents to enroll their childern in these schools. Once, enrolled they keep attending

Table 4.29: Certain salient findings of the village study regarding school education

Sl. No.	*Village Name*	*Year*	*Average class strength Govt.s*		*Absence %*		*Salient observations made in the report*
			M	*F*	*M*	*F*	
1.	Edakkad	2005	20	17	Average drop-out rate 4%		No school fees; SC/ST get Rs. 155 scholarship annually, fishermen Rs. 95 and Muslim girls Rs. 80 and in HS this ranges from Rs. 250-1000; Under SSA, girls/SC/ST students are given books, pencils and slates and Rs. 600/year for disabled children. Yet, girls are lesser in UP and HS.
2.	Kizhakk-ambalam	2006	11	9	0.04	0.05	No fees in government/aided schools. School going became a habit for children. Intake in aided schools is high compared to government schools (41); the dress, discipline and enthusiasm seems better in UA schools. English medium is an attraction in UA schools. The preference to government schools is waning despite the provision of mid-day meal consists of rice 'kanji' (a kind of raw pudding) of 60 gms, green gram 30 gms per day and 1 egg per week. On festivals like Onam, Xmas, Ramzan 5 kg rice also given free.
3.	Elankua-nnapuzha	2007	16	13	0	0	
4.	Ramana-ttukara	2009	13	12	4.95	4.26	Large scale student exodus from government schools to private schools where English medium is an attraction
5.	Kizhzakke Kallada	2010			No drop-out		Student-Teacher ratio varies from school to school and the range across schools—was 9.02 to 28.14, which is very low when compared to Indian level (42). There is quest for English medium schools, if family economy permits. Better discipline and quality is the attraction in private institutions. Even parents who depend on MGNREGS for work do not prefer schools with Malayalam medium. Also, even the children of agricultural labourers engage private tuition for their children for which they have to spend about Rs 500 per month. These children feel that private tuition is essential as their class mates also engage private tuition to add to their competency.
6.	Feroke	2010					The strength of public system of education is deteriorating
7.	Avinisserry	2010			Drop-out rate-negligible		Teacher-Non-teacher ratio 32:5; Only children of the poorest of the poor families get enrolled in the government school.
8.	Mayyanad	2011	Boy-girl ratio is 236: 207. 100% enrollment:				Students from BPL families are more in number. Well-qualified teachers. Mid-day meal: 30 gm rice, 15 g pulses in pre-primary classes; 100g rice and 30 g pulses for LPS (1-5); 150 g rice and 30-50 gm pulses for UPS (6-8);
9.	Kodancherry	2011			Attendance good. But enrollment is poor in governemnt schools		Illiterates are mostly tribals. Tribal children do not go to schools and Anganwadi workers find it difficult to get the children to school.

Source: Village reports.

the schools without showing much absenteeism. Preference of the children to get themselves enrolled in private un-aided schools to the government/aided system is a very worrying point that was made in all the reports. Better infrastructure, other amenities in these schools, higher qualification of teachers in government schools, better teacher-student ratio, better coordination and networking between them in a much more responsible and accoutable way, all make the performance level still better.

However, the perception of the parents seems to have changed a lot in favour of private un-aided schools, where they find better discipline and higher scope of getting their children 'English-speaking'. Speaking English, ability of singing English rhymes, wearing colour uniform, and in some cases even the neck-ties, carrying the school bag, taking the children in school-vans etc. have all great commercial value in school system in Kerala. Therefore, the un-aided private schools which are being run by the fees collected from the students (in many cases, at exorbitant rates, and includes the heavy profits the management expropriates), give much priority to these exhibitive elements. This pays off well even in villages. Even the agricultural labourers, MGNREGA workers, many of whom could never go to school in their childhood though they realized the value of education by now, prefer to send their children to un-aided schools. The teachers in these private schools are said to be not of adequate quality and up-dated skill levels, and are paid pathetically lesser than their counterparts in the government/aided schools. This not only affects the quality of teaching in the schools but also makes the whole pedagogy uncertain in these institutions, as the risk of these teachers leaving their jobs without notice is very high. The merit of the government schools and the offers they make to attract children and facilitate their over all development go un-noticed, or crowded out, in the pomp and glitter of catchment techniques of un-aided schools.

Incidence of Morbidity and Healthcare in Villages

Despite the reported high attainments of social development and well-being of people in the State, the village reports highlighted the relatively higher incidence of morbidity and malnourishment. Table 4.30 lists the diseases being commonly reported and the village-wise incidence thereof. This data is collected from the hospital records while the investigators visited the hospitals of the village of their choice. In that sense, these figures have great value as the data based on primary investigation. Kerala being located in the humid tropical region with two annual monsoons leading to heavy downpour during 5-6 months of the year, the incidence of water-borne, vector-borne seasonal diseases would be high, and the hospitals record a large number of such diseases in these months. Moreover, higher social and economic attainments have led to higher standard of living of the people, and this in turn resulted in the higher incidence of the so called life-style diseases. Life-style diseases, though require regular monitoring and check-ups, do not warrant frequent hospital visits. The incidence of these diseases are hence not being reflected in the hospital records, though it amounts to spending a considerable income from monthly revenue of the people.

Table 4.30: Common diseases reported in villages

Villager	*Diseases reported*
Edakkad	Diarrhoea, chicken pox, TB, cancer, diabetes and BP.
Kizhakkambalam	Upper respiratory infections, acute diarrhoea, intestinal worm infection, lymphatic filariasis and scabies; seasonal diseases like Leptospirosis and Dengue and general nutrient deficiency like iron, vitamins.
Kumbalangy	Respiratory problems, Diarrhoea, lymphatic filariasis. chikungunya was severe in 2006-07. Malnutrition was also prevalent
Eruthempathy	In 2008 the number of patients with communicable diseases reported: Diarrhoea (387), chicken pox (52), mumps (13), Hepatitis (10), Leptospairosis (9), Typhoid (4), Dengue (3), Measles (1), Malaria (1)
Chellanam	In 2009 the number of patients with communicable diseases reported: Diarrhoea (145), chicken pox (35), mumps (13), Hepatitis (10), Leptospirosis (9), viral fever (69), Typhoid (4), Dengue (10), Measles (1), Malaria (10)
Feroke	In 2008 the number of patients with communicable diseases reported: Diarrhoea (387), chicken pox (52), mumps (13), Hepatitis (10), Leptospairosis (9), Typhoid (4), Dengue (3), Measles (1), Malaria (1)
Elankuannapuzha	In 2010 the number of patients with communicable diseases reported: Acute Diarrhoeal Diseases ADD (235), chicken pox (22), mumps (9), Hepatitis (10), Leptospirosis (14), Typhoid (4), Dengue (3), Measles (1), Malaria (1)

Source: Village reports.

It has already been pointed out that the human development indicators in Kerala are very high, compared to the all-India level. Kerala ranked first in HDI and recorded a far higher value than the immediate follower. Life expectancy ratio, child mortality, among other things, are important determinants of human development. Table 4.31 shows the village-wise data (wherever reported) on these two parametres, and the infrastructure facilities instituted in the villages to manage issues of health care.

Table 4.31: Certain salient findings of the village study regarding Public Health

Village		*Life expectancy—Female*	*IMR*	*Average No. of field staff in a PHC*	*Average number of out-patients in PHC per day*
Edakkad	2005			11	30-80
Kizhakkambalam	2006	73	16		
Kumbalangy	2008	73	16		
Eruthempathy	2008	73	16		
Chellanam	2010	73	18		
Feroke	2010				
Avinisserry	2010		17	20	About 40
Elankuannapuzha	2011		16		
Mayyanad	2011				

Source: Village reports.

Ever since the launching of ICDS programme in India in early 1980s, in Kerala, *anganwadis* have come to be great institutions of health care and provider of essential preventives against diseases generated from malnourishment of mothers and children. Some salient observations on the performance of *aganwadis* being operated in the respective villages and the major problems faced by them during the course of their working, are made in the some village reports. These observations are listed below.

Problems faced by the PHCs and Anganwadis in the Villages

Edakkad

Low paid staff, declining facility, Attendance decreasing due to the opening up of private centres with same service.

Kizhakkambalam

Decreasing preference to government systems.

Kumbalangy

Less preference to government systems of health care.

Chellanam

No sewerage system. But the common practice by poor people of defecating in open was almost fully done away with, thanks to the subsidy to BPL families of Rs. 5000 to construct toilet with septic tanks.

Feroke

Forty seven trained ASHAs; source reduction activities for mosquito eradication; chlorination; regular water quality assessment and cleaning of canals by NREGP workers; mass health education programmes; medical camps and observation camps and routine inspection of hotels, eateries.

SUMMING UP

> "I will give you a talisman. Whenever you are in doubt, or when the self becomes too much with you, apply the following test:
> Recall the face of the poorest and the weakest man whom you may have seen, and ask yourself, if the step you contemplate is going to be of any use to him. Will he gain anything by it? Will it restore him to a control over his own life and destiny? In other words, will it lead to *Swaraj* for the hungry and spiritually starving millions?
> Then you will find your doubts and your self melt away."
>
> — *M.K. Gandhi*

As part of the village study, the probationers have not only visited all the important institutions in the village through which the public, especially the common men, were offered services and other benefits that the government intended to deliver. They have also visited a couple individuals/citizen-groups who could not be reached earlier by government programmes for the poor, but are currently on the thick of running a public service or utility, like self-help groups. In some cases, a women panchayat member, or in others, a *kutumbasree* unit (a self-help group) was also covered. These case studies serve as divine examples to emulate from. Some of the probationers closely observed the living conditions of one or more persons who had been found to be very poor or deeply deprived. Such "hungry and spiritually starving millions" deserve to be heard and attended to by the people in power. Such cases of the 'poorest of the poor' in the village give a profound insight into the backwardness of the poor in the village, so that the planners could take cues and chalk out plans to rehabilitate them out of the vicious situation they were got entangled in. The report of the case studies made by the probationers is given verbatim in this section.

In the village reports cases of participation of women panchayat members have been recorded in positive way, a poor women cheated by an employment agency is also mentioned in one village. The role of women SHG, positive role of MNREGA, IAY, Comparison of two aganwadi centres and catering activities of women SHG (*Kutumbasree*) make the reports very useful. The working of PRIs, devolution of finances, functions and functionaries have made Kerala a leading state in decentralized governance. Although over the period of time the transfers to the PRIs has declined slightly a real and proportionate terms yet the State has out-performed over other States in the country. The higher level of literacy, very low level of dropout rates of children from the schools, high consciousness and awareness among the people and above all greater mobilization at grassroots level put Kerala on the top in HDI. There is further scope for improvement in paying greater attention towards the needs of tribal population. Notwithstanding, these limitations the State is a model for social and economic transformation for a large number of States in India.

5

The Socio-Economic Situation of Andhra Pradesh and Telengana

T. PRABHAKARA REDDY*

INTRODUCTION

Andhra Pradesh is blessed with a bounty of natural resources, endowed with fertile land, water and conducive agro-climatic conditions and it is an agriculturally prosperous state. It ranks among the largest producers of foodgrains, fruits, vegtables, cotton, maize, dairy and poultry products in the country. It is the leading state in several agro-based industries such as sugar, edible oil, seafood etc.

Andhra Pradesh is a mineral rich state ranked second in India containing a vast variety of mineral wealth. There is still untapped and under-utilized mineral wealth throwing up many opportunities for the new entrepreneurs in the field. The State accounts for considerable reserves of important minerals in the country.

NEED FOR STUDY

The socio-economic study of a village helps in understanding the status of a village in terms of availability of resources such as land

* Director, Vidya Bhawan Institute of Local Self-Governance and Responsible Citizenship, Udaipur, Rajasthan.

for cultivation and grazing, livestock, forests, tanks, canals and rivers and the functioning of a Gram Panchayat in terms of economic development and the land revenue system existing in a village among others. Therefore, studies of this nature would bring out a wide variety of insights and help in formulating proper policies by the Government.

LAND-USE PATTERN

The land-use pattern of Andhra Pradesh state represented a sort of skewed distribution of area which is given below:

Table 5.1: Land-Use Pattern* in Andhra Pradesh

Region	*Forest*	*Barren plus waste*	*Non-agricultural*	*Pasture*	*Fallow*	*Agriculture*
Coastal Andhra	21	11	13	2	8	45
Telengana	24	7	7	3	23	36
Rayalaseema	22	13	9	1	15	40

* We have taken the data of 2003 to compare with individual villages under study.

Source: A. Amarendar Reddy, 2003.

In Telengana, only 36 per cent of the total geographical area is used for agriculture and a large portion is fallow land (23%) (cultivable, but not cultivated in the reporting year). The large area of fallow land in Telengana is a sign of the neglect of the agricultural sector and a lack of investment in land development measures over the last five decades. As a matter of fact, agricultural development of a region is dependent on the investments made in development of irrigation facilities. The higher irrigated area in coastal Andhra can be attributed to higher public investments in irrigation which is facilitated by lower gradient and higher rainfall among others.

On the other hand, Rayalaseema which is a drought prone area registered 40 per cent of land used for agriculture while only 15 per cent are fallows. Coastal Andhra has shown 45 per cent of land used for agriculture and 8 per cent fallows while 13 per cent land to put to non-agricultural purpose reflecting industrialization that is happening in a big way in the region.

EXISTING SITUATION

As regards the existing situation of land use pattern in Warangal district during 2004-05 revealed that 32 per cent has been used for cultivation. 29 per cent of the area has been under forest coverage while 11.5 per cent designated as other fallows and 9 per cent current fallows needs to be probed for policy purposes. About 5 per cent of the land in the district has been put to non-agricultural use while 4.2 per cent of the area has been declared as barren and un-cultivated. About 4 per cent of the area has been under permanent pastures and other grazing lands. As a matter of fact, the land under grazing has been on the decline in the state over a period of time causing concern to the livestock and the communities dependent on livestock for their livelihoods.

On the other hand, it was found that the villages in Guntur district are agriculturally prosperous and nearly 90 per cent of the land is cultivated with assured irrigation from Nagarjunasagar canal. However, we find some are landless and leasing-in land from landlords in the villages. It was reported that the land distribution continued to be skewed and considerable number of families are landless or having a meagre amount of landholding. Though thc district of Guntur is advanced in agriculture cultivating commercial crops such as cotton and chilies mainly, still there are agricultural families who are adopting traditional agricultural practices and incurring losses (Babu, A.). As a result, it was reported that some of the farmers who became indebted heavily have committed suicide in the district of Guntur (T. Prabhakara Reddy).

The land use pattern in the district revealed that the net sown area is 32 per cent, while current fallows are 27 per cent which causes concern to all. On the other hand, other fallows are to the extent of 12 per cent which is another important ratio that needs to be attended to immediately. The issue is that why the current fallows are so high? What should be done to bring them under cultivation in the district? The forests are limited to 6 per cent which, in fact, is less. The source of data is relatively new referring to Agricultural Census 2009-10.

Further, the land use pattern of Penakacherla village in Anantapur district revealed that the fallow lands are substantial and net sown area is limited due to less than average rainfall experienced by the area. On the contrary, Vekanuru in Avanigadda mandal of Krishna district showed a different land use pattern wherein the entire land in village has been cultivated as it has been irrigated by Krishna canal. A small portion of land is observed as fallow land due to water stagnation and low lying area.

LAND AND AGRICULTURE

Irrigation is the main input for agriculture in any part of the country while larger the irrigation higher the productivity, other things being equal. In fact, irrigation is a major difficulty for farmers as the rainfall (752 millimetres normal rainfall) is less than national and state average in Nalgonda district. Though there are three irrigation dams, viz. Nagarjunasagar, Dindi and Musi in the district the farmers are deprived of irrigation due to political and other reasons as a result of which many times they protested during general elections. In fact, there are quite a few rivers such as Krishna, Musi, Alair, Pedavagu, Dindi, Ahalya and Kanagal which are flowing for a long distance in the district which can be utilized if properly planned by constructing medium and small dams across it. On the other hand, the Vekanuru village of Krishna district registered assured irrigation resulting in very good productivity from agriculture reflecting the State's assistance benefiting farmers.

As regards the composition of irrigation sources, it is clear that the tanks are also equally an important source of irrigation in Nalgonda district. There are 421 large tanks with three to four thousand acres of ayacut while small tanks are about 4000 with less than 100 acres of ayacut. It is important to mention that the tubewells are also substantial in number (1,25,680) which is providing irrigation to agriculture in the district.

Historically, canal irrigation has been very unevenly distributed across the State. In addition, the decline of surface water sources (especially tanks) because of neglect and other factors has led to greater reliance on the exploitation of groundwater, which entails substantial costs on individual cultivators in the form of digging bore-wells etc. In addition, there are very large differentials in access to assured irrigation across districts in the State. A remarkable feature of the State is that districts (Nellore and West Godavari) with higher normal rainfall are also those more likely to have higher levels of assured irrigation. At the same time, assured water in the command areas does not encourage water conservation, especially with a flat charge per acre for water use needs to be looked into.

The uneven distribution and unequal access to canal irrigation and the decline of other surface water sources have led to greater reliance on the exploitation of ground water which entails substantial costs on individual cultivators. Therefore, it is recommended that a massive programme for restoration of tanks and other minor water bodies must be taken up giving priority to the drought affected regions. Further, the State Government should evolve a water policy with an emphasis on equity in the spatial distribution of surface water resources in the state and on the conjunctive use of surface and ground water.

CROPPING PATTERN

The cropping pattern is still the traditional one and water intensive (Paddy, Maize, Jowar, Groundnut, Greengram, Redgram, Bajra, Sesamum). However, there are some farmers who are cultivating cotton and other commercial crops in Nalgonda district. Of course, compared to the field study period to today the agriculture has undergone dramatic changes in terms of cropping pattern which is in favour of commercial crops cultivation. Besides, it needs to be mentioned that the village Penakacherla in Anantapur district has depicted cultivation of two crops only, *viz.* paddy and groundnut. The village has about 10 per cent of the land which is irrigated wherein paddy is cultivated as a single crop during a year. On the other hand, groundnut is cultivated on un-irrigated lands to a great extent.

The cropping pattern in coastal Andhra is different as they grow mainly paddy followed by other crops such as black gram, mangoes, vegtables, turmeric, banana and fodder in some areas in a limited way. In fact, it reflected the commercial agriculture exclusively for market resulting in profits to the farmers. As a result, the profits accrued from agriculture have been transferred from agriculture to industry and services sectors during seventies leading to a shift in the pattern of regional development.

On the contrary, the cropping pattern in other districts has underwent drastic changes reflecting the cultivation of commercial crops such as cotton, chillies and turmeric at the cost of millets and pulses deteriorating the quality of nutritious food in the villages which had severe repercussions among the poorer sections especially women and children. On the other hand, the farmers who have taken up commercial crops in dry areas experienced losses due to various reasons and finally, there are instances wherein they committed suicides.

LAND REFORMS AND TENANCY

Land is the main source of livelihood for many of the rural people especially the poor. The land reforms implemented in the State have brought about a sea change in the rural structure in so far as assigning land to the poor and improving their livelihoods substantially. However, there are some cases wherein the land has been assigned to the poor but, they are unable to possess and make use of it further for their livelihoods. It was reported from Guntur district, which is agriculturally sound, that the land allotted to poor has been alienated from them in villages, viz. Konduru and Pathammallayam because of benami holder.

In Konduru village the process of alienation of land from allottees has taken place due to a middleman who got the lands transferred in the name of benamies. The middle man has taken illegal agreements from gullible poor with a *malafide* intention couple of years back. At the time of study, it was reported that the middleman has executed documents by the declarants in favour of strangers resulting in alienation of land. As a result, the small farmers became agricultural labour and working in others' field for wages losing status and livelihoods.

Similarly, lotheru village report revealed that the tribal land alienation continues unabated despite the legislations that are supposed to protect the interests of tribal people. The land alienation is of two types; one is land of tribals taken over by non-tribals through various means and unethical practices, second important type of land alienation is state acquiring land of tribals in the name of private industries, development projects like mining, hydro-electric projects, tourism and other projects. Research studies, NGOs and local tribal revolts and campaigns have clearly brought out the evidence that these projects have not benefited the tribals in any form of economic, social or political empowerment. Therefore, there are several complex issues which need to be resolved in this connection (Gaurav Uppal).

Finally, the following suggestions are made in village report to control the tribal land alienation in the schedule areas:

- The transparency and access to land records to tribals at the village level in local language not in English only;
- Speedy disposal of cases where tribals are involved and oral evidence is to be considered where records are absent; and
- Tribals and NGOs should be allowed to participate in the process of survey of lands (Gaurav Uppal).

It has been observed from the process of land relations which have been deteriorated over time resulting in cultivators becoming agricultural labourers and their occupational pattern changed especially among tribal communities (due to land transfers from tribal to non-tribals). It is also relevant to a great extent in the plains wherein the small and marginal farmers incurred losses due to lack of irrigation and other facilities and continued agriculture in unviable landholdings. As a result, there is a marked shift in the occupational pattern of farming communities in the villages which is clearly seen in Palem village of Nalgonda district.

It was observed that the number of agricultural labourers are twice higher than the cultivators in Palem is a testimony of the situation. There are about 81 per cent of small and marginal farmers belonging to Palem village who prefer to work for others for wages rather than cultivating their own plot of land which does not have irrigation, investment for inputs like seeds, fertilizers and pesticides etc. Though some modern farmers began talking about organic farming in the district it is confined to well to do section of farming community only.

• THE SITUATION OF TENANCY

Land relations in Andhra Pradesh are extremely complicated and this complexity has contributed significantly to the problems facing actual cultivators in the state. Unregistered cultivators, tenants and tribal cultivators all face difficulties in accessing institutional credit and other facilities available to farmers with land titles. Hence, the immediate priority is to record and register actual cultivators including tenants and women cultivators and provide passbooks to them to ensure that they gain access to institutional credit and other inputs.

Tenancy is not only practiced, but it is on the rise in the villages of Guntur in a big way as the lands are leased out by landlords who reside elsewhere which is known as 'absentee landlordism'. The oral agreement entered into between the landlord and the tenants is the main reason behind the vulnerable position of tenants. The insecure tenancy is resulting in 'uncertainty' about the control and continuance of his/her cultivation in a parcel of land. Secondly, given the uncertainty the tenant is restricted in so far as undertaking durable investment on the land which can result in higher productivity. Thirdly, the form of tenancy is 'fixed cash rent' in majority cases which is decided unilaterally by the landlord which is exorbitant. However, some are also following the share cropping method in the State.

In the absence of written agreement the tenant is at the receiving end if any natural calamity or drought occurs. Having made advance payment of fixed cash rent the tenant is supposed to pool up resources for fertilizers, pesticides and other agricultural activities. Added to it, if there is any natural calamity the burden on the tenant is so many folds that he/she may not cope with the situation as they are economically poor.

There are instances wherein the poor tenants have taken lands on lease with an expectation that the canal water will provide them irrigation to their fields. Contrary to their expectation, the farmers who are in the tail end region of irrigation canal could not receive the water resulting in loss of crops and finally, farmers are indebted heavily. The village studies have corroborated the fact that the tenants are at loss due to various reasons. Therefore, it was opined that there is a need for fresh initiative for modifications in respect of tenancy legislations to respond to field realities. The need to either correct the existing tenancy laws or to evolve new ones based on an understanding of three aspects of the land lease market. They are the extent of tenancy, efficiency and exploitation of tenants. Hence, it was rightly pointed out in Guntur village study that probing the following would give us a solution.

- What percentage of tenancy is informal?;
- What percentage of poor are tenant farmers?;
- How entering into a tenancy agreement affects the landlord?; and

- How the existing acts of tenancy are responsible for the existing state of affairs?

Further, it was opined that in spite of the absence of written agreement the problem can be overcome if the revenue machinery at the grassroots level that is village servant and Panchayat secretary reflects the ground level realities in the *Adangal*. Besides, the financial institutions may be requested to extend the financial assistance to tenants on production of an *adangal* copy issued by the revenue authorities.

While supporting the same idea, it was opined that the tenancy legislations have to be modified reflecting the ground realities. Besides it was suggested that the tenancy has to be recognized officially without sacrificing the interests of the landlords and the tenants. It means the landlord is not losing his/her title over land while the tenant will get a piece of land to cultivate for a reasonable price. Hence, it was suggested to adopt the West Bengal model for tenancy legislation.

As a matter of fact, the State Government has come out with a pioneering tenant friendly act known as Land Licensed Cultivators Act, 2012 and tried to protect the interests of both the parties by issuing a loan eligibility card to tenants. But there are problems in the implementation of Act due to apprehensions of landlords that if the tenant is not repaying the bank loan the banks will confiscate their lands. Further, they expressed doubts that they may not get loans on the basis of lands as has already been taken by a tenant. Hence it was suggested that clearing the doubts and educating the landlords would go a long way in improving the land relations and productivity in agriculture.

EDUCATION, HEALTH AND SANITATION

In some of the villages (studied) the literacy is less than national average and more so the female literacy is less. However, in some areas the situation is better. The commonality observed among many of the villages is that although the schools are running there is a shortage of teachers and if teachers are there the commitment is lacking. Further, many schools are identified with lack of toilets especially for girls. There is a lack of classrooms which is a common phenomenon in most of the schools in the villages. Thanks to SSA programme under which these facilities are provided to all schools in the recent past making schools functional.

As regards the health care facilities it was observed in majority of the villages they are minimal and a pathetic situation existed. In many villages under study, PHCs and SCs are away from the villages and hamlets causing real hardship to the people with an exception of Penakacherla village which is closer to the hospital of RDT a local NGO. Consequently, the IMR and MMR and other health indicators depicted a bleak picture in the state. The villages which are closer to the district and mandal headquarters are relatively better off in terms of having health care facilities.

In fact, health care is poor with very few PHCs, SCs and staff, while the doctors and nurses per 1000 population are at low. As a result, it was observed that the 'out of pocket expenses' have registered high levels of expenditure in a family's budget. It is a fact that the health and poverty are interlinked in so far as affecting their financial position hence out of pocket expenses affects adversely the families who are below poverty line.

Sanitation as a public health issue is posing challenges to the government and the people that need to be focused in planning in the villages. Most of the people are still resorting to open defecation more importantly in coastal Andhra region followed by Rayalaseema. However, it is little better in Telengana region as people are used to individual latrines for quite some time. The poor sanitation in villages is due to lack of awareness, adequate water, proper implementation of programmes like Central Sanitation Programme, Nirmal Bharat among others.

On the contrary, the Vekanuru village of Krishna district had relatively good infrastructure facilities like 100 per cent electrification, good roads, five government primary schools and one high school, PHC and safe drinking water. However, it was identified with low literacy rate which is below national and state average (55%) coupled with dropouts. On the other hand the village has an adult literacy centre and literacy campaign is taken up in a big way.

POVERTY ALLEVIATION PROGRAMMES

The Government of Andhra Pradesh has implemented various poverty alleviation programmes all over the state with a commitment to reduce the population below the poverty line and improve their standard of living. They include the following:

- Swarnajayanti Gram Swarozgar Yojana (SGSY);
- Housing under INDIRAMMA scheme;
- Pensions to old age, widows, disabled and weavers etc.;
- SHGs and Pavalavaddi which is known as interest subsidy scheme;
- Mahatma Gandhi National Rural Employment Guarantee Scheme (MGNREGS);
- Rajiv Arogyasri;
- Scholarships and fee reimbursement;
- Rs. 2 per kg for all white card holders;
- Free power to the small and marginal farmers; and
- Issue of *patta* of assigned land to the landless.

In fact, the above initiatives have benefited immensely the BPL population in obtaining the facilities like housing, employment and health among others. It was found from the village reports that under SGSY self-help groups are formed, nurtured and finally, linked to banks for obtaining the loan for livelihood purposes. It was reported that the SHGs are functioning like a movement in all the villages of the State and resulting in women empowerment in terms of their freedom in taking decisions, spending their earnings and saving for the future etc.

Andhra Pradesh is known for SHG movement which has displayed sustainable models in poverty alleviation that are worth emulating by other states in the country. The strength of strategy of poverty alleviation is social mobilization with sensitive support structure and community resource person which has been adjudged as the best in the country.

As a matter of fact, social mobilization and building sustainable institutions of the poor has been proved to be a good strategy in reducing poverty in the State. Andhra Pradesh has a history of vibrant SHG movement beginning from the days of DWCRA activities. The positive effect of SHGs has been observed from areas of Velugu mandals initially and subsequently all the mandals have been covered under IKP.

To begin with, the State Government has embarked upon poverty alleviation programme in three districts with the assistance of UNDP in the name of Andhra Pradesh South Asia Poverty Alleviation Programme (SAPAP) and later District Poverty Initiatives Programme (DPIP) and finally, Rural Poverty Reduction Project (RPRP) were taken up in a mission mode. On seeing the success of SAPAP in Kurnool, Mahabubnagar and Anantapur districts which are relatively poverty stricken the government of Andhra Pradesh has implemented DPIP in 16 districts and later on covered all the 22 districts under RPRP.

By and large the programmes have shown positive results in reducing the absolute poverty levels and improving the awareness levels of people especially women who are members in SHGs. The impact assessment studies conducted in this context have unequivocally appreciated the efforts of the government and pointed out certain grey areas of implementation such as leadership on rotation, continuation of sensitive support structure, bank linkage for livelihoods purpose, and formation of social committees to address the social issues.

It was reported that the SHG activity in the district of Guntur has given a fillip to the local communities. The group approach in poverty alleviation programmes has made a great impact in the livelihoods of many villagers and it has to be taken up with a great vigour. It was felt that the group activity should become self-sustaining and they should be self-reliant over a period of time.

Pavalavaddi which is known as 'interest subsidy' scheme has been implemented for poor women members of SHG who repaid the loan promptly. This as incentive many groups availed Pavalavaddi by ensuring 100 per cent repayment of loans after utilizing it for livelihood and other purposes. The model has been emulated by the MEPMA in urban areas which is a great success and benefited many poor women.

MGNREGS

Another important area that needs to mention is the implementation of National Rural Employment Guarantee Scheme (NREGS) in all over the state which helped in arresting the distress migration especially in districts like Anantapur in Rayalaseema region apart from providing wage employment (100 days) and income to the BPL families. It was observed that the drought prone district like Anantapur has been able to utilize the opportunity of NREGS and awarded the best performing district under MGNREGS during 2008-09 and the annual expenditure in 2009-10 was almost Rs. 350 crore (S. Ahmad).

There are studies which proved that the bargaining power of the labourers has improved and equal wages are paid to men and women. In some areas the ground water Table has improved as a result of watershed works taken up under the programme. Besides, SC and ST families have received benefit substantially in terms of desiltation and deepening of wells, and land clearance among others. Road connectivity improved, afforestation took place, and tanks are renovated improving the irrigation efficiency under its ayacut area significantly.

Further, it was noticed that under MGNREGS water conservation and harvesting, tree plantation and micro irrigation works are taken up in a big way in Krishnapuram village of Bukkapatnam mandal in Anantapur district that have yielded positive results. Similarly, Penakacherla village in Garladinne mandal of Anantapur district also utilized the scheme to a great extent in providing wage employment to the labourers and controlling the migration to other places. It was emphasized that the type of works and selection of labourers (job card holders) for the same has been done in gram sabha in a transparent manner.

However, it was found that the fake muster rolls are created and monies are siphoned off in Palem village while bank accounts are not opened in many cases causing great hardship to the wage seekers. Besides, the quality of works is minimal and inspection is conspicuously absent resulting in misuse of funds. In fact, the farmers' organisations have opposed the implementation of the programme during harvesting and sowing season as it affected their agriculture adversely leading to increase in wages and shortage of labour for agriculture.

Nevertheless, it was observed from Takkolu village of Sidhout mandal in Kadapa that the MGNREGS works have been taken up in the residential areas of Ex-Sarpanch and OC habitations not in the SC/ST habitations. Of course, subsequently the issue has been addressed when raised in the meetings. Further, it was reported that the labour turn out is good and women are actively taking part and earning good money compared to earlier situation. It was also mentioned that the use of technology and ICT in the implementation of such programmes made fool proof and how a programme evolved with changes over time has been demonstrated very well.

The performance of MGNREGS in *Telengana* proved to be interesting for the reason that the farmers of Pandurangapuram village in Khammam district began complaining about the hike in wages to the labourers who demanded for the same back in agricultural fields (K.M. Raj). It showed that the bargaining power of the labourers has improved dramatically and equal wages for both women and men are also sought. A noteworthy aspect of the programme is that the poor realized that they can demand for work as a 'right' which consequently empowered them to some extent in the villages.

As regards the implementation of MGNREGS in coastal Andhra region it is mixed response. Lotheru village study of Araku valley revealed that the impact of poverty alleviation programmes is less than expectation. Proper implementation of wage employment is recommended in the village and corruption should be curtailed at the grassroots level. It was also found that there is corruption in the distribution of old age pension too.

Under Indira Kranthi Patham (IKP) youth are trained, but without ascertaining their interest and aptitude in it. Further, it was mentioned that the placements should be cent per cent after successful completion of training. The youth should be motivated to take up jobs even at a far off place.

Palem village study from Nalgonda district revealed that the villages are in bad shape in so far as lack of infrastructural facilities such as drinking water, roads and the impact of poverty alleviation programmes at the grassroot, level. It was emphasized that the provision of drinking water is a major problem in the district as it has flourosis content in many parts of the district.

HOUSING AND PENSIONS

Although housing has been provided to many BPL families under INDIRAMMA it was reported that there were irregularities in the implementation. There occurred inclusion and exclusion errors in terms of selection of beneficiaries in villages which was reported in the village studies. For instance, the households who are supposed to be included in the beneficiary list did not get registered while APL population figured in the list of BPL list for housing unit. The distribution of pensions in villages is delayed either for one reason or other causing great inconvenience to old people, disabled and others.

FUNCTIONING OF GRAM PANCHAYATS

Deepening democracy and strengthening decentralized governance from below is the key theme in bringing about change in the life of people. The argument for greater devolution is based on the demonstrated experience that the transfer of funds, functions and functionaries is central to more successful decentralization. The emergence of strong, democratic sub-national governments is a precondition for successful planning and implementation of economic development programmes in any country. Therefore, decentralization is seen as essential by the community, governments and international partners in most countries especially in a larger democracy like India (T. Prabhakar Reddy).

In fact, it was opined that the Panchayati Raj System has to be made a reality in its ideal form. The planning process has to begin from the village with the active participation of people and finally, the village situation analysis has to happen. Further, these plans can be vetted with the help of subject matter specialists. Besides, the village plans have to be pooled at the mandal level and in turn all mandal plans have to be merged and prepared a district plan. The District Planning Committee can supervise the entire operations in such a way that the plan prepared at the village level is a comprehensive plan consisting of aspirations of the people.

It was emphasized that at least 40 per cent of the State budget has to flow down to different tiers of Panchayat. Besides, the planning process should be preceded by one year rigorous capacity-building of officials, CSOs, NGOs and the community so that the exercise is done efficiently (Babu, A.).

Further, Article 40 of the Constitution of India requires that "the State shall take steps to organize village Panchayats and endow them with such power and authority as may be necessary to enable them to function as units of local self-government."

In Ninth Five Year Plan, democratic decentralization has been given a boost with the enactment of the 73rd and 74th Constitutional

Amendments which are milestones in the history of democracy wherein several steps have been taken to rejuvenate the Panchayati Raj Institutions and Urban Local Bodies by assigning necessary powers to them. Consequently, most of the State Governments/UTs have enacted enabling legislations, providing for elected bodies at the village, intermediate (taluka) and district levels with adequate representation from the weaker sections and of women. Most of the states have constituted State Election Commissions and State Finance Commissions as stipulated in the Constitutional Amendment Acts.

Under Panchayati Raj System there are three tiers, viz. Gram Panchayat, Mandal Panchayat and Zilla Panchayat in the State, of which the GP is an important institution which is meant for planning and economic development of the village. As per 73rd Constitutional Amendment Act the local self-governing institution at the village level is responsible for ensuring the delivery of services to the people and, thus improving the quality of life of people. Therefore, the village study assumes significance in understanding the level of development and the socio-economic background of the people.

The village studies thus, conducted by probationers of all-India civil services have collected data and information about the Gram Panchayat and tried to analyze the functioning of it in terms of planning and implementation of programmes for economic development and working in coordination with the government functionaries. It was observed from the reports that the coordination between the Panchayat and the government functionaries is good in Karimnagar district while it is a mixed response in other districts. However, it was stressed in a subtle manner that the coordination needs to be improved between the government functionaries and the elected representatives in villages.

FINANCIAL STATUS OF PANCHAYATS

Besides, effective, responsive local governments that are engaged with empowered communities are needed to ensure the accoutable, transparent and efficient uses of public money and the effective delivery of local public services. Their creation and consolidation should be supported by Central Government institutions that adhere to 'principle of subsidiarity' without sacrificing national fiscal balance or overall policy coherence.

The sources of revenue for the Panchayat are many. The main source for revenue of the Panchayat is the funds from the centrally sponsored schemes, Central Finance Commission, transfers from State Government. Nonetheless, they have their own sources of revenue like house tax, stamp duty, profession tax among others. Apart from the above sources the Panchayat also gets funding from schemes like MGNREGS and others.

It is heartening to note that the GP of Nidigonda village of Raghunathpalli mandal in Warangal district has registered a surplus balance of Rs. 1,62,099 for the year ending March 31, 2010 is a *sin qua non* of strengthened GPs. The GP has collected taxes and fees for issuing permission of new construction that resulted in a surplus budget after meeting their expenditure towards development in the village. It is a worth noting case wherein the Gram Panchayat has received funds under BRGF, Twelfth Finance Commission, and tax revenue locally and able to meet its expenditure and show a surplus budget. Hence, it is important to mention that the tax compliance at the grassroots level is crucial in improving the financial status of GP while receiving the funds under various heads from above.

Similarly, the villages from Guntur district also showed that the tax collection has given them an edge over to others by maintaining surplus budget of the Panchayat. The fact is that wherever the taxes are collected from the people the Panchayat has been able to manage it effectively. Hence, it is a thumb rule that the Panchayats are supposed to collect the taxes and maintain the civic amenities properly in the interest of people (Babu, A.).

It was noticed from village reports that the participation of people is less than expectation in the villages though they are politically active and there existed *de facto* sarpanches who are running the show on behalf of others in Panchayats (Sujata Sharma). The brother/husband/father of a lady Sarpanch is managing the whole show and attending meetings in panchayat has been observed in some of the places is detrimental to the decentralized governance at the grassroots level. The gram sabha is not adequately empowered to take a decision which will be in favour of marginalized sections of society.

As regards the functioning of the Gram Panchayats in Visakhapatnam district most of them are interior villages and it was revealed that they do not conduct regular meetings. It was observed in village reports that the elected representatives are not showing interest in attending the Gram Panchayat meetings because all of them end up with skirmishes and arguments rather than finding a solution for the problem. All the meetings are closed after discussion about the problems but never been able to find the solution. However, it was reported that the Seekari Panchayat is conducting Panchayat meetings in a formal way. The reason could be that the village is well connected with RTC and private buses and jeeps and vans everyday plying between Paderu and Seekari. Seekari Gram Panchayat's financial position is also good. In fact, the villages with good transportation have an understanding of the Panchayat and its implications in order to utilize the same for development.

However, it was concluded that the village Seekari needs telephone connection from BSNL. As regards education the administration is lacking focus. Regular visit of ANM should be enforced by following HN days strictly. Drinking water should be chlorinated by using Panchayat funds. Nutrition content of people is dismal especially the women and children, therefore, it needs immediate attention. Self-employment under Rajiv Yuva Shakti should be encouraged. Pensions should be disbursed on the first of every month and SGSY has to be monitored by Village Organization. Nevertheless, other villages also need attention towards health care facilities in the village, physical infrastructure like electricity, roads, school buildings, Anganwadi centres, toilets and setting-up of local shandy among others (Ronald Rose).

Gram Sabha (the village assembly) is not conducted in a manner it is expected to be organized and the participation of the people is minimal. It was reported from village studies that the villages of Visakhapatnam need a big push in so far as strengthening Panchayati Raj System and following the nitty gritty of Panchayat (Gaurav Uppal, Pradyumna, Ronald Rose). Part of the problem could be due to lack of education among elected representatives and hence, it was felt that a well-designed programme working with the ERs would improve the functioning of the Constitutionally recognized bodies at the grassroots level. As a result, the participation of people can be ensured in tribal areas and subsequently PESA can be implemented gradually.

Lotheru village (Visakhapatnam district) study revealed that the Gram Panchayat meetings should be held regularly. The ward members should be motivated adequately to take part in the meetings actively with a special focus on women elected representatives. Proper monitoring of the welfare schemes right from the identification of beneficiaries to throughout the implementation of the scheme is essential for ensuring poorest of the poor benefit from it.

CONCLUSION

From the foregoing discussion it is clear that the State of Andhra Pradesh is known as granary of foodgrains particularly for rice production followed by maize and others which became possible through state's assistance in terms of irrigation dams etc. Despite the land use pattern which reflected substantial current fallows and barren plus waste lands the farmers have been able to produce adequate amount of foodgrains. Further, the cropping pattern has changed towards commercialization and crops like cotton, chillies and turmeric are grown in areas of assured irrigation in the State contributing to the State GDP significantly. However, cases of farmer suicides are discussed due to lack of irrigation and other inputs and cultivation of commercial crops in dry areas.

As regards the land relations there existed tenancy which continued unabated orally making tenants vulnerable and their continuation uncertain in a piece of land. However, The Land Licensed Cultivators' Act, 2012 implemented by the Government with some modifications would help in giving a status and loan from banks to the tenants. Further, it was suggested that the research into tenancy would help benefit in understanding the issues like extent of tenancy, efficiency and exploitation of tenants so that the existing Acts can be modified in favour of tenants whose productivity would go up drastically in agriculture.

Education, health and sanitation status is a cause of concern though the institutions exist but their functioning is not satisfactory resulting in hardship to the people. More importantly, the out of pocket expenses have added to the burden of common people in the villages. However, Arogyasri has saved many lives which was started by late Y. S. Rajashekar Reddy, the former Chief Minister of Andhra Pradesh.

The assessment of poverty alleviation programmes depicted that it is a mixed response in so far as performance is concerned. MGNREGS has, by and large, enabled labourers to improve their bargaining capacity for higher wages and equality in wages to men and women. Many activities pertaining to irrigation and water conservation have been taken up under the scheme and the SC, ST communities and others benefited immensely. It is also observed that the distress migration has been controlled in many parts of the State.

It was mentioned that many BPL families have been benefited under housing programmes such as IAY, INDIRAMMA and pensions, Pavalavaddi and Arogyasri in study villages. It was also observed that the students got scholarships and farmers received free power which is something acclaimed as the pro-poor policy from the point of view of agrarian crisis experienced by the farmers in the State.

The functioning of gram panchayats is again varying from village to village depending on various factors. The financial status of some panchayats is good as they had shown surplus budget because of tax compliance of the people. On the other hand, some panchayats in Telengana region are finding it difficult in the absence of adequate funding for taking up development works. Secondly, whatever they raise through taxes is also inadequate as against the needs of the people in the villages. Therefore, it is worth mentioning that some of the study reports succinctly put the need for devolution of funds from State Government to the panchayats and making them effective and efficient local self-governing institutions.

Table 5.2: The Framework of Socio-Economic Indicators and Summary

Indicators of socio-economic situation	*Telengana*	*Coastal Andhra*	*Rayalaseema*
Demography	The villages under study are of reasonable size in terms of population	The villages are relatively big with many hamlets	The villages are big with many hamlets reflecting the concentration of development in GP village only
Educational status	The situation is mixed as some places are good while others are bad without any teachers and buildings etc.	Relatively good	Relatively poor
Health and sanitation	Health care facilities are poor registering heavy out of pocket expenses.	Health care is good, however, OPE are substantial	Health care is poor with very few PHCs, SCs and staff, the doctors and nurses per 1000 population is at low.
Land-use and agriculture	Land use pattern is skewed and net sown area is limited. Because there is no proper irrigation facility in the region.	Land used for agriculture is large as there is assured irrigation and farmers are used to commercial farming for quite some time.	Land use pattern is skewed and net sown area is limited. Because there is no proper irrigation facility in the region.

(*Contd.*)

Indicators of socio-economic situation	*Telengana*	*Coastal Andhra*	*Rayalaseema*
Land relations and tenancy	Tenancy is in vogue and it is oral. There is a threat of eviction to the tenant who is vulnerable. Fixed cash rent and share cropping is followed. The government introduced Land Licensed Cultivators' Act in 2012 with a view to protect the interests of the tenants by issuing a loan eligibility card.	Tenancy is in vogue and it is oral. There is a threat of eviction to the tenant who is vulnerable. Mostly it is fixed cash rent which is followed in the region.	Tenancy is in vogue and it is oral. There is a threat of eviction to the tenant who is vulnerable. Fixed cash rent and share cropping is followed.
Tribal land alienation and legislations	Tribal land alienation continues unabated despite the legislations to protect the interests of tribals in the region which comes under schedule V area.	Tribal land alienation continues unabated despite the legislations to protect the interests of tribals in the region which comes under schedule V area.	No tribal area in the region.
Assessment of poverty alleviation programmes	SHGs are formed but capacity-building is limited; bank linkage is provided but financial counselling is absent; it is a mixed picture in so far as poverty reduction in the area. Pensions are distributed to many in the region.	The performance of group activity is good due to high awareness levels of people; and some have taken up social issues such as anti-liquor movement; poverty reduction among SC, ST families is good. Pensions are distributed to many in the region	Groups are formed and doing well, however, it needs follow up and adequate capacity-building; absolute poverty levels have come down in some areas while in other areas it is not. Pensions are distributed to many in the region
Functioning of gram panchayat	It is dominated by upper caste and *defacto* representatives. Women's participation is limited. Though it is an advanced region in the state devolution is yet to take place. Gram Sabha is effective in some places reflecting the participation of people while it is not in other areas.	To some extent the marginalized sections are enjoying the power in the LSGIs. Women's participation is relatively good. Though it is an advanced region in the state devolution is yet to take place. Gram sabha is effective in some places reflecting the participation of people while it is not in other areas.	It is dominated by upper caste and *defacto* representatives. Women's participation is limited. Devolution is yet to take place despite so many years lapsed after 73rd CAA. Gram sabha is effective in some places reflecting the participation of people while it is not in other areas.

Appendix

THE LIST OF VILLAGES STUDIED IN ANDHRA PRADESH

Sl. No.	District	Mandal	Village	No. of villages
		Telengana Region		
1.	Adilabad	Jainath	Kura	1
2.	Karimnagar	Sircilla	Chintaltana	1
3.	Khammam	Paloncha	Pandurangapuram	1
4.	Medak	Kangti (Narayanaked)	Gajulapadu	1
5.	Nalgonda	Nakrekal	Palem	1
6.	Warangal	Sangem	Elguru Rangampet	3
		Raghunathapalli	Nidigonda	
		Atmakur	Ladella	
		Rayalaseema Region		
7.	Cuddapah	Sidhout	Takkolu	1
8.	Anantapur	Bukkapatnam	Krishnapuram	2
		Garladinne	Penakacherla	
		Coastal Andhra Region		
9.	Krishna	Gudur	Kappaladoddi	3
		Machilipatnam	Bogireddipalli	
		Avanigadda	Vekanuru	
10.	East Godavari	Biccavolu	Balabhadrapuram	2
		Gollaprolu	Chendurthi	
11.	Guntur	Duggirala	Godavarru	3
		Prathipadu	Pathamallayapalem	
		Amarthallur	Konduru	
12.	Visakhapatnam	Anakapalle	Kunchangi	4
		Kotapadu	Singannadorapalem	
		Pedabayalu	Seekari	
		Araku valley	Lotheru	
13.	West Godavari	Unguturu	Vellamelli	1
			Total villages	**24**

Source: Compiled from the reports of probationers of all-India Civil Servants.

REFERENCES

1. A. Amarendar Reddy and M.C.S. Bantilan (2011) *In Perspective; Regional Disparities in Andhra Pradesh, India*, ICRISAT, Hyderabad.
2. *Report of the Commission on Farmers' Welfare*, (2004) Government of Andhra Pradesh, Hyderabad.

3. P. Sainath, (2008) NREGA, A fine balance, www.indiatogether.com, 13 July.
4. T. Prabhakara Reddy (2010) "Decentralized District Planning in Madhya Pradesh; A Study of Mandla and Rajgarh districts". Report submitted to UNDP, New Delhi, mimeo.
5. T. Prabhakara Reddy (2010) "Distress and the Deceased; An Analysis of Farmers' Suicides in Andhra Pradesh" in *Agrarian Crisis and Farmer Suicides, Land Reforms in India*, Vol. 12, LBSNAA, Mussorie, ed. by R.S. Deshpande and Saroj Arora, Sage Publications, New Delhi.
6. T. Prabhakara Reddy and K. Pratap Reddy (2008) "Social Mobilisation and Poverty Eradication", A. Vinayak Reddy and Yadagiracharyulu (ed.) *Rural Development in India, Policies and Initiatives*, New Century Publications, New Delhi, June.
7. *Report on Census of Land Holdings in Andhra Pradesh (2009-10)*, Directorate of Economics and Statistics, Government of Andhra Pradesh, Hyderabad.
8. Surjit Bhalla, (2010), Does NREGA really work? *The Business Standard*, 27th March.
9. Yamini Aiyar and Salimah Samji; (2009), *Transparency and Accountability in NREGA: A Case Study of Andhra Pradesh*, Centre for Policy Research, New Delhi.
10. Hanumantha Rao, C.H. and S. Mahendra Dev (2003). *Andhra Pradesh Development: Economic Reforms and the Challenges Ahead*, CESS, Hyderabad.

6

Socio-Economic Profile of Rural Bihar

QAMAR AHSAN*

INTRODUCTION

Bihar was created as a separated political entity on 1st April, 1912 after bifurcating the then Province of Bengal. The new state was rich in mineral wealth and other natural resources such as fertile land and water. These along with large human and natural resource, had attracted considerable investment in mineral based and agro-processing industries in the newly created state. The state's rich cultural heritage, young demographic profile and good governance enabled Bihar to emerge as one of the fast growing states in the country on the eve of Independence. However, two further bifurcations of the State in 1935 (Orissa) and in 2000 (Jharkhand) deprived Bihar of its economic edge. The state lost most of its mineral and forest wealth first to Orissa and then to (Jharkhand) while over two-third of its population remained in the residual area accounting for less than half of its original size. Deprived of its vital economic resources, the state's economy underwent a long period of retrogression. The present state had inherited a largely semi-feudal agrarian economy even after abolition of an exploitative system of *zamindari* which was introduced in 1793 by Cornwallis. Poor implementation of land reform measures

* Professor of Economics Magadh University and former Vice Chancellor of B.N. Mandal University, Madhepura.

in the post-Independence era, led to economic impoverishment of rural masses and break up of social order in the rural areas. A new phase of caste and class conflict ensued changing social relations and land ownership pattern which has changed in favour of upper and middle castes. This gave rise to new social alignment having a far reaching social and political ramification.

The regression in the economic activities in the state did not start due to the failure of the state to govern. Rather, it is the outcome of the structural changes brought about due to planning and shift in the policy of state controls to achieve faster growth rate. Bihar was one of the economically viable states and was also singled out as better governed state than many others in the early years of Independence. However, the policies and the process of planning made a negative impact of the state's development. Bihar was singled out to subsidise infrastructure and power development for the rest of the country through the policy of freight equalization, which meant transportation of vital raw materials to distant states from the source at a highly subsidized rate. This naturally negated the locational advantage of the State. Now power, steel and other metal and metallurgical industries were being set-up at places where in the absence of raw material such industries could not be set-up earlier. Similarly, the Industrial Licensing Policy also neutralized the advantage of the state in resource endowment. Industrial houses like Tatas and Birlas invested mainly in the state due to its locational advantage, started investing in other states due to industrial licensing and freight equalization policy. The loss on account of freight equalization also one in steel alone in calculated to be over 1 lakh crore. Some say that the "Drain Theory-continued to be in operation for Bihar except that the centre of exploitation was shifted from London to New Delhi!"

THE STATE OF ECONOMY

Bihar is the Twelfth largest state in the country occupying an area of 94,163 square kilometre or nearly 3 per cent of the total area of the country. However, in terms of population it has 103.8 million or 8.5 per cent of the total population of India. Hence, it has a very high population density in the country which stands at 1,102 persons per square kilometre as against Indian average of 382. The State's population growth is estimated at 25 per cent as per 2011 Census.

Trapping of large population in a relatively small geographical area has resulted in demographic pressure which has triggered the process of economic and social retrogression in the absence of progressive economic, social and institutional factors which generally underline the development pattern in other states.

Gross State Domestic Product (GSDP) is an important indicator of development. The transition of an economy from the state of underdevelopment to a developed one involves changes in sectoral composition which contributes to GSDP over a period of time. In the state of underdevelopment primary sector is predominant, but as the process of development proceeds, the secondary and the tertiary sectors start becoming major contributors to the GSDP. The share of primary sector is declining in GSDP and the shares of secondary and tertiary sectors are increasing on a continued basis in Bihar, there are still till over 88 per cent population who live in the rural areas and their livelihood is dependent primarily upon agricultural and allied activities.

The share of primary sector in Bihar which was 63.34 per cent in 1950-51 declined to 51.77 per cent in 1979-80 and it further declined to 36.5 per cent in 2003-04. It stood at 22.1 per cent in 2008-11. The decline in the share of Secondary Sector is mainly due to the fact that Bihar underwent a phase of de-industrialisation on account of division of the state in 2000, when most of the industries went to the new

Table 6.1: A Comparative Sectoral Contribution to Growth of Bihar, Andhra Pradesh and India

Sectors	*1999-2000*			*2004-05*		
	Bihar	*AP*	*India*	*Bihar*	*AP*	*India*
1. Agriculture and Allied Activities	30.5	18.4	5.9	2.5	13.6	6.0
2. Industry (Construction)	9.0 (10.3)	25.0 (9.5)	31.6 (11.5)	32.3 (28.8)	27.3 (12.9)	28.4 (8.3)
3. Services (Trade, Hotels and Restaurant)	60.5 (40.1)	56.6 (13.8)	62.5 (21.0)	65.3 (36.8)	69.1 (12.7)	65.6 (17.0)

Source: Paper presented on Growth and Poverty Reduction: Bihar and AP, D.N. Reddy *et al.* at IHD, New Delhi, 2013. For this Table, Note is needed, (i) whether figures are in percentage or number, and (ii) what figures stand for in the brackets/parenthesis?

State of Jharkhand. The share of tertiary sector has however increased considerably from 24.68 per cent to 25.80 per cent and 61.3 per cent during the same period. The trend in sectoral distribution of GSDP largely follows the All India trend, but in a skewed manner. The direct implication of this trend is reflected in worsening of the economic position of a vast mass of rural population who are dependent on farm and allied activities. This has led to disparity in income distribution of the rural population and has also increased the rural-urban divide. This can be understood from the fact that the worsening of the economic situation is taking place primarily from a standard subsistence.

Per Capita Income of the State which is a measure of economic growth has been one of the lowest in the country standing at just around Rs. 16,119 in 2009-10 as against Rs. 46,492 for All India during the same period. The per capita income of Bihar works out to only 32.2 per cent of All India average. This ratio has actually declined from 60 per cent in 1960 and 40 per cent during 1993-94. The low per capita income along with stagnant economy has resulted in economic deprivation of a large segment of population. The Tendulkar Committee in 2004-05 had estimated that 54.5 per cent populations in the state lived below the poverty line. The levels of rural and urban poverty in the state was estimated to be 55.7 per cent and 43.7 per cent respectively. The relative deprivation of rural area has been on account of distorted pattern of income distribution, poor rural investment and in effectiveness of the institutional framework and agrarian transformation.

Growth Rate of the State which had been mired in stagnation and under development since late sixties is now showing some positive signs of change. The growth rate has started accelerating and there has been some serious efforts to alleviate poverty by providing opportunities for increased income and employment in the State. The economy of the State grew at 11.36 per cent between 2004-05 to 2010-11. This turn around in growth rate is termed as revival of a stagnant economy. Though, there has been appreciable increase in the growth rate, there also has been wide inter-sectoral variation which affect the socio-economic stabilization process. The impact of inter-sectoral variation has been most pronounced on the rural economy which has remained an area of concern for the policy-maker and implementation agencies.

The State Report is based on the Village Study Assignments of IAS Officer Trainees in the State of Bihar. It covers 38 villages covering districts of the State (List given in Annexure I). These villages are spread over diverse economic and agro-climatic zones and give a representative profile of the rural economy in the State. The Village Study Assignment is based on sample selection of villages and structured questionnaire to obtain information. These individual reports cover the following aspects of a Villages under study:

(a) Rural Infrastructure,
(b) Agrarian Relations,
(c) Social Structure,
(d) Economic Activities,
(e) Anti-Poverty and Rural Development Programmes, and
(f) Panchayati Raj System.

These different aspects of study help in understanding the socio-economic status, issues and programmes of Rural Economy in the State. These also provide an insight with respect to social and agrarian relations, functioning of grassroots institutions, democratization, stake-holders participation, delivery mechanism and the adequacy or insufficiency of outcome of the state sponsored intervention programmes.

AGRARIAN AND SOCIAL FRAMEWORK

Harmonious agrarian society is a pre-condition of inclusive growth in a predominantly rural economy. The low level of investment in agriculture and rural production has been a major cause of stagnant rural economy. The burden of underdevelopment is felt primarily by the rural poor. Economic liberalization since 1991 has further deteriorated the condition because of the worsening of terms of trade between agriculture and industry as well as widening rural urban divide. This had adverse impact of social and agrarian structure in the rural areas resulting in deprivation of the poor and aggravation of caste and class system often resulting in increasing rural violence.

AGRARIAN RELATION

The exploitative agrarian relation born out of the regressive land settlement and failure of the political system to implement the equity based land reform policies has not only deepend rural poverty but has impacted the economic and social behaviour of the rural society. It has been observed that the overall pattern of landholding is gradually changing and the old landowning class is declining, however, there has emerged a new land owning class drawn from intermediate castes or OBCs. Landlessness has not only increased but is now concentrated among the Scheduled Castes, extremely backward and lower caste Muslims. It is a matter of concern that more than half of the rural population in the State has become landless. This has serious ramification on the harmony and stability of the rural society. In rural Bihar the place of a person in society is dependent upon his ownership of land and hence the landless are at the lowest rung of society and are unable to share the fruit of development equitably with others on a higher rungs of social order. Assetlessness makes them most vulnerable and are unable to guard against the tyranny of rural rich and neo rich. An important outcome of the increasing size of disadvantaged group has been the widening of the ranks of peasantry which now consists of several castes drawn from SC, OBC, EBC and Muslims. This has also led to mobilization of poor peasants and landless in rural areas and increased migration in other parts of the State or country in search of employment.

Agrarian relation in the State is dependent upon land ownership pattern among the different castes and classes in the villages. Kuldip Narain (Borbara, Muzaffarpur) report that majority of the landholding is less than 5 acres and 17.7 per cent of the population is landless. Over 60 per cent *raiyat* have too small landholding to be remunerative. Further, the landholding is also highly skewed in favour of upper castes and OBCs who own 90 per cent of the land. Most of the small and marginal farmers come from EBCs or SC category who own 1 acre or less which is not sufficient even for subsistence. Ajay Yadav (Shivhar, Mokama, Patna) reports that land ownership contributes not only to livelihood, but also determines the status of the individuals in Socio-cultural hierarchy. The landholding pattern of Shivhar is heavily tilted towards forward castes and OBCs and there is only a marginal land ownership with lower and Scheduled Castes. He also reports that the competition for bigger share between forward castes and OBCs has led to deepening of Social fissure and there is polarization of under-privileged. Bala Murngan D. (Amari, Purna) also finds shared landholding pattern in favour of OBCs while the SC are mostly landless. Palka Sahni (Maheshpur, Katihar) reports huge asymmetry in land relations and ownership pattern in the village under study. Most of the land in the village is owned by middle castes such as Kushwaha and Chaurasias. The emergence of middle castes as a major land owning class has also contributed to the social unrest between the land owners and landless farm workers. The castes, therefore, also signifies the class in the villages. Bandna Preyashi (Matukpur, Bhojpur) also reports asymmetry in land relation. Most of the land is owned by the Kaysthas (a forward caste) and the Yadvas who are categorized as OBC. The SC and EBCs serve as farm labour or petty trade. This is the class which is generally prone to migration in search of employment during non-farm season.

Although Bihar was one of the first state to announce abolition of Zamidari system yet land reforms in the state present a dismal picture on account of stiff resistance from landed gentry who exercised great influence over legislature and higher bureaucracy. However, there have been considerable changes in the ownership pattern of land in the villages. With the rise in population the size of operational landholding, has declined and coupled with fragmentation of landholdings a vast number of marginal farms have either been sold out or leased out resulting in pauperization of the peasants (Sharma 2005). An important factor that affects the agrarian framework is not only the land ownership pattern, but also the question, who cultivate the farms? It has been found that only a small proportion of large land owners among the upper and OBCs actually cultivate the land themselves and the rest lease out to share croppers who are themselves small and marginal famers. But unfortunately the share cropping agreement is mostly verbal and not written. This deprives the share croppers of many benefits from governmental intervention programmes and creates uncertainty of lease period. This has in many ways acted as obstacle to private investment in agriculture. Dharmendra Singh (Budhav, Madhepura) reports that the land under ownership cultivation mostly belongs to marginal and small farmers. The upper caste land owners mostly rent out land while the OBCs and other small landowning castes rent in land. Share cropping in villages is a dominant economic activity and to some extent it is also influencing agrarian relationship. Low agricultural investment uncertainty of lease and poor economic condition has aggravated social unrest between the land owners, lease holders on the one hand and landless labourers on the other. The landless labourers who are at the bottom of class and caste ladder are getting polarized and thus often results in violent struggle between the land owners and landless farm workers, prevalent in more than 60 per cent of the districts in the State.

SOCIAL STRUCTURE

The village society is bound by primordial identities of religion, castes and gender-caste is not only a strong social organization which determines social interaction, but it also directs the level of participation in the economic decision-making at the local level. Ajay Yadav (Shivhar, Patna) reports that it has also found wider acceptance in the modern political system in the state. Despite afirmative action under the Constitution to neutralize its regressive effect it has continued to be an important tool of polarization of society and has yielded rich political dividend to several political parties. All most all the reports confirm total segregation of houses on the basis of castes in the villages and the different castes are found living to their caste based *tolas*. They do not mix generally with other castes Scheduled Castes are the most segregated ones who do not participate in social activities except for working as labour for odd jobs. Caste segregation is also affecting development work in rural areas. Jai Singh (Nonhi, Gaya) reports that the rivalry between upper caste and the most disadvantaged communities has stalled development work in the SC *Totals*. Vinod Singh Gujniyal (Behranwa, Patna) reports that even the BPL Survey has become a tool of exploitation of weaker section in the hands of politically empowered upper and intermediate castes. Caste based rivalries and conflicts have also been an important cause of emergence of caste based private armies like Ranvir Sena, Sunlight Sena, Lorik Sena etc. On the other hand the SCs and EBC Castes organized the defence through numerous Maoist outfits. Rural violence caused by Caste and Class rivalries has its negative impact on process of rural development and social integration.

Historically speaking, the social structure, consisting of caste groups with distinct social hierarchies, has been the most important element in determining the distribution of benefits arising out of development initiatives of the Government. However, there has been significant change with regard to social hierarchy and alignment or realignment of castes with respect to cornering political power or economic benefits arising out of state sponsored development programmes. It has been reported by most of the field reports that the traditional caste hierarchy is undergoing a change as the middle castes like Yadavas have now emerged as large land owners. Castes under OBC category like Kurmis and Korries have also benefited although to a lesser extent. The improvement in their socio-economic indicators has been because of affirmative action and political ascendancy. While the position of upper castes has declined due to changing asset ownership pattern, the position of middle castes has rather improved. The emergence of powerful middle castes have now led to multiple hierarchies which has impact aggravated conflicts in the villages. In between the two the position of lower castes has even worsened.

Pauperization of marginalized people have also been influenced by disappearance of village commons which supplemented, supported their economic well-being. Ramesh Kumar (Khutwara, Darbhanga) reports that village common property resources consisting of pasture, forest grazing ground, small water bodies etc., is lost due to increasing population, encroachment, setting-up of mobile tower and even private housing. Manoj Kr. Singh (Jagganathpur, Purnia) also reports that population pressure and rural infrastructure development along with other factors have eroded common property resources in the village. The disappearance of village commons has deprived the poor of their income as due to lack of grazing ground, small animal rearing like goats, sheep and even milk animal has become difficult for them. With the disappearance of small water bodies, the source of natural fishing has also disappeared.

In case of village Social and Agrarian profile, it is observed that while the traditional systems have been breaking down, but modern systems have not yet been securely found (Arvind N. Das, 1987). It has also been brought out that regressive nature of social structure in the State has in fact been a major contributory factor to the rural under development.

RURAL INFRASTRUCTURE

Rural infrastructure directly influences the productive activities of the economy which in turn help in reducing interregional and intra regicnal disparity. In a predominantly agrarian economy which is also categorized among the 'Least Developed' state, investment in infrastructure is considered precondition for initiating, accelerating and sustaining the process of growth. While exploring the right strategy for agricultural growth in eastern states in India, it was observed that "The basic strategy for inducing agricultural practices has to be through infrastructure development. Unless it is improved through investment of adequate capital the scope for technological progress will remain limited.

RURAL CONNECTIVITY AND ELECTRICITY

In Bihar over 88 per cent live in rural areas and derives its livelihood from agriculture and allied activities. If the State desires to exploit the potential for growth in the rural sector it will have to push investment in expanding infrastructural facilities vigorously. This also becomes important from the point of view of the fact that two-third of the geographical area of the state suffers from recurring floods from the rivers originating from the valleys of Himalayas. So, investment is not just a one time affair, but adequate funds have to be made available for repairs, reconstruction and rehabilitation, if the facilities are to be used purposefully for long-term.

The village field studies have examined the availability and sufficiency of rural basic infrastructure such as connectivity, electricity and drinking water in the respective villages under study.

In Bihar rural road network is inadequate in proportion to population and because of disrepair most of the *kuccha* roads and partially the *pucca* roads are not motorable. The all-weather roads cover a small network and require proper maintenance. The Rural Works Department is engaged in providing construction of new roads, strengthening and maintenance of existing roads has not been able to rise up to the expectation. There is multiplicity of rural roads schemes like Pradhan Mantri Gram Sadak Yojana (PMGSY), Mukhyamantri Gram Sadak Yojana (MMGSY), Apki Sarkar Apke Dwar (ASAD). Minimum needs programme (MNP), NABARD sponsored Rural Infrastructure Development Fund (RIDF) and Border Area Development Programme (BADP). The Multiplicity of Scheme is one of the reason for ineffective targeting, allocation and implementation due to paucity of funds and delay in decision-making. This is the reasons that only 13,705.18 kms of new rural roads could be constructed during 2006-2010. Another factor which severely affects connectivity is the absence of bridges as the State has a serpentine network of rivers and canals. Adequate planning and allocation is also needed to overcome this problem.

Despite the increased allocation and implementation of new scheme, the total road length was 94.0 thousand km in 2010 in which the share of NH is a mere 3 per cent. State Highways account for 4,857 km or 22 per cent. The major district roads have witnessed a decline of 5 per cent as many of these have been declared state highways. The rural road network accounts for mere 13.7 thousand km despite the large number of rural road schemes under the Central and State sectors.

The availability of all-weather roads in the villages is essential for the development of the village economy. This is the basic infrastructure and acts as arteries of connectivity with the market and towns, and has a bearing on the quality of life of the population. The state of rural roads in Bihar is a matter of serious concern. Not only the per capita/availability of road is very low, but the quality is also extremely poor. In the absence of all-weather roads the villages located in remote areas become isolated during monsoon in most parts of the State. This is more so in the case of villages in North Bihar and those located at greater distance from the national highway or the State Highways. Ashish Vachhni (village Lagma, Khagaria) reports that all village roads are in bad condition and mostly *kuccha*, which becomes almost unusable during the monsoon. Similarly, Dharmendra Singh (Budhaw, Madhepura) also reports poor connectivity of the village despite being closer to District main road. Palka Sahani (Maheshpur, Katihar) also reports that the biggest hindrance is the poor village connectivity with the town and the market is the all-weather roads. The roads become almost non-usable during monsoon. This has restricted agricultural growth as the farmers have to sell their produce locally at low price. He also points out that poor connectivity has led to rise in the number of quacks in and around the villages. The villagers in the absence of connectivity, are compelled to rely on alternative system. Gopal Meena (Khizirpur, East Champaran), Manoj Kumar Singh (Jagannathpur, Purnia) and Cherry Malik (Singhaul, Gaya) too report that rural roads are in shamble and a hindrance to the development of village economy. Most of these villages under study fall in the North Bihar which are severly affected by the havoc of flood almost every year. Recurring floods from the rivers originating from the Himalayas pose serious problem of damage to physical infrastructure, cattle and human lives. However, some village studies in the western and southern part of the States covering the Districts of Patna, Begusarai, Gaya, Rohtas and Bhojpur, have reported better road connectivity. Ramandeep Chaudhary (Sonhar, Rohtas) and R. Lakshmanan (Simariya-1, Begusarai) have reported better connectivity. Similarly, villages located nearer to district headquarters or National or State Highways too have reasonably good connectivity even though the incidence of flood is high in the area. Kumar Ravi (Mohadipur, West Champaran), Kuldip Narain (Borbara, Muzaffarpur), and Raman Kumar (Khutwara, Darbhanga) have reported better connectivity despite these villages falling in the districts of North Bihar.

Electricity is not only important from the point of agricultural operation and allied economic activities, but also from the point of view of quality of life. Till 2011-12 a total of 17,363 villages were connected under Rajiv Gandhi Grameen Vidyutikaran Yojana (RGGVY). Under this scheme 171 power substation have been charged and 1,976 thousand BPL families were provided electrical connection. But looking at the vast rural population the progress appears to be highly inadequate. Secondly, the availability of power specially during agricultural season remains inadequate and erratic. Electrical connection is now available in 65 per cent of the reported villages, but the availability or the irregularity of electricity supply renders such connectivity useless as reported by Gopal Meena (Khizirpur, East Champaran), Ashish Bachani (Lagma, Khagaria), Raman Deep Choudhary (Sonhar, Rohtas).

The condition of power supply is usually worse during the summer season. Agricultural operation becomes costlier if the farmer has to resort to diesel pumpsets due to high cost of diesel. It has been observed that the villages nearer to large towns or district headquarters have somewhat better power supply than the remotely located villages. In the villages electricity connection is mostly in the *pucca* house of those belonging to the upper castes or the landed OBCs. The SCs and the non-land owing labourers usually have very low or no-electric connection in their houses.

Safe drinking water is another major problem of the rural Bihar. There has been significant advances with regard to availability of drinking water through the intervention of the administration. Hand pumps remain the major source of safe drinking water but in the North-Eastern part the quality of underground water is very poor. But in several villages the water is collected from common wells and ponds. Dharmendra Singh (Budhaw, Madhepura) has reported that the villagers have to travel long distance to fetch water. There is no hand pump available in the village. In the Kosi area ground water quality is also not good because of the presence of high iron content. Non-availability of safe drinking water in this area is also posing serious health problems.

EDUCATION

The pace of economic development is often determined by the level and quality of education. The region of Bihar, once the fountainhead of knowledge with the Nalanda and Vikramshila Universities in the region started loosing its supremacy with the decline of Gupta Empire. The State was later in history, made a part of the province of Bengal. The vernacular schools like Pathshalas and Madrsah during the medieval period were few and these were open to the elites from the upper strata of population. With the advent of British rule public schools started coming up in the district towns and later in the smaller towns and *kasbas*. The real thrust to education was, however, received only after the state acquired a separate entity in 1912. However, the level of literacy and education remained very low specially among the socially, economically and geographically disadvantaged groups like women, SC, ST and minorities.

The literacy rate in the state remains one of the lowest in the country. The literacy rate in Bihar, as per the 2011 census is 63.8 per cent as compared to 47.0 per cent in 2001 while the All India literacy is recorded as 74.0 per cent and 64.8 per cent during the same period. Not only the literacy rate is low, but there also exists a very wide gender gap. In 2011 the gender-wise literacy rate were 73.4 per cent for male and 53.3 per cent for female which implies a 20.1 per cent gap between male and female. Bihar will still have to wait for 2-3 decades to achieve universal literacy in the state.

Bihar, in the last two decades has been able to significantly reduce the gender gap in literacy yet it is besieged with a very high intra-state literacy rate. In 2011 while Rohtas had 75.6 per cent literacy rate for Purnea it was just 52.5 per cent. The decadal growth in literacy was very high in the districts where earlier the literacy was low. It has also been a matter of satisfaction that the rural urban differential in literacy has considerably lowered down at 61.8 per cent for rural areas and 78.8 per cent for the urban areas. The narrowing of the rural urban differential at 17.9 per cent shows some positive trend.

Table 6.2: Trends in Literacy rates in India and Bihar

Year	*India*			*Bihar*			*Gender Gap*	
	Male	*Female*	*Total*	*Male*	*Female*	*Total*	*India*	*Bihar*
1961	40.4	15.4	28.3	35.2	8.2	22.0	25.1	27.0
1971	46.0	42.0	34.5	35.8	10.2	23.2	24.0	25.5
1981	56.4	29.8	43.6	43.8	15.8	32.3	26.6	28.0
1991	64.1	39.3	52.2	52.5	22.9	37.5	24.8	29.6
2001	73.3	53.7	64.8	60.3	33.6	47.0	21.6	26.7
2011	82.1	65.5	74.0	73.4	53.3	63.8	16.6	20.1

Source: *Economic Survey*, 2011-12, Government of Bihar Finance Department, Patna, p. 189.

Cherry Malik (Singhaul, Gaya) reports that education is a low priority area for the SC and OBCs. Low rate of literacy is especially in the villages where the dominant population is of OBCs and SCs. The villages with mixed caste structure have recorded higher male literacy as found by R. Lakshmanan (Simarya, Begusarai). But the female literacy remains low even in such villages. Anupam Kumar (Harpur, Muzaffarpur) also reports highest incidence of illiteracy from the OBCs and Scheduled Castes. In contrast, the upper castes have considerably higher literacy and educational status. In far-flung areas like Jagannathpur, Purnia, Manoj Kumar reports that people do realize the importance of literacy and education. Yet the village has a very poor literacy rate, specially the female literacy which is a matter of great concern.

The progress in elementary education in the villages of the State is slow and tardy resulting in large number of children in the age group of 0-14 remaining outside the school. Progress in expansion of elementary education implies greater access and inclusion of rural population in the mainstream educational system. The state has a total number of 42,307 primary schools and 27,958 upper primary schools. With the combined number of 70,640 schools the State aims at providing universal education to children 0-14 age group whose total population far exceeds the capacity created in these government schools. It is an important reason for large number of children remaining outside the school.

Another major hurdle in expansion of literacy and education in the state has been school enrollment and dropout rate. The situation has, however, improved considerably in the last 15 years with the increased central flow under DPEP and later through Sarva Shiksha Abhiyan. The improvement in enrollment is evenly recorded in all region and all social groups. However, school dropout rate is greatly influenced by the social and economic disadvantages, especially among the OBCs, Scheduled Castes and minorities. The annual rate of increase in enrollment in all the 38 districts of the state during 2009-10, has been a matter of some satisfaction. It has been found the rate of enrollment has been higher in the districts where the rate of literacy was lower during 2001-02. Most of these low literacy rate districts fall in the North and North-Eastern districts of the State. For instance the upper primary enrollment in districts like Kishanganj (29.4%), East Champaran (30.7%) and West Champaran (34.9%) have recorded very high growth rate. Similarly, for the primary education the growth rate of enrollment in Purnia, Araria and East Champaran varied between 12.3 per cent to 15.2 per cent. This is more than the increase in enrollment in the developed districts like Patna, Muzaffarpur, Bhagalpur and others. The rate of increase in enrollment is confirmed by the findings of the village field studies also. The Bihar's Annual Economic Survey 2009-10 has listed the important development in education as: (i) there has been increase in enrollment in all districts, regions, gender and social groups; (ii) the rate of increase for enrollment for the Scheduled Castes is not at par with the general category at the primary level, but it increases over the rate of enrollment of general section, at the upper primary level; and (iii) the enrollment of girls is increasing at a faster rate than boys. Similar trend has also been observed from students belonging to the disadvantaged categories. These are indeed positive developments in expansion and infusion of population which was out of school system in the State.

Enrollment rate does not mean that anyone who is enrolled in a school received a minimum required years of schooling. The dropout rate in the state is also alarmingly high and thus neutralizing the gains from the increasing enrollment. The dropout rate in the state in the primary level (I to V) recorded at 42.5 in 2009-10. Although it has come down from 61.6 in 2001-02, yet if effective measure is not taken, this may negate the objective of universal education. The dropout rate in upper primary level is extremely high at 58.8 per cent. The field reports have also observed the dropout phenomenon especially among the disadvantage groups and girl child indicating gender and caste as important elements in dropout in the villages under the study.

Birendra Prasad Yadav (Sonaru, Patna) has observed that although the enrollment in primary school is very high due to drive by administration and government yet there is also considerable dropout between 0-14 age group of which two-third consists of girls. Most of the dropouts belong to OBCs and Scheduled Castes. Raman Kumar, (Darbhanga), (Khutwara, Sadar Block), also has the similar finding that despite high enrollment the dropout rate of girl students is very high due to social and economic conditions of the population, specially among the weaker sections. Saket Kumar (Latra, Bhagalpur) also arrives at the similar conclusion that although enrollment is high yet there are significant cases of dropouts and out of school children. Manish Kumar (Rahatpur, Begusarai) blames the rigidity of caste structure and low social awareness for poor enrollment and high drop out rate of girl child. The high figure of enrollment does not really mean actual attendance or learning achievement.

These studies make some important findings such as: (i) parents do not consider the schools as useful learning centres due mainly to absenteeism among teachers, their teaching ability and school environment; (ii) Social and economic environment at home which encourages, specially the girls to stay back at home and help in domestic or income related work; and (iii) Deficiencies in school infrastructure. The field study has also reported on the poor quality of education in the village schools which is also a major contributory factor for dropouts.

Asangba, Chumba AO (Madhubani Tol, Madhubani) and Raman Kumar (Khutwara, Sadar Block) have observed that the quality of education in government schools is a matter of concern. The level of learning achievement is poor and the teachers by and large emphasize rote learning. Saket Kumar (Latra, Bhagalpur) blames irregularity of teachers as a major factor contributing to low learning achievement. Abhay Kumar Singh (Nonhar, Rohtas) has observed that there is general apathy towards school curriculum. Free meals and books do attract the students but student, absenteeism is also very high as they have to support their parents in their economic pursuit. Nundan Kumar (Raziganj, Purnia) reports that despite the high enrollment, the attendance reflected the teaching learning programme. Partly this is also due to the irregularity of teachers in the school and partly this is due to poor environment at home. In villages where private schools are in operation, have registered better attendance and education even when sending their children to the school means additional cost. This facility is, however, for the economically better off sections.

Inadequacy of school infrastructure is another factor that discourages retention in the school. As an important component of enrollment and retention the infrastructure facilities like school buildings, furniture, classrooms, toilets, playground and drinking water are major source of attraction to school. In the absence of such facilities the dropout rate is bound to increase.

Asangba Chuba AO (Madhubani Tol, Madhubani) laments poor infrastructure specially with regard to classrooms, drinking water and toilets. Lokesh Kr. Singh (Navada, Patna) has also found that inadequacy of school infrastructure does not motivate the students to complete school education. The distance of the village from the local school is also a discouraging factor. Kundan Kumar (Raziganj, Purnia) reports that although the school occupies large piece of land, yet the school building and essential facilities like drinking water and toilets are inadequate. School building is also in dire need of repair and renovation.

All these factors have thus worked as a hurdle in achieving the target of universal primary education. While the economically well off and specially the Upper Castes send their children to private schools mushrooming in villages and smaller towns, the poor and the disadvantaged group are generally deprived of quality education and eventually dropout from the school system.

HEALTH SANITATION AND NUTRITION

Bihar has been accorded a priority state status under the National Health Mission (NRHM) as the State has alarmingly low indicators related to primary health care infrastructure and as also in terms of reproductive and child health care. The major health indicators such Infant Mortality Ratio (IMR), Maternal Mortality Ratio (MMR) and Total Fertility Rate (TFR), are among the highest in the country and taken together, these indicators give a clear signal of the level of deprivation and vulnerability of a large section of population mainly falling within in the Scheduled Caste, Scheduled Tribe and Minority Communities.

According to the 2011 Census the total population of Bihar stood at 103.8 million accounting for 8.58 per cent of the total population of the country. The State has a very high density of population and an extremely slow pace of urbanization. The rural population formed 88.7 per cent and the rate of urbanization was 11.3 per cent. With a large rural population, State is required to put in place an appropriate rural health infrastructure to meet the requirement of growing population.

Table 6.3: Selected Health Indicator for Bihar (2004-2010)

Year	*Crude Birth Rate*		*Crude Death Rate*		*Total Fertility Rate (TFR)*		*Infant Mortality Rate (IMR)*	
	India	*Bihar*	*India*	*Bihar*	*India*	*Bihar*	*India*	*Bihar*
2004	24.1	30.2	7.5	8.1	2.9	4.3	58	61
2005	23.8	30.4	7.6	8.1	2.9	4.3	58	61
2006	23.5	29.9	7.5	7.7	2.8	4.2	57	60
2007	23.1	29.4	7.4	7.5	2.7	3.9	55	58
2008	22.8	28.9	7.4	7.3	2.6	3.9	53	56
2009	22.5	28.5	7.3	7.0	2.6	3.9	50	52
2010	22.1	28.1	7.2	6.8	—	—	47	48

Note: Figures in this Table are per thousand population.

Source: Sample Registration System (SRS), Office of the Registrar General of India, Ministry of Home Affairs, New Delhi.

Despite the severe limitations in expanding health infrastructure, there has been some positive trend in health care in the recent years. IMR and MMR have shown significant improvement between 2004-2007. In fact the Crude Death Rate (CDR) has now come down below the national average. In 2004 the CDR for India was 7.5 and for Bihar it was 8.1 in 2010 the CDR come down significantly to 7.2 and 6.8 for India and Bihar respectively. TFR has also come down from 4.3 in 2004 to 3.9 in 2009. The pace of gradual decline in state TFR has caught up with all-India average. These improvements are made out to be the result of increase in coverage of immunization, institutional delivers, better use of health care facilities and increased investment, flow from NRHM and other schemes in the State.

However, the most significant factor which has not yet been properly quantified and documented is the private expenditure on health by the rural families in the absence of adequacy of public health care services (PHC) or social health insurance coverage despite of the state being categorized as 'priority state' for the NRHM intervention. The resource constraints and large infrastructural gaps in health service delivery has further aggravated the situation resulting in disappointing scenario specially in far-flung rural areas of the State. Even at the places where primary health services are available, these fail to serve effectively because of poorly equipped facilities as found by Pranav Kumar (Etuarpur, Vaishali). A similar observation of inadequacy of facilities is raised by Manoj Kumar (Sonhar, Rohtas). Kumar Ravi (Mohajdipur, West Champaran) has found that even with the presence of a PHC, people have a dominant bias for private practitioners and some of them even visit quacks too. Bandna Preyashi (Matukpur, Bhojpur) has found out that family expenditure on health is minimal, but if there is major illness or child birth the expenditure rises drastically and the services are generally obtained from the private practitioners in nearby towns. Only a handful of Scheduled Caste and OBCs visit PHC. Most of the expenditure on health services is financed out of the family savings or loan from relatives. But, there is also significant borrowing from the money-lenders in medical emergencies. Loans from local money-lenders is largely resorted to by the poor and OBCs.

The success of health care services, to a great extent depends upon: (i) the health functionaries, at the PHC level; and (ii) the functional elements such as adequacy and availability of medicines and other services at the centre. It has been found that high degree of absenteeism among the health workers specially the doctors compel the people to seek services of quacks or alternative medical practitioners. They go out to nearby town or to bigger cities in case of major health problem, Palka Sahani (Maheshpur, Katihar) further finds out the role of ground level health workers is critical in view of the low literacy and awareness among the rural poor about immunization, male sterilization. The role of ANMs, ASHA or the Para-Medical workers who are supposed to fill up this awareness gap have also not been up to expectation and hence there is gap in target and achievement.

SANITATION

In all the studies it has been pointed out that the sanitary condition in the villages even after 65 years of Independence is a matter of not only concern for the administration but a major source of spread of diseases. Lokesh Kr. Singh (Navada, Patna) has found that the village under study being closer to Patna has better rural infrastructure, but toilets, both community and individual are woefully absent. Barring a few well off the practice of open defecation is widespread. Ajay Yadav (Shivhar, Barh) has pointed out that most of the toilets constructed under IAY are unused either because of poor constructions or because of the social habit of population. He comes up with an interesting finding that poor sanitation facility is not particularly a class phenomenon, as a number of well to do households are also without toilets. In some areas it is a 'gender problem' as the men in the household do not feel the need for a *pucca* toilet and prefer to continue with the old age practice. This unhygienic practice of open defecation has also been a major source of disease and spread of infection. Poor sanitary condition is influenced by social conditioning, lack of awareness and the cost of toilets specially for the poor household. Apart from the intervention programme, improvement in sanitary condition also needs a sustained social campaign specially by the women organizations. There is need to promote community based latrine in villages to makes it more acceptable from the point of view of the poor household and maintenance of the facility. But this would required hygienic conditions and proper maintenance of the facility to be useful to the rural folk. Significant achievements in health status cannot be achieved in the absence of improved water supply and sanitation services. Mere fulfilment of target under various schemes is meaningless unless these services could properly be maintained on a sustained basis.

Poor health and sanitation condition is reflected in widespread diseases such as acute diarrhoea (4.46 lakhs), Bacillary dysentery (2.33 lakhs), viral hepatitis (0.12 lakh), enteric fever, Malaria and fever of unknown origin (11.5 lakh) were reported in Bihar in 2010-11. The burden of inadequacies in health services is borne by the rural population who have to pay for the treatment from their own sources. Things have now, however, started looking up after some state sponsored schemes and intensive awareness campaign in the rural areas.

ANGANWADI AND ICDS

The State has achieved a better record in pursuance of National Policy for Children which emphasizes integrated delivery of health services to expectant mothers and children under ICDS. The programme targets children between 0-6 years age group and their mothers, for growth, monitoring, immunization, health checkups, supplementary feeding as well as nutrition and health education. There were 544 ICDS Projects in the state covering all the blocks in 38 districts in 2010. A total of 86,237 Anganwadi centres (AWC) and 5,540 mini AWCs were functioning under these 544 ICDS projects in 2011. In addition to this SABLA scheme was launched in 12 districts as 100 per cent centrally sponsored scheme which is targeted at adolescent girls in the age group of 11-18 years for improving their nutritional and health status, upgradation of home skill and vocational skill. The scheme is being implemented using the platforms of ICDS and AWCs.

ICDS-AWC centre provides a package of six basic health services such as immunization, supplementary feeding, referral services, non-formal preschool health and nutritional education to the target group. It has been noticed that in the absence of trained and motivated manpower, monitoring and financial allocation the objective remains largely unfulfilled in the areas covered under the study of Ajay Yadav (Shivhar, Barh). Inadequacy of ICDS-AWC is attributed to the selection process of field workers, and woeful lack of infrastructure specially in the areas inhabited by lower castes. Further, Gopal Meena (Khizirpura, East Champaran) also found that the higher caste *sevikas* sub-let the several strenuous jobs to women belonging to lower castes as she found the work below her 'dignity'.

The field reports have clearly established that despite the best of the efforts of the Government to increase institutional health care in the rural areas, the health services remain in very poor shape. PHCs have not been effective and the health care based on referral system has allowed the quakes and private practitioners to mushroom in the rural areas. Financing of the health problems has also been a contributing factor for the indebtedness of the rural poor as they resort to private money-lenders for meeting heavy medical expenses in private clinics and hospitals. The state initiative has failed to address the health problems of rural population.

ANTI-POVERTY AND RURAL DEVELOPMENT PROGRAMME

Poverty is multi-dimensional phenomenon and it cannot be estimated by calories intake alone. The level of deprivation is also dependent upon food quality, housing, drinking water supply, sanitation, clothing and education. Taken together these components can give a good indication of the state of social exclusion or group vulnerability. However, all the available estimates on the basis of which poverty alleviation programmes are worked out are based on the calorie consumption. According to the Tendulkar Committee (relating to 2004-05) 55.7 per cent of rural households and 43.7 per cent of the urban households in Bihar fall below the poverty line. This naturally implies a poverty ratio of 54.4 per cent which was much higher than 41.8 per cent of all-India figure. With only 11 per cent of India's rural population is located in Bihar, fifteen per cent of the India's poor reside in the State. The poverty count becomes more complex as there also exists regional variation in the level of deprivation within the State. For instance poverty is more acute in North Bihar and Seemanchal area than in Central and Western Bihar.

The level of deprivation becomes acute wherein the monthly per capita consumption expenditure (MPCE) is taken into account. The National Sample Survey Office (NSSO) in its 66th round (2010) for the country as a whole shows that MPCE in rural areas in India is Rs. 1054 and for the urban areas it is Rs. 1984. In case of Bihar it has been worked out at Rs. 780 and Rs. 1283 respectively for the rural and urban areas. Of this meagre expenditure the rural Bihar spends as much as 64.7 per cent of MPCE on food component as compared to 52.9 per cent in urban areas. This indicates that due to spending of the major portion of household income little is left for meeting non-food needs such as fuel, clothing, housing, nutritional supplement or healthcare which could bring about improvement in the quality of their lives. It is also revealed that incidence of poverty and deprivation is very high among the Scheduled Castes, extremely backward classes, Muslims and landless labourers. Higher poverty and vulnerability have worsened the human development indicators. It is also pertinent to note that while the national poverty ratio shows a declining trend, the same has registered a rising trend in Bihar.

These indicator and trends demand State intervention to a moderate poverty in the rural areas. A number of poverty alleviation and rural development programmes has been initiated of which most are centrally sponsored schemes. The village field reports have attempted to examine adequacy and suitability of some of the rural development programmes. It is a fact that poverty and unemployment are intertwined with agriculture in rural areas with dismal growth in agriculture, low productivity and subsistence nature of agriculture which keep the wages low. Besides agricultural operation is spread over only 6-9 months in a year. There is also few jobs outside the agricultural operation in the villages. This has created problem of unemployment and under-employment. Considering the complex nature of rural poverty, different types of rural poverty alleviation programmes have been organized, i.e. wage employment, asset creation, capacity-building and welfare schemes.

The Swarnajayanti Gramin Swarozgar Yojana (SGSY) was created by restructuring the earlier scheme called Integrated Rural Development Programme (IRDP) launched in 1999. SGSY aims at capacity-building among the rural poor so that they can access self-employment opportunities. The scheme operates by creating income generating assets through bank credit and governmental support and beneficiaries are organized into Self-Help Groups (SHGs). Nearly, 0.27 lakh members of SHGs are reported during 2011-12 which is, however, far less than 1.84 lakh members during the previous year. The number of SHGs has also decreased to 12,017 in 2011-12 as compared to 31,453 during the previous year. Another dismal picture is poor fund utilization which comes about to just 48 per cent of the sanctioned amount. The fund utilization is specially less than the state average in backward and minority concentration districts of Seemanchal. The poor performance of the SGRY is also reflected in the village field studies of most of the IAS Trainees.

Bandna Preyashi reports that women were completely left out from all the six schemes undertaken in Matukpur village (Bhojpur). She blames it on ineffective Mahatma Gandhi National Rural Employment Guarantee Schemes (MGNREGS). The earlier National Rural Employment Guarantee Programme (NREGP) has restructured and renamed as MGNREGS. The Scheme is designed to ensure a 100 days of employment to each rural household demanding employment. It also endeavours to create community assets in rural areas so as to increase livelihood options and improve social and economic infrastructure. Further, it enhances bargaining power of agriculture labour and checks distress migration. The Scheme is of great significance for Bihar which has a very high proportion of rural poor and landless labourers. However, the scheme has performed poorly as only about 20 per cent of the rural poor who have been issued job cards were given some employment and only 5.1 per cent of job card holders were given 100 days of employment. The total employment generated also came down from 1,597 lakh person, days in the previous year to 866.36 lakh person, days 2010-11. This presents a disappointing picture of the flagship scheme for poverty reduction in the state. Dharmendra Singh (Budhwe, Madhepura) has reported that although the intensity of employment is less than desired yet demand for wage employment has increased and it has to some extent checked distress migration.

Indira Awas Yojana (IAY) is another Scheme of the Central Government which aims at providing financial assistance to BPL households in rural areas for construction or upgradation of their houses. The Scheme aims at providing and enhancing basic amenities in rural areas. The state has, however, failed to achieve annual physical target and the share of SCs in total beneficiaries has also come down significantly. Ashish Vachhani (Latra, Bhagalpur) reports unsatisfactory performance of the scheme due to wide spread corruption and emergence of intermediaries. In one of the case at least the money meant for house construction was diverted for expenditure on medical need of the beneficiary.

Besides these three important employment and rural development schemes, the State also has sponsored a number of social and welfare programmes which cover women empowerment, healthcare, old age pension, education, sanitation and other such welfare schemes. However, it is disappointing to note that the two flagship schemes targeted at the weaker section below poverty line (BPL), i.e. SGSY and MGNREGS have performed very poorly in most of the villages which were surveyed. The impact of these flagship scheme is very low because of poor targeting, large scale corruption, insufficient monitoring and surveillance.

PANCHAYATI RAJ SYSTEM

The 73rd Constitutional Amendment has ushered in the era of grassroots democracy in India. However, it took over 22 years for the State to introduce democratic governance at the grassroots in the State through the Bihar Act, 2006. Panchayati Raj Institutions (PRIs) are considered third tier of the government which are empowered to oversee and implement of various schemes and programmes in their jurisdiction. In Bihar, the statutory provisions of the PRI have gone one step further to provide reservation to women and other marginalized groups, such as SC, ST, extremely backward castes. The 3-tier PRIs consist of Gram Panchayat at the lowest level, Panchayat Samiti at Block level and Zila Parishad at District Level. Presently there are 38 Zila Parishads, 531 Panchayat Samitis and 8,442 Gram Panchayats. The Act incorporates provision for 50 per cent reservation for women including the reservation on single posts.

The Financial flow to PRIs is categorized as: (i) Grant amount through transfer of net taxes of the State through the recommendations of the State Finance Commission. This amount is meant for such priority works as provision for drinking water, drainage, *Kuccha* road, brick soiling, cleaning of roads, drains, ponds, wells etc., (ii) United grant is given to the PRIs to ensure maintenance of account and capacity-building of the 3-tier institutions.

With the introduction of PRIs in the State there has been greater awareness among the different sections in the rural areas and the level of their participation in development work has increased. However, the field study tells a different story. Bandana Preyashi (Matukpur, Bhojpur) reports that the government has entrusted the local bodies with planning and implementation of schemes through PRI, yet hardly any proper planning takes place. The implementation of the schemes is through the nexus of heads of the PRIs at different levels, the BDOs, contractors and junior engineers of the line department. All important decisions are taken unilaterally and corruption is rampant.

Another important aspect is the identification of beneficiary by Gram Sabha. Kundan Kumar (Raziganj, Purnia) reports that the main interest of the members of Panchayat has been selection of their supporters on the beneficiary list under various schemes. Vinod Singh Gunjiyal (Behranwar, Patna) has mentioned BPL survey created a lot of controversy in the village due to *malafide* and subjective assessment was done by the Panchayat Supervisor. BPL inclusion identification is dependent on a 13-point score and this has become a tool in the hand of local political class to favour their followers and relatives.

Despite the best of intentions the Gram Sabha has not lived up to the expectations of the local community. The objective of strengthening grassroots democracy is yet to be realized fully for the marginalized sections of the village community to have greater say in the affairs of the PRIs. However, the positive aspect is increased level of participation of women and SCs in the Panchayati Raj System and gradually it will allow their greater space. The role of the government functionaries becomes important in realizing the objectives.

ECONOMIC ACTIVITIES

Economic activities in rural Bihar are largely dependent upon the scope and opportunities in the primary sector which continues to be the dominant source of livelihood. The potential of rural development, therefore, depends upon the activities of existing institutions, schemes and opportunities of investment in agricultural and allied activities. The village reports of the IAS Trainees have examined the various aspects of the economic activities categorized under the following heads:

(i) Agriculture (farming on own land or leased land),
(ii) Farm labourer,
(iii) Non-farm labourer,
(iv) Petty traders and craftsmen/craftswomen, and
(v) Migrant workers

Agriculture is the main source of income and employment of the rural population. In the State majority population engaged in agriculture, 29 per cent belong to the cultivator category and about 48 per cent are agricultural labourer. The poor agricultural situation is attributed to the existence of large, number of marginal and small cultivators.

The average size of landholding is 0.75 hectares which is less than half of All India holding size of 1.57 hectares. Over 80 per cent farmers have less than 0.30 hectares as a result of which small and marginal cultivators constitute 91 per cent of total landholdings. A large number of small and marginal cultivators fall below the poverty line. Not only the farm size is low, but there are serious problems of fragmentation of landholdings, poor land records, poor consolidation of landholdings and inadequacy of rural infrastructure. The above factors taken together with the uneconomic size of landholdings, restrict the financial access for farm modernization. Besides, the agriculture in the State has the high risk of flood, water logging and drought. Recurring natural disasters have severely affected the life and livelihood of the rural population in the State.

The village reports also present a similar picture which is in close proximity of the state averages. Ajay Yadav (Shivhar), Patna, reports that in a village land ownership pattern is the main factor that determines the identity of a person in the village. The size of landholding not only contributes to family income, but also the place of that person in socio-cultural hierarchy. The landholding pattern in Shivhar is highly tilted towards the traditional forward castes and OBCs. There exists competition among the forward castes and the neo rich OBCs for acquiring greater share in landholding which has also led the significant social fissure at the local level.

Agriculture being the main occupation it is the mainstay of income and employment. A very small number of rural household have economic size of landholding. But the owner of larger units usually do not cultivate the farm themselves but they lease it out to the tenants who are mostly smaller marginal land owners. By and large tenancy is not recorded for the fear of landlords losing their land rights. In the absence of written contract investment on land is also low due to uncertainty of tenancy. This is also a contributory factor for low farm productivity. Further, even the village level workers (*Halka Karamchari*) do not report the incidence of tenancy. Maintaining proper land record is the key to efficient land management. Only Kundan Kumar (Razigan) Parkia, and Manishankar (Rahatpur, Begusarai) have reported recorded tenancy. Tenants have to bear the entire cost of production and land revenue even in a highly uncertain environment.

Apart from agriculture, animal husbandry is the most important occupation of a large number of rural population. Procurement by milk cooperatives and increasing demand of milk in urban areas has encouraged animal husbandry in the villages. This occupation is largely undertaken by the OBCs and there are large incidence of rearing of milch cow on '*Bataidari*' as reported by Jai Singh (Noni, Gaya).

Bihar has a history of low labour force participation specially for the weaker section and women. Despite the increase in wage, there has been worsening of employment situation in rural areas both in terms of quantity and quality. The deficiencies of the labour market is most pronounced in the agricultural sector which absorbs over 78 per cent of the labour force. Despite providing large employment, the contribution of agriculture is around a fifth of the State Domestic Product (SDP) which has worsened the economic situation of workers. The agricultural wage rate in the State is much lower than the neighbouring states and the national average. Jai Singh (Noni, Gaya) reports that prevailing wage rate was between Rs. 60-70 per day which is below the minimum wage rate fixed by the State. Further, agriculture employment is mostly during the sowing and harvesting and therefore, total employment seldom increases above 120 days. In such a situation the most affected are the landless labourers.

Thus, during non-agricultural reason the landless labourers tend to migrate to urban areas or other States where employment for unskilled workers is available in construction and farm sector activities. Sanjay Kr. Singh (Berua, Muzaffarpur), Cherry Malik (Singhaul, Gaya) reports that there is an exodus of labour mostly young to other areas for employment and only old, women and children are left behind in the villages. Outmigration not only provides higher income in non-agricultural season, but is also seen an upward mobility. However, most of the migration takes place among the economically better off groups and the most disadvantaged groups stay back for not affording to bear the cost of travel and residence in urban areas or outside the state.

However, MGNREGA has some positive effect on increase in income and employment opportunities. This has been of significant help to the people below poverty line. MGNREGA has also been instrumental in lowering out-migration of landless laboures from the village.

CONCLUSION

The basic objective of village study has been to understand the factors underlying the socio-economic dimensions of rural communities. Although each village has distinct and unique characteristics, but the report of 38 villages taken together gives a clear picture of the socio-economic situation in the rural areas in Bihar. It has also given an opportunity to the IAS Trainees to experience the major issues in the rural development.

There is no doubt that the rural areas in the state suffer severe socio-economic deficiencies yet there is sufficient scope of mitigating the problems like poverty, health and education through proper and efficient execution of rural development schemes. Village studies have been an opportunity to identify the main problems in rural connectivity health, education, agricultural operation, village infrastucture and implementation of schemes like NREGA, IAY, SGSY and improving the functioning of Panchayati Raj Institutions. The development of rural economy can be achieved through convergence among the various government schemes. There is also the need to cover the gap in capabilities of the rural community on a sustainable basis through horizontal and vertical integration of available resources.

An important area which could hold key to the rural development is universal access to a range of financial services. This requires greater financial inclusion through organized banking sector and micro-finance institutions. Although the incidence of rural indebtedness is low in the State yet greater access and inclusion will encourage larger investment and economic activities.

A serious problem that has been encountered in the survey is poor status of land and crop records. "*Halka Karamchari*" who is responsible for maintaining crop statistics in the area, has not been discharging his duties efficiently. This is because of the lack of proper supervision and monitoring. The quality and reliability of agricultural statistics has in fact deteriorated over the years.

Implementation of Government sponsored schemes have been another area of concern. Success of poverty alleviation programmes depend upon appropriate identification of the beneficiary and ensuring effective delivery mechanism. However, most of the village reports indicate large incidence of corruption and administrative apathy. Further, the PRIs which were supposed to the usher in grassroots democracy and allow greater peoples participation in decision-making at the local level, have been marred with controversies and inefficiency. Despite of the obvious gaps in achievement level, significant progress has been witnessed in transformation of rural economy in the State.

BIBLIOGRAPHY

Books

Agro-Economic Research Centre (1982), *Agricultural Development in Bihar* (1951-52 to 1977-78), Vishwa Bharti, Shantiniketan.

Ahsan, Qamar and I. Ahmed (2009) *Bihar: An Introduction* (Bihar EK Parichay), National Publication, Patna.

Arora, R.C. (1986), *Integrated Rural Development*, S. Chand & Co., New Delhi.

Barik, P.K. (2007) *Land and Caste Politics in Bihar*, Shipra Publication, New Delhi.

Chakravarty, Anand (2001) *Social Power and Every Day Class Relations: Agrarian Transformation in North Bihar*, Sage Publications, New Delhi.

Chaudhary, Amiya K., (2010), *Contemporary Politics and Changing Economy of Bihar*, Shipra Publication, New Delhi.

Das, A.N. (1983), *Agrarian Unrest and Socio-Economic Change in Bihar* (1900-1980), Manohar, New Delhi.

D. Narayan and P. Petesch (Ed.) (2001), *From-Many Land Voices of the Poor* (Gains and Stagnation in Bihar and Andhra Pradesh), World Bank and OUP, New York.

Haq, M.A. (1976) *The Poverty Curtain*, Columbia University Press.

Imam Hassan and Joe Kalapura (2009), *Resistance in Dalit Folk Tales* (*Dalit Gathaon Mein Pratirodh*), Daanish Books, New Delhi.

Jha, Usha (2003) *Land, Labour and Power: Agrarian Crisis and the State of Bihar*, Aakar Publication, New Delhi.

Janunnzi, F.T. (1974) *Agrarian Crisis in India: The Case of Bihar*, Sangam Books, Delhi.

Kumar, Arun (2001), *Rewritting the Language of Politics: Kisans in Colonial Bihar*, Anthem Press, New Delhi.

Kumar, S. and Pravesh Jha (2001) *Development of Bihar and Jharkhand: Problems and Prospects*, Shipra Publication, New Delhi.

Khan, A.R. and E. Lee (ed.) 1983, *Poverty in Rural Asia*, ARTEP, Bangkok.

Mazumdar, M.L. (2005), *Emerging Grass Roots Power: A Critique to Elections to Panchayats and Municipalities in Bihar*, Concept Publishing Co., New Delhi.

Mishra, R., (Ed.) (2002), *Region in History: Perspectivising Bihar*, Janki Prakashan, Patna.

Ramchandran, V.K. and Swaminathan. M., (Ed.) (2002) *Agrarian Studies, Agrarian Relations in Less Developed Countries*, Talika Books, New Delhi.

Nambisan, Vijay (2000) *Bihar in the Eyes of Beholder*, Viking, New Delhi.

Narayan, J.P. (1970), *Face to Face*, Navchetna Prakashan, Varanasi.

Ozler, B.G. Datt and M. Ravallion (1996), *A Database on Poverty and Growth in India Policy Research Department* World Bank.

P.K. (2009) *Grassroots Democracy at Work: A Study of Panchayat Elections*, Mahaveer Sons Publication, New Delhi.

Prasad, Arun Shankar (2005), *The Mushars*, Janki Prakashan, Patna.

Prasad, Pradhan H. and Merra Dutt (2001), *Bihar in the Grip of Globalization (Vaishvikaran ke Chapet mein Bihar)*, Bihar Hindi Granth Academy, Patna.

Pandey, M.P. (1979), *Land Records and Agrarian Situation in Bihar*, ANSISS, Patna.

Prasad, K.N., (1972) *Economics of Backward Region in a Backward Economy*, Scientific Book Agency, Kolkata.

Sachchidanand (2006), *Empowerment of Elected SC Members Through PRLS in Bihar*, Sulabh Institute of Development Studies, New Delhi.

Sachchidanand and B. Mandal (2009), *Crisis of Good Governance: The Case of Bihar*, Serial Publications, New Delhi.

Sharma and Gupta (1987) *Bihar Stagnation or Growth*, Spectrum Publishing, Patna.

Sahay, G.R. (2001) *Village Studies in India*, Rawat Publication, New Delhi.

Saurabh, A. (2007) *Agricultural Development and Investment: Patterns in Bihar*, Janki Prakashan, Patna.

Singh, K.S., *People of India: Bihar including Jharkhand*, Seagnll, Kolkata.

Journals

Alan, Md. Sanjeer and S. Raju (2007) Contextualising Inter-Intra Religions and Gendered Literacy and Educational Disparities in Rural Bihar, *EPW*, Vol. No. 42 (18).

Ahsan, Qamar, and M. Quddoos (2000) Rationale of Land Reform under the New Economic Policy: With Special Reference to the Progress and Problems of Land Ceiling in Bihar, *Social Profile*, Vol. IV, No. 1, June 2000.

Badal, P.S. and R.P. Singh (2001) Technology Change in Maize Production: A case study of Bihar, *Indian Journal of Agricultural Economics*, Vol. 56, No. 2, April-June.

Bhatt, M., G.S. Rao, P. Manjushree and V. Bhanurthy (2010) Space Based Disaster Management of 2008 Kosi Floods, North Bihar, India. *Journal of Society for Remote Sensing,* Vol. No. 28.

Bhattacharya, D., Bihar After Bifurcation: A Challenging Future, *EPW*, Vol. No. 35 (44/45).

Bhattacharya, D., (2009), Intra-State Disparity in Government Expenditure: An Analysis, *EPW*, Vol. No. 44 (26/27).

Baerlaet, M., Meheus, Singh, Valerberghe, Messen, and Sundar (2009), The Poorest of the Poor: A Poverty Appraisal of Households Affected by Visceral Leishmaniasis in Bihar, India, *Topical Medicine and International Health*, Vol. No. 14 (6).

Chaudhri, Kaushik and Sushmita Roy (2009) Gender Gap in Educational Attainment: Evidence from Rural India, *Education Economics*, Vol. 17 (2).

Carbribdge, Stuart *et al*., (2003) How the Local State Works in Rural Bihar Jharkhand and West Bengal, *EPW*, Vol. 38 (4).

Der'ze A., A. Sen (1995) *India: Economic Development and Social Opportunity*, Oxford University Press, Oxford.

Dettan, A. (2002) Migration Livelihoods in Bihar, India, *Journal of Development Studies,* Vol. No. 38 (5).

Diwakar, D.M. (2004) Livelihood Constraints: Options and Strategies for Survival of Agricultural Labour in North Bihar, *Social Action*, Vol. 54, No. 9.

Gupta, S. (2001), Bihar: New Panchayats and Subaltern Resurgence, *EPW*, Vol. 36 (29).

Kishore, Avinash (2004), Understanding Agrarian Impasse in Bihar, *EPW*, Vol. 35 (19).

Kumar, Girish (2001), Bihar-Panchayat Elections: Overcoming States Resistance, *EPW*, Vol. No. 36 (20).

Kumar, Niraj (2005), Land Reforms in Bihar: An Appraisal, *IASSI Quarterly*, Vol. 229, No. 2.

Kumari, V. and R.K.P. Singh (2006), Food Security in Rural Bihar: A Village Level Study, *Journal of Rural Development*, Vol. 25, No. 4.

Lal, Manohar (2004), Primary Education and Health in Bihar, *Journal of Social and Economic Studies*, Vol. 16, No. 1.

Singh, J.P. (2001), Problems of Population and Health in Bihar, *Journal of Social and Economic Studies*, Vol. No. 16 (1).

Singh, R.K.P. and S. Nasir (2003), Agricultural Credit Flow in Bihar: An Economic Analysis, *Indian Journal of Agricultural Economics*, Vol. No. 58 (1).

Thakur, Jawahar *et al.*., Rural Income Distribution and Poverty in Bihar, *EPW*, Vol. No. 35 (52-53).

Wilson, Kalpana (2002), Small Cultivators in Bihar and "New" Technology, Choice or Compulsion, *EPW*, Vol. No. 37 (13).

Yuko Tsujida, Hoda and P. Ghosh (2010), Development and Intra State Disparities in Bihar, *EPW*, Vol. No. XLV (50).

Reports

Annual Economic Survey (2005 to 2011) Department. of Finance, Government of Bihar, Patna.

Government of India (2004) Economics of Bamboo Boring: A Case Study if North-East Region of Bihar, 601, New Delhi.

Government of Bihar (2009) Towards Accelerated Agricultural Development in Bihar, Report of Steering Group, G.O.B., Patna.

International Fund for Agricultural Development (2003), A Study on Rural Poverty in Gangatic Plain: Profile of Detainments.

Kaushal, S., S. Patra (2009). *Elementary Education in Bihar.*

Mandal R.B. (2006) Water Resource Management 11 PA, New Delhi.

Resurgent Bihar—A Development Vision (2009), Report of the Special Task Force on Bihar Government of India, New Delhi.

Singh R.K.P. (2009) Performance of Agriculture credit system in Bihar: Some Experial Evidences, State Farmers Commission, Patna.

World Bank (2005) Bihar Towards a Development Strategy, World Bank, New Delhi.

Annexure-I

List of the IAS Trainees who participated in the Village Survey: Bihar

Sl. No.	*Name of Officer Trainees*	*District*	*Village*	*Batch*
1.	Bandana Preyashi	Bhojpur	Matukpur	2003
2.	Asangba, Chuba A.O.	Madhubani	Madhubani Tol	
3.	Anupam Kumar	Muzaffarpur	Harpur Krishna	
4.	Lokesh Kumar Singh	Patna	Navada	
5.	R. Lakshmanan	Begusarai	Simariya-I	2004
6.	Cherry Malik	Gaya	Singhaul	
7.	Palka Sahni	Katihar	Maheshpur	
8.	Birendra Prasad Yadav	Patna	Sonaru	
9.	Kundan Kumar	Purnia	Razigunj	
10.	Abhay Kumar Singh	Rohtas	Nonhar	
11.	Manish Kumar	Begusarai	Rahatpur	2005
12.	Kumar Ravi	Champaran	Majhualia	
13.	Divesh Sehara	Gaya	Singhaul	
14.	Kuldip Narayan	Muzaffarpur	Borbara	
15.	Ajay Yadav	Patna	Shivhar	
16.	Balamurugan D.	Purnia	Amari	
17.	Adesh Titarnare	Jehanabad	Nonhi	2006
18.	Ashwini D. Thakare (Ms)	Patna	Tineri	
19.	Daya Nidhan Pandey	Bhojpur	Mahadev Chak	
20.	Dharmendra Singh	Madhepura	Budhawe	
21.	Sandeepkumar, R.P.	Madhubani	Parohi	
22.	Deepak Anand	Bhagalpur	Belthu	2007
23.	Neeraj Kharwal	Jehanabad	Sikariya	
24.	Gopal Meena	East Champaran	Khizrpura	
25.	Vinod Singh Gunjiyal	Patna	Behranwa	
26.	Jai Singh	Gaya	Noni	
27.	Manoj Kumar	Gopalganj	Manjha	
28.	Sanjay Kumar Singh	Muzaffarpur	Berua	
29	Ashima Jain (Ms.)	Bhagalpur	Bagri	2008
30.	Buddhabhatti Kartikey D.	Gaya	Suraj Mandal	
31.	Giriwar Dayal Singh	Purnea	Lakhna	
32.	Pranav Kumar	Vaishali	Etwarpur Sisaula	
33.	Ramandeep Choudhary	Rohtas	Sonhar	
34.	M. Ramachandrudu	Khagaria	Lagma	2009
35.	Manoj Kumar Singh	Purnea	Jagannathpur	
36.	Raman Kumar	Darbhanga	Khutwara	
37.	Saket Kumar	Bhagalpur	Latra	
38.	Seema Tripathi (Ms.)	Jehanabad	Kako	

Annexure-II

	States	Index
1.	**Relatively Developed States**	
	1.1 Haryana	0.395
	1.2 Uttarakhand	0.383
	1.3 Maharashtra	0.352
	1.4 Punjab	0.345
	1.5 Tamil Nadu	0.341
	1.6 Kerala	0.095
	1.7 Goa	0.045
2.	**Less Developed States**	
	2.1 Manipur	0.571
	2.2 West Bengal	0.551
	2.3 Nagaland	0.546
	2.4 Andhra Pradesh	0.521
	2.5 Jammu & Kashmir	0.504
	2.6 Mizoram	0.495
	2.7 Gujarat	0.491
	2.8 Tripura	0.474
	2.9 Karnataka	0.453
	2.10 Sikkim	0.443
	2.11 Himachal Pradesh	0.404
3.	**Least Developed States**	
	3.1 Odisha	0.798
	3.2 Bihar	0.765
	3.3 Madhya Pradesh	0.759
	3.4 Chhattisgarh	0.752
	3.5 Jharkhand	0.746
	3.6 Arunachal Pradesh	0.729
	3.7 Assam	0.707
	3.8 Meghalya	0.693
	3.9 Uttar Pradesh	0.638
	3.10 Rajasthan	0.626

Source: Based on the Raghuram Ranjan Committee Report, Ministry of Finance, GoI, New Delhi, 2013.

7

Conclusion and Recommendations

SUCHA SINGH GILL

This volume brings out that the rural development is picking up in the country in the wake of socio-economic process of development and policy interventions from the Union Government as well as the State Governments. But the state level papers bring out that the rural areas are lagging behind the urban areas both in income and employment generation as well as in civic and social amenities. This gap needs to be narrowed by faking concerted efforts for upliftment of the rural areas. The chapters also bring out of a lot of spatial variations in the socio-economic development and profile of the rural areas. On one extreme one finds the state of Kerala where rural development especially decentralized rural governance has reached grassroots level where are the state Bihar lags far behind other states. The other States in the country fall between these extremes. But both the extremes are showing the sign of changes especially in the recent years. Within each state there are districts and within those districts villages which have done much better than other districts and villages within them. In forward districts there are backward villages and in backward districts there are forward villages. The spatial differentials bring out the rural development in a village is dependent on its location either close to a highway or close to a city or subjective factors like mobilization at village level due to involvement of some NGO or a political party committed to decentralization of rural development or enlightened local leadership (village sarpanch) imbibed in welfare of the people. Wherever such factors become favourable rural development picks up. In locations where such factors are not favourable rural development becomes a casualty. The villages which become faction ridden due to rivalries among different political parties also suffer on this count. In situations where rivalries based on caste or communal are prevalent, the rural development suffers. It has also been observed in some villages that an outside intervention (by NRIs in case of Punjab) have proved beneficial both in terms of mobilization of resources as well as a reconciliation factors to promote rural development. The chapters in this volume bring some useful lessons which can be listed as policy recommendations. These recommendations can help in acceleration of the rural development not only in the states about which chapters have included in this book but also in the other states of the country. The recommendations are as follows:

1. The rural development can pick up in big way if adequate funds are made available every year. The village panchayat must know in the first week of April every year the amount allocated to them. The Kerala experience provides a good illustration of this.
2. The village panchayats need to be empowered to collect some taxes at local level to improve their financial position. This accompanied by transfer of functions, functionaries and finances as envisioned in the 73rd Amendment of Constitution can accelerate the process of rural development.
3. As stated above there is a large spatial variations in the rural development among the villages. The forward districts have backward villages and backward districts have forward villages. There is need to identify backward region in each district and cluster of villages where rural development has not picked up. The district administration can be instructed to pay special attention for development of such villages. In order to promote development of those villages specific constraints can be identified for corrective measures.
4. It has been found that villages which are close to national or state highways experience better development. It is, therefore, necessary to pay special attention towards the villages which are in the interior areas/hinterland of the State. It is from

such villages that distress migration of labour takes place. The location of some modern economic enterprises in those villages based on agro-processing can be extremely useful to check distress migration and regenerate their socio-economic development.

5. It has been observed that the improvement in connectivity at village level helps in improvement of agriculture and allied activities both in acquisition of inputs as well as disposal of output. This needs to strengthened under PMGSY and regular repair of such roads must be undertaken. This will also encourage some agro-processing units to be located in those villages for generation of rural non-farm (RNF) employment. This will also check distress migration of labour from the villages where jobs are shrinking due to mechanization of agriculture.
6. It is a common experience that the villages where mobilization of beneficiaries has been done by some individuals or NGOs or political parties, the rural development has moved forward. There has been better utilization of the government funds, greater accountability and benefits reach the target groups. It is necessary component for the rural development. This also ensures regular holding of gram sabha. The Government must encourage such individuals and NGOs or local unions to mobilise people in the rural areas for rural development and decentralized governance.
7. In order to make mobilization of the rural people for decentralized development and regeneration of the rural economy awareness among the people is a necessary condition. The process of awareness in the rural areas can be initiated by organization of training programme of elected representative of PRIs. The awareness programme can include the need for mobilization of people and need for holding gram sabha for approval of various programmes, duties and functions of elected representatives of PRIs and details of programmes administered through PRIs. Through the training and orientation of the elected representatives of PRIs awareness can reach quickly to the village level. It can also create good ground for individuals and NGOs involved

in mobilization of the people around rural development programmes.

These recommendations can be implemented depending on the specific requirement of the each village. The picking up of the villages and districts on priority basis which are lagging behind can help in bridging the gap between the villages placed at different geographical locations especially with disadvantage in connectivity. These steps can go a long way in making rural development programmes a success in the villages in different parts of the country.

Index